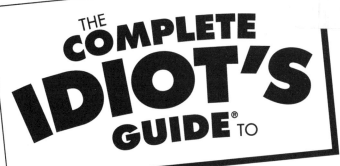

Native American History

by Walter C. Fleming

ALPHA

Penguin Group (USA) Inc.

This book is dedicated to my wife, Shelley, my children, Jennifer, Travis, Les, Kaleena, and Tristyn, as well as my grandchildren, Jacob and Kjersten, and all Indian children and grandchildren. Also, to Indian parents, like mine, who raised their children with pride and dignity. This is my gift to all of you, even unto the next seven generations to come.

Most Alpha books are available at special quantity discounts for bulk purchases for sales promotions, premiums, fund-raising, or educational use. Special books, or book excerpts, can also be created to fit specific needs.

For details, write: Special Markets; Alpha Books, 375 Hudson Street, New York, NY 10014.

Publisher: *Marie Butler-Knight*
Product Manager: *Phil Kitchel*
Senior Managing Editor: *Jennifer Chisholm*
Acquisitions Editor: *Gary Goldstein*
Development Editor: *Jennifer Moore*
Copy Editor: *Jan Zunkel*
Illustrator: *Chris Eliopoulos*
Cover/Book Designer: *Trina Wurst*
Indexer: *Heather McNeil*
Layout/Proofreading: *Angela Calvert, Mary Hunt*

Contents at a Glance

Contents

Appendixes

Foreword

In *The Complete Idiot's Guide to Native American History*, Walter C. Fleming, a member of the Kickapoo tribe, presents an alternative view of history—one that you won't find in most history books. With words as his palette, he paints an earth-colored tapestry of Native American people—creating a portrait of Indians that challenges the reader to see them not as warriors, not as oppressed people, and not as savages (noble or otherwise), but as people, plain and simple, who have suffered great injustices yet have survived. They have faced the trauma of removal as, nation by nation, the U.S. government encroached upon their tribal homelands in the name of Manifest Destiny. They have been dishonored by broken treaties as well as federal policies of assimilation that forced many tribes to adopt white practices at the expense of their own traditional cultures.

Given their treatment by early European explorers and colonizers and, eventually, the U.S. government, Native survival into this millennium is nothing short of a miracle. But to thrive, Native Americans must overcome the continuing racism and bigotry that's a byproduct of ignorance about them and their rich culture. For although Native Americans have been locked in a cycle of poverty for several centuries, they are *culturally* wealthy. And to their credit, they have shared this wealth with other Americans. To take just a single example, the creators of the U.S. Constitution used the Iroquois model of representative government in designing the legislature.

Native Americans are also a *spiritually* wealthy people who continue to observe their ceremonies as the keepers of earth. They strive to be at peace in their minds, hearts, spirits, and bodies. They understand the importance of love, respect for all relations, generosity, forgiveness, and most important, the value of living peacefully upon the earth. These valuable life lessons are crucial for all humanity at this juncture of history.

Native Americans also cherish knowledge and understanding. It is this wonderful gift of understanding that Walter Fleming has given his readers in *The Complete Idiot's Guide to Native American History*.

Henrietta Mann, Ph.D.

Henrietta Mann, Ph.D., is a Cheyenne, enrolled with the Cheyenne and Arapaho tribes of Oklahoma; Endowed Chair in Native American Studies, Montana State University—Bozeman.

Introduction

According to the 2002 census, there are more than 2 million American Indians, Eskimos, and Alaska Natives in the United States. By 2050, the Census Bureau estimates that the number will increase to approximately 4 million, continuing a growth trend that started back in the 1850s. At that time, the population levels were at their lowest, as the Indians had suffered the ravaging effects of disease and violent encounters with Euro-Americans.

Behind these numbers are individual and tribal stories of survival, of overcoming the challenges that come with conflict.

A hundred years ago, American Indians were taught to be ashamed of their identity. Their parents were encouraged to assimilate into non-Indian society and to forget about Native languages and cultures. Such relics of the past, they were told, interfere with progress and becoming "civilized." Generations of Native people were taught that their ancestors were barriers to western expansion and were savage killers.

In the 1970s, as a product of the awakening ethnic-pride movements, many young Native peoples began to reclaim their culture and study their history. When they did, they discovered several realities. First, their tribal histories, in some cases, were incomplete or nonexistent. They also learned that the histories they did have were often told from a non-Indian perspective. And they learned of the horrors that their ancestors endured since whites first stepped foot on their lands.

In many cases, this new-found appreciation for their histories gave American Indians a sense of pride in their identities. But this knowledge also angered them. How can one not be enraged upon learning of the terrible tragedies, of massacres, and relocation, suffered by one's ancestors? The question many young Indians asked was, "why didn't we learn *this* history in school?"

Why Should Anyone Care?

Today, many non-Indians, in this country and around the world, have discovered an interest in and appreciation for Native peoples and their cultures. And when they become aware of the sad chronicle of events that Native peoples have suffered, they, too, ask, "Why didn't we learn this history in school?" The answer is obvious: We are all studying from the same textbooks. These are books written by the dominant society to tell mainstream history. Native history is relegated to the footnotes or sidebars, trivialized and ignored.

As a college professor, I encounter students who are products of this kind of exposure to history every day. Most are appreciative and respectful, properly horrified when they learn just how inhumane people can be to one another. Once in a while, however, a student will ask, "Why should I care? I didn't steal Indian land. My ancestors came to this country after all this happened. I am not responsible for the actions of the past."

Those students are making cynical, but valid, observations. Why should non-Indians care about Native American history?

The answer is complex, but goes something like this:

When we all learn about our collective pasts, we can better understand ourselves, because we are all a product of that past. Our lives are intertwined and dependent.

Felix S. Cohen, an eminent scholar of American Indian law, described Native peoples as this country's miner's canary—the bird that miners used to carry in a small wooden cage deep into the heart of mountains to detect methane gas. If the canary survived, the miner knew he was safe; if the canary died, the miner would know to exit the mine because poison was present. Cohen noted that "like the miner's canary, the Indian marks the shift from fresh air to poison gas in our political atmosphere; and our treatment of Indians … reflects the rise and fall in our democratic faith." If Native peoples and cultures cannot survive into the future, then there is little hope for other cultures—for America and all of its traditions.

I will try, in this book, to present the Native points of view about Native *and* American history. I promise not to be overly academic. I will try to be entertaining without being trite. Occasionally I will attempt to amuse you, but please recognize that Native American history is filled with woe. It is also an inspiration, and we need to honor that as well.

And Here's How I'll Do It

This book is divided into four parts that explore Native American history from creation to the present.

Part 1, "America B.C. (Before Columbus)," is an introduction to Native American peoples. You'll learn some of the terminology Native peoples use to identify themselves (you've already encountered several of the terms in this introduction!) and become acquainted with various theories—including Native peoples' own explanations—about how the ancestors of today's Native people came to be in the Americas. You'll also learn about some of the oldest cultures in the Americas and the characteristics of people who live in the 10 Native culture areas of North America.

Part 2, "There Goes the Neighborhood," describes some of the earliest European explorations of the so-called "New World." Chapters in this section cover the English, Spanish, and French colonial relationships with Native tribes and how European in-fighting impacted tribal affairs in the colonies. You'll find out about the federal government's policies toward Indian tribes and how western expansion forever changed Indian lives.

Part 3, "Reservations and Resistance," tells the sad story of how tribes came to be put on reservations and how they adjusted to that new environment. You'll find out about the Indian wars out West, and meet some of the American Indian leaders who resisted the attempts by the American government to conquer Native peoples. Finally, you'll learn what policies the federal government enacted to "civilize" the American Indian and break up the reservations.

Part 4, "Modern Indians, Modern Challenges," examines contemporary trials that Indian tribes face. After explaining the contemporary relationship between Native tribes and the American government and what rights tribal governments possess, we will explore hunting and fishing rights and the history of the education of Native peoples. You'll read about the challenges Indian people face in health care and in developing a reservation economic base. Finally, you'll learn about Native spirituality and the modern practices of Native American religious beliefs.

Wait, There's More!

To help keep things lively, you'll find the following sidebars throughout the chapters:

Tribal Truths

These boxes contain fascinating facts about Indian culture, people, and perspectives—including some of my own.

Native Voices

It is important that Native peoples participate in the telling of their own history. In these boxes, their "voices" shall be heard—in the form of quotes, sayings, and observations by Native peoples.

Ancient Tales

Our ancestors often spoke words of great wisdom, which I relay to you in these boxes.

Code Talking

During World War II, a number of Native soldiers helped the Allies achieve victory by using Indian languages to transmit vital messages. While the Navajo Code Talkers are the best known, the Choctaw, Comanche, Sioux, and Crow languages, among others, were also used. I do a little of my own "code talking" in these boxes by defining words and concepts that you might not have heard of.

Acknowledgments

Thanks first to my wife, Shelley Fleming, who listened to my musings and contributed importantly to the section on Indian gaming. Also to the staff and faculty of the Center for Native American Studies, Montana State University, who offered helpful guidance all along the way. Any errors, however, are all mine.

Special Thanks to the Technical Reviewer

The Complete Idiot's Guide to Native American History was reviewed by an expert who double-checked the accuracy of what you'll learn here, to help us ensure that this book gives you everything you need to know about the history of American Indians. Special thanks are extended to Henrietta Mann, Ph.D.

Trademarks

All terms mentioned in this book that are known to be or are suspected of being trademarks or service marks have been appropriately capitalized. Alpha Books and Penguin Group (USA) Inc. cannot attest to the accuracy of this information. Use of a term in this book should not be regarded as affecting the validity of any trademark or service mark.

Part 1

America B.C. (Before Columbus)

Some Native peoples believe we have always lived where we do now, that we were created in this place called North America, America, or Kansas. Scholars, however, tell us that we came across the Bering Strait from Asia, about 20,000 years ago.

Part 1 introduces you to the earliest ancestors of those called American Indians or Native Americans and offers you a glimpse into their earliest histories. We don't know exactly what happened to these people, but their blood remains in all tribal peoples.

Chapter 1

Who (and What) Is an American Indian?

In This Chapter

- What to call the first Americans
- How American Indians define themselves
- Tribes, bands, and clans
- The language of the people

Probably no other group in the United States is and has been so misunderstood as Native Americans. Many people, for example, believe that Native Americans constitute one race, which shares one culture and one history. This is dead wrong.

Here's another one: People mistakenly believe that American Indians are a dying race. The myth of the "Vanishing Red Man" is still a prominent misconception when in fact the Native American population has been growing, not only steadily, but dramatically, for the past 40 years. Along with this false impression, a lot of folks refer to Native culture in the past tense, as if Natives no longer practice their ways. While much has been lost, much of the traditions are very much alive.

To make matters worse, people's "knowledge" of Native history and culture often comes from popular literature and western movies. You know—the ones where the "Red Man" is bloodthirsty, stupid, or drunk. Or, in a complete reversal, he's portrayed as a noble savage—in which the Indian is as a child of the forest, at one with nature, and walking softly upon the earth. This representation is equally as damaging as that of the savage, because it creates an image that is impossible for American Indians to live up to. In neither case are Indian people permitted to be human.

So if all of these characterizations are incorrect, who are *Native Americans?* Well, let's start with what they are called, by themselves and by others.

An Indian by Any Other Name ...

Because what you call yourself plays a large part in determining who you are, the first thing I'll tackle is how the people who are the topic of this book like to be called. I'll give you one hint: It's not *Tonto*.

Code Talking

Native Americans are people who lived in the Americas before the coming of Europeans; the term also refers to the ancestors of those original inhabitants.

Didn't You Used to Be ...?

Of course, 500 years ago, how to refer to Native peoples wasn't an issue. Tribes had their own names for themselves, often names that translated to mean "The People" or "The Original Ones." The Cheyenne knew themselves as *Tsististas*, or "The People." It was the Dakota, a neighboring tribe, who called them *Shahiyena*, meaning "People Who Talk Differently." So the name Cheyenne is not theirs.

Tribal Truths

The name "Sioux" can be a little misleading, because there is no one group or tribe of Sioux. That term is a garbled version of an Ojibwa (Chippewa) name meaning "the Lesser Adders." In linguistic terms, the Sioux can be divided into the Lakota, or Western Sioux; the Nakota, or Central Sioux; and the Dakota, or Eastern Sioux. While they all speak the same language, there are dialectic differences, as evidenced by their pronunciation of Lakota, Nakota, and Dakota. The westernmost Sioux, or Teton Lakota, are perhaps best known by their band names, Oglala, Hunkpapa, Miniconjou, and so on. Sitting Bull, Black Elk, and Crazy Horse were Lakota Sioux.

Some Navajo prefer *Diné*, which in their language means "The People." The Papago are now formally known as the *Tohono O'odham* (Desert People) and the Pima have reclaimed the name *Akimel O'odham* (River People).

This current renaming trend may seem confusing and, to some, even ridiculous. However, these tribes are asserting control of their own identities, to try to revive pride in their heritage and history. Most important, however, they are correcting the errors of the past.

I'm Glad Columbus Wasn't Looking for Turkey!

Some Native peoples take issue with being called an "Indian" or "American Indian" for a lot of good reasons. First, "Indians" was a misnomer, a product of Christopher Columbus's mistaken belief that he had reached the East Indies. Second, people from India are also called "Indians." "American Indian" doesn't help much, as a person from India who lives in the United States could well be termed an "American Indian."

The term "Native American," although it is probably the most commonly used expression, still causes some confusion. There are non-Indian people who quite proudly proclaim, "I'm an American and I'm native to this country, so I'm a Native American, too!"

Others prefer the term "Native." In Canada, "Native peoples" has long been used to refer to the indigenous people in that country. In Alaska, the phrase "Alaska Natives" refers to American Indians, Eskimos, and Aleuts. Eskimos and Aleuts are culturally and historically distinctive peoples and are, understandably, sensitive to being considered "Indian."

Tribal Truths

One Native wit observed that Columbus called us "Indians" because he was looking for India. Good thing he wasn't looking for Turkey!

To confuse things further, Native scholars have recently begun to promote and use the terms "first nations people" or "indigenous peoples." It's not likely that these terms will replace either Native American or American Indian in the popular lexicon any time soon, but they are preferred by some Native peoples.

I've resolved the issue by using the term "Native American" or "Native" in more formal situations, such as when I'm writing for the public or giving speeches. In the classroom, and in other more informal situations, I will more often use the term "American Indian" or just "Indian."

The best answer avoids all the awkward options. When asked, "What are you?" most Native Americans respond by giving their tribal affiliation. Thus, one might respond, "I'm a Kickapoo," or "I'm Cheyenne."

Tribes, Bands, or Clans

When someone calls him or herself Kickapoo, that person is identifying his or her tribal affiliation. But what, exactly, a *tribe* is depends on whom you ask.

Code Talking

A **tribe** is a social group, bound by common culture and history. A tribe is also a political organization, a group of people recognized by the federal government as a political entity. The term tribe has also come to mean "peoples" or "nations," as in the Crow Nation, and so on.

Ethnologists, folks who study cultures, define a tribe as a group of indigenous people, bound by blood ties, who are socially, politically, and religiously organized according to the tenets of their own culture, who live together, occupying a definite territory, and who speak a common language or dialect.

The Supreme Court, in a 1901 decision, said that "[b]y a 'tribe' we understand a body of Indians of the same or similar race, united in a community under one leadership or government, and inhabiting a particular though sometimes ill-defined territory." Lots of help, huh?

Tribal Truths

Some Native groups that aren't currently recognized by the federal government as tribes believe that they are entitled to be considered as such. To gain federal recognition, a tribe must go through a long and complicated process wherein it must meet many criteria, including the following:

♦ The group petitioning for recognition must prove that it has been identified as an American Indian entity since 1900.

♦ The group's members must be descendants of an historical Indian tribe that functioned as an autonomous political entity.

♦ The group must have maintained political influence over its members from historical times to the present.

Presently, approximately 230 tribes are seeking federal recognition.

According to the federal government, there are more than 560 federally recognized tribes in the United States, including 223 village groups in Alaska. These federally recognized tribes and groups have a special, legal relationship with the U.S. government. This relationship is referred to as a government-to-government relationship and was established historically through the treaty-making process (see Chapter 8 for more on treaties).

I'm a Card-Carrying Indian!

The American Indian is the only ethnic group in the United States that must prove its ethnicity. That is a product of their relationship with the federal government. They often signed treaties with the government and were promised specific rights. Tribes ceded millions of acres of land in exchange for those rights. To make sure the right people are afforded those rights, the government must have criteria for defining who is an Indian. Some government agencies require proof of a certain amount of Native ancestry, or Native blood, to determine eligibility for services. In some cases, Natives must have a *blood quantum* of one quarter Native blood in order to be considered an Indian. For other agencies, such as the U.S. Bureau of Census, one only needs to declare oneself a Native American to count as one.

Code Talking

Blood quantum is a criterion for determining who is an Indian based on ancestry. For example, a blood quantum of one quarter Native blood (meaning that at least one grandparent is of 100 percent Native ancestry) is usually required to count as a member of a tribe.

Tribes also determine who are or are not members. A person must apply for membership—a process called enrollment—and must provide proof of Indian ancestry, according to specific criteria. When you are enrolled with a tribe, you have met established standards and are legally a member of that tribe. No one is ever "registered" with a tribe, however—we're not members of the American Kennel Club, you know!

For example, for enrollment for the Cherokee tribe in Oklahoma, one must be able to trace their ancestry to a descendent who appears on the Dawes Rolls in the early 1900s. The Kickapoo Tribe of Kansas requires the applicant to have at least one quarter Kickapoo blood.

So there you have it: There is no single definition of a tribe. Some groups can be recognized by the federal government as tribes for one purpose and not for another. Some tribes are considered to be so by the states in which they reside, while still others are recognized only by other Native American groups. There are even "tribes" that are only recognized by the members themselves!

Being in a Band

A *band* is a political subdivision of a tribe. Among some tribal groups, a band is a residential subdivision, like a village or town. For mobile tribes on the American plains,

Code Talking

A **band** is a subdivision of a tribe. It is a local group of people jointly in search of subsistence and can be made up of related families.

A **clan** is kinship reckoning through a line of common descent, either through the mother's side (matrilineal) or father's side (patrilineal).

a band was a group of people jointly traveling in search of subsistence. The band may be made up of several extended families under the loose leadership of a patriarch or headman.

Hatfields and the McCoys?

A *clan* is an extended family unit, one that usually shares a common line of descent. In a matrilineal clan system, a person becomes a member of his or her mother's clan, and in a patrilineal system, he or she is a member of the father's clan.

The origins of the clan systems are unknown, although in a given tribe there may be a story of the origin of a specific clan. A typical story might relate how the clan—let's call it the Bear Clan—was created by the union between a mortal woman and the spirit of the bear in mythical times. Generally, matrilineal clan systems seem to be identified with horticultural tribes in which women farmed, perhaps as a system to determine property rights to garden plots. Patrilineal systems may relate to rights to rule, usually determined through male descendency.

Clan affiliation is so important among the Crow Indians of Montana and the Diné (Navajo) of the American Southwest that such membership is identified as a part of the greeting. In the case of the Crow, one would say, "I am a member of the Whistling Water clan and a child of the Greasy Mouths (father's clan)." The Diné identify themselves by stating their "Born To" clan, or mother's clan, and their "Born For" clan, their father's clan. Clans are almost always exogamous; that is, one has to marry outside of one's own clan, and, therefore, identifying clan affiliations eliminates violations of incest taboos.

Code Talking

A **language family** is a group of languages that show close historical connections. For example, Spanish, French, Portuguese, and Italian are all Romance languages. They may share a common ancestry and may have derived from the same mother tongue but are not mutually intelligible.

Do You Speak Indian?

As you've probably figured out by now, there is no single Indian language. As a matter of fact, it has been estimated that in 1492 more than 400 Native languages were spoken in North America. Most of these languages were mutually unintelligible, that is, only understood by those who speak it.

Linguists have grouped Native languages into *language families* based upon similarities. For example, Cree, Cheyenne, and Passamaquoddy are classified as Algonquian languages. Scholars believe that these languages derived from the same mother tongue. The major language families in North America include Algonquian, Athapascan, Siouan, Iroquoian, and Eskimo-Aleut.

What's Your Sign?

Because there were so many different languages, communicating with one another was a challenge for individuals of different tribes. The Plains tribes created a universal sign language to help in trade and other intertribal situations. Some of the signs are logical. Hands on both sides of the head with your fingers outspread is the sign for a deer. The sign for a woman or female is to put one's hands on either side of the head, at ear level, palms down, fingers facing back, and then lowering the hands to indicate long hair. Tribal names were indicated by combining the sign for "Indian," rubbing the back of the left hand with the right, and adding a sign for that tribe. The Cheyenne, for example, were known by the sign representing the cutting off of fingers, indicated by drawing one index finger across the other.

Other groups, like the Iroquois tribes in the northeast of the United States, used beaded wampum belts to communicate. The symbols or designs beaded into the belt represented words and concepts.

> **Tribal Truths**
>
> Wampum beads are white and purple disk-shape beads fashioned from clamshells found along New Jersey and Long Island beaches. They were exchanged as gifts during important ceremonies, so Europeans mistakenly assumed that wampum represented a form of currency among the northeastern tribes.

Death of a Language

Unfortunately, more than one half of the Native North American languages are now extinct, and many others are nearly extinct, because there are so few speakers and these speakers tend to be elders.

Many indigenous people don't speak a Native language for a variety of reasons. Some, like myself, had parents who were from different tribes. For others, perhaps they were raised at a time when Native peoples were discouraged from and even punished for speaking their own language (see Chapter 16). This can be a source of shame for some individuals, while others are quite comfortable speaking only English. Some who do not speak their own language are attempting to learn. Good for them!

Some Indigenous Languages

Speakers	Language	Location
148,530	Navajo	Arizona; Utah; New Mexico; Utah
35,000	Ojibwa	Montana; Wisconsin; North Dakota
20,355	Dakota	Nebraska; Minnesota; North Dakota; South Dakota
17,890	Choctaw	Oklahoma
12,693	Apache	Arizona
11,905	Cherokee	Oklahoma; North Carolina
11,819	Papago-Pima	Arizona
10,000	Yupik (Eskimo)	Alaska
6,413	Zuni	New Mexico

Native languages are important elements of Indian identification and culture, and their loss has profound effects. Without Native languages, for example, tribes lose the ability to transmit knowledge, philosophy, beliefs, and other aspects of culture. Still, speaking an Indian language does not make one a Native American any more than *not* speaking one makes one any less of an Indian. An Indian is someone who identifies him or herself as an Indian and whom the community accepts as an Indian. That can only come from the heart.

The Least You Need to Know

- Native Americans are indigenous to the Americas.
- Individual Indian people use many different terms to identify themselves, so when in doubt, ask.
- Native Americans are members of a tribe, and that is their primary way of identifying themselves.
- A Native person may or may not be able to speak his or her native language.

2

We Were Here First: Populating Turtle Island

In This Chapter

- ◆ The Bering Strait theory of migration
- ◆ Some "not-so-scientific" origin stories
- ◆ How Natives remember their origins

Ever since Columbus got lost and Native peoples of the Americas found him, people have speculated about the origins of the original inhabitants of Turtle Island, as many Native peoples called this continent. Many early European explorers could not imagine a world of other people with skin colors different from their own. And so, when casting about for explanations for the presence of Native peoples, Europeans concluded that the Natives of North America must have been, in their distant past, Europeans or descendents of other peoples about whom they knew.

Keeping Your Bearings Straight

For the scientific community, the question of the origin of humans in the Americas is not a question of "From where?" but rather "When?"

Scientific evidence points to a fairly clear path: Ancestors of the first Americans crossed the Bering Strait from Asia. The Bering Strait, the body of water separating Siberia from Alaska, is only 56 miles wide and 180 feet deep. The prevailing theory holds that during the last ice age, when the sea levels were as much as 300 feet below current levels, *Paleo-Indians* were able to walk from Siberia to Alaska across the Bering Land Bridge. (Scientists call this area, which is now under water, *Beringia*.)

Code Talking

Archaeologists use the term **Paleo-Indians** to refer to the first human beings to arrive in the New World from Asia. *Paleo* is from the Greek word meaning "ancient."

Beringia is the name scientists use to refer to the land bridge, now under water, between Siberia and Alaska.

Early, Earlier, Earliest

It's likely that, rather than one single migration across the Bering Strait, people migrated in a series of little movements, some originating in northern Asia, others in southern Asia (or in even specific regions, like Japan or Korea). Because of this Asiatic origin, Native Americans are classified as "Mongoloid." This classification, though, is outdated, based on the nineteenth-century notion that there are three human races: Caucasoid, Mongoloid, and Negroid. More conventional thinking holds that there is only one race—the Human Race!

The Second Wave

A second migration is thought to have occurred approximately 8,000 years ago. These people are the Na-Dene (from an Athabaskan term meaning "The People"), tribes that now make up the Athabaskan language family. Contemporary tribes, such as the Haida and Tlingit of Alaska, and the Navajo and Apache of the American Southwest, may be descendents of this second wave of migration.

These first two waves of migration account for the American Indians but not all Natives.

Last but Not Least

Four to six thousand years ago, people once again started moving to the Americas. The descendants of this last group are now known as the Eskimo (or *Inuit*, meaning "The People") and the Aleut, cultural relatives of the Eskimo. The Eskimo and Aleut most closely physically resemble some Asian peoples, evidence, to some, of their eastern Asian roots.

When?

Okay, so the answer to the "From where?" question is still not conclusive. But neither is the "When?" question. America's oldest humanly altered artifact is a 27,000-year-old caribou-bone scraper found in the Yukon, so we know that people were in North America at least by then. How much earlier than that they may have arrived is not known, although researchers have employed a number of methods to try to narrow in on the answer.

It's All in the Genes

Nearly all Native American groups carry one of four distinct DNA lineages in cellular structures called *mitochondria*. These lines of descent have been compared between Native peoples in Asia and the Americas. Genes diversify at a predictable rate, so genetic differences between populations provide a gauge of how long they've been apart. The theory is that the more variation you find between two groups, the longer they've been apart. Using genetic variation between Native peoples of Asia and the Americas, scholars have calculated that 20,000 to 40,000 years had elapsed since North American and Asian groups shared a common ancestor.

Code Talking

Mitochondria are small energy-producing organelles found in cells. Unlike nuclear DNA that is equally inherited from both father and mother, mitochondrial DNA is inherited only from the mother. In theory, science can trace common female ancestry in individuals through genetic testing.

How Old Is Old?

Archaeologists have discovered hundreds of Paleo-Indian sites in the Americas and have employed numerous dating techniques to try to answer the question "When did humans first come to this continent?" The answers vary from 20,000 years ago to 100,000 years ago, depending on the site and the scholar making the interpretations of the data.

So why can't scholars be more precise? Much of the research depends on dating techniques, like *carbon-14* (C-14) testing that, until recently, hasn't

Code Talking

Carbon-14 is a radioactive isotope of carbon produced in the upper atmosphere by radiation from the sun. The C-14 will undergo radioactive decay, and after 5,730 years, half of it will be gone. Eventually, all of it will be gone. So if we find an object, the amount of C-14 in it will tell us how long ago it was alive.

been very dependable. C-14 dating measures existing radioactive carbon in an organic artifact to yield an approximate time when that organism lived. The difficulty is that after about 60,000 years, the amount of C-14 remaining is so small that the fossil can't be dated reliably.

To date, the oldest human remains in North America are a woman's bones found on the Channel Islands, in southern California, that have been tentatively dated at 13,000 years old. Given that no one has found more ancient remains than this, the evidence supports the theory that humans didn't evolve in the Americas but, rather, migrated here. Some scholars in South America disagree, suggesting that humans evolved in the Americas and migrated out. This is not, however, a very popular theory.

Tribal Truths

America's oldest artifact is a 27,000-year-old caribou-bone scraper, its edges still intact, found in the Yukon.

Reed Boats and Lost Tribes

Euro-Americans came to a number of conclusions about the "true" origins of the Native peoples of the Americas. These conclusions are naturally filtered through the bias and knowledge (or lack of it) of the time. As such, they seem strange, even laughable, to many people today, but each was, and is, an explanation long held by one group or another.

Where's My Mummy?

American Indians must be, thought some, descendents of Phoenician seafarers or Egyptian sailors. How else can the pyramids of South America be explained? Surely, "ignorant savages" are incapable of such engineering genius! Pop anthropologist Thor Heyerdahl sailed a reed boat across the Atlantic, proving, at least to himself, that contact between the ancient Egyptians and South and Central Americans was possible. If these people were not truly Egyptian, they must have learned everything they knew from visitors from across the Atlantic.

Oy Vey! (And Greek, Too!)

The Church of Jesus Christ of Latter-Day Saints suggests that American Indians descend from one of the lost tribes of Israel and call Natives *Lamanites*. The *Book of Mormon* declares that when Lehi's sons, Laman and Lemuel, rebelled, God cursed them and their Native American descendants with a dark skin. According to this theory, the indigenous peoples of the Americas are Hebrew.

Other theories state that the ancestors of the American Indians are the survivors of the lost empire of Atlantis, or the Pacific version, the lost continent of Mu.

Welsh Rarebits

One of the most persistent and oldest theories concerns a Welsh prince by the name of Madog or Madoc, who got lost while exploring new worlds, and who beat out even the Vikings as the earliest European visitors to North America. Early visitors on the Plains speculated that the Mandan Indians living in what is now North Dakota were the descendents of these Welsh explorers, as some of the Mandan had light skin and fair features. When Lewis and Clark encountered the Salish people in 1805 in what is now Montana, they speculated that these might be "the Welsh Indians," Madoc's progeny.

These "not-so-scientific" theories for the origin of humans in the Americas reflect a certain ethnocentrism: If the Natives were not descended from European or northern Africans, so the thinking goes, they were certainly influenced by them.

Ancient Tales
The Crow or *Absarokee* people of Montana tell of a time when their ancestors were trapped in a world of ice and snow. They were unable to go to the warm, green lands to the south because of the great sheets of ice that surrounded them. These ancient peoples appealed to the bison for help. Seven buffalo bulls each took turns ramming the sheets of ice until a corridor opened, enabling the Absarokee to enter into the green lands to the south.

Indian Genesis

Native peoples have their own answer to the question "Where did we come from?" Scholars have not given these theories much credibility as valid explanations for the peopling of the Americas. So these accounts are classified as *myths* or folklore, studied by scholars of literature. Yet for many tribal people, the story of their own creation and migration are often as real as any scientific explanation.

There is no single creation story among Native tribes. Each nation has an account of the creation of Earth and her inhabitants. Although each tribe's story is unique and special to that tribe, similarities and common motifs do exist among the various accounts.

Code Talking

A **myth** in folklore is a story about the deeds and doings of supernatural characters.

Earth Divers

Many stories involve a Creator or supernatural being, who completes the world with the help of an *Earth Diver.* According to these accounts, a great ocean originally covered this world. The Creator first made the beings that lived under the water and then the animals that lived on the water. Then, a water bird or a water animal dove to the bottom of the ocean to retrieve mud or a stick to complete the creation of Earth.

Ancient Tales

In the beginning, according to the Cheyenne, there was nothing except Maheo. With his power he created a vast ocean. "There should be water beings," Maheo told his Power.

So he created the snow goose and other birds. One day they said to the creator, "We grow tired swimming all day." Maheo commanded, "Then fly."

One day they called to Maheo, saying, "We need a place to build our nests, to raise our young." Creator told them, "Dive to the bottom and bring me what you find."

The water coot told the Creator, "I am small and cannot swim well, but I would like to try to reach the bottom and bring you what I find."

So the water coot dove into the water and swam as deep as he could. When he came to the surface, he had a ball of mud in his mouth. Creator rolled this mud in his hands, and as he did, the ball grew. Creator put the ball on the back of Grandmother Turtle.

Code Talking

Earth Diver myths are creation stories in which the earth is made from a substance brought to the surface by a water bird such as a duck or animal like a beaver or an otter.
Emergence creation stories entail humans coming from earlier worlds.

Worlds Before

Another type of creation story, the *emergence* story, tells of the creation, destruction, and recreation of many worlds. In these stories, the people were unable to live according to the Creator's plan, so the world had to be destroyed and remade. Only those who were faithful to the Creator's instructions were spared and journeyed to the next world.

Whatever the story, these creation myths address the first questions humanity must have had, even before they could form the words to ask, "Where did we come from?" and "Why are we here?"

Ancient Tales

When the Creator first made humans, he made four kinds, from red, black, white, and yellow clay. But he could not decide who should live here. Whoever lived here must be strong, hardy, and brave.

To decide, Creator devised a test. He commanded that each run through a gauntlet of arrows. The yellow, black, and white clay people, afraid of what might happen, refused. The Creator told them, "You do not have to do this. But you cannot live here, where life will be difficult. I have another place for you; a place that is more pleasant."

When at last came the turn of the red clay people, they did not hesitate but instead ran through the arrows. When they emerged out the other side, the Creator told them, "You have proven your bravery. This shall be your lands from now on."

So the Plains Indians have lived there ever since.

The Least You Need to Know

◆ The scientific community believes that the ancestors of Native Americans came across the Bering Strait from Asia.

◆ Other theories hold that American Indians came from Europe, Africa, or continents now lost.

◆ Each tribe has an account of their creation.

The Most Ancient Ones

In This Chapter

- What Paleo-Indian cultures were like
- Cultures in the Old Southwest
- Who built the mounds in the Midwest

Once the ancestors of the contemporary Natives got to this continent (by whatever theory you accept), they developed lifestyles and livelihoods that became unique to the Americas. The Native American cultures of today are built on cultures and civilizations that have arisen and fallen over thousands of years.

Often, the level of development of a people is measured by the technology that they possess. Historians chronicle the ages of "civilization" by referring to the "Stone Age," "Iron Age," and the "Bronze Age." People who use stone tools are often referred to as "primitive" in the most negative sense of that word—backward and brutish. However, simply because people use a more simple technology by no means makes them intellectually inferior.

Although the first residents of the Americas, the Paleo-Indians, used stone tools and weapons, they were far from primitive. Their skill at tool making, for example, was so sophisticated that no one today can reproduce the flint stone, obsidian blades, and projectile points they made. In this chapter, we'll uncover the history of some of these very early Natives.

Pass the Mammoth, Please

Some of the most ancient sites in North America belong to a Paleo-Indian *culture* called Clovis, after a site in New Mexico. These people lived some 11,000 years ago. The Clovis were big game hunters—and when you think big game, think *big!* They hunted mammoths, mastodons, giant bison, and camels, using spears tipped with finely crafted, fluted points that are now referred to as Clovis points.

Code Talking _____

A **culture** consists of beliefs, values, attitudes, and morals that a group of people holds in common.

Tribal Truths _____

Finding evidence of ancient cultures can be as easy as looking down at the ground! Lots of people collect "arrowheads" without knowing that these points are actually spear points or dart points (*not* arrowheads) and are more ancient than they think. More properly, these sharp stone tools are called "projectile points." The bow and arrow didn't show up in the Americas until 1,000 years ago.

Hunting 101: It's a Group Thing

The Paleo-Indian culture of the Folsom people (after a site near Folsom, New Mexico) became dominant about 8,000 B.C.E. Folsom hunters were still after the same game as the Clovis people, but the larger mammals were beginning to die out. They also developed new hunting techniques such as stampeding herds over cliffs or into swamps for easier kills. Also Folsom hunters used the atlatl, a spear-thrower consisting of a wooden stick about two feet in length that served as an extension of the hunter's arm, thereby giving greater distance and force to the throw.

Tribal Truths _____

The huge beasts, or mega-fauna, hunted by early humans included mammoths standing 14 feet high at the shoulders, slightly smaller mastodons, horses, super-size bison, and camels. Humans in the Americas competed with other meat eaters, such as the dire wolf, saber-tooth tiger, and bears bigger than any that now exist. Humans were both consumer and consumed.

These early people were followed by the rise and fall of other cultures, but little evidence remains of who these people were and what became of them. We do know that the large game they hunted became extinct, and other hunting groups that followed found life in North America difficult. Smaller foraging groups replaced the Paleo-Indian hunters, and these early Natives spread out over the landscape.

Ancient Civilizations—the Old Southwest

One of the most culturally rich areas in North America in ancient times was the American Southwest. This area includes present-day southern Utah, Colorado, Arizona, New Mexico, western Texas, and northern Mexico. Although many cultures made this region home, the most significant were the Mogollon, Hohokam, and the Anasazi.

Tribal Truths _____

In about 5000 B.C.E., maize (corn) was first cultivated in the Tehuacán Valley in central Mexico.

Newspaper Rock in Utah is a petroglyph panel etched in sandstone that records perhaps 2,000 years of human activity in the area.

(© Corbis)

The Mountain People of the Desert

The Mogollons ("Mountain People") are considered to be the first Southwestern people to adopt agriculture, house building, and pottery making. The heart of Mogollon (pronounced *muggy-own*) territory is the Mogollon range of mountains on the southern Arizona and New Mexico border. Mogollon culture began around 250 B.C.E. and ended about 1450 C.E. They are best known for their pit houses—semi-subterranean structures that included ceremonial centers called *kivas*. The Mogollon are also known for their Mimbres, or black-on-white pottery and textiles. Although scholars are not certain, they think that the present-day Zuni Indians may be, at least in part, composed of Mogollon descendants.

> **Code Talking** _____
>
> A **kiva** is a ceremonial structure used by the Indians of the Southwest, often built underground. A young man joined a kiva, where he learned the secrets of the religious society to which he now belonged. Men retired to the kiva for prayer and to prepare for their roles in community ceremonies.

Bringing Water to the Desert

The Hohokam (meaning "Vanished Ones" in the Pima language) were centered in the Gila and Salt River valleys of present-day Arizona. Their culture thrived from about 300 to around 1500 C.E. The Hohokam are best known for their use of irrigation. They built a system of canals to bring water to their fields of corn, beans, squash, tobacco, and cotton. They were such expert engineers that the city of Phoenix, Arizona, uses virtually the identical Hohokam plan for diverting water from the Salt River. For unknown reasons, the Hohokam abandoned their villages and scattered into small groups. It is thought that these small groups became the ancestors of the Pima and Tohono O'odham (Papago) peoples.

> **Code Talking** _____
>
> The **Anasazi** (from the Navajo or Diné language meaning "Ancient Ones") are one of the oldest cultures in the American Southwest. They are perhaps best known for their cliff dwellings, the most famous of these being Mesa Verde in Colorado.

> **Tribal Truths** _____
>
> In the present-day Four Corners area, more than 50,000 sites have been identified as Anasazi sites, with two great centers at Chaco Canyon and Mesa Verde.

City-Dwelling Desert People

Imagine an apartment complex with 800 rooms and home to 1,200 people. Where are you? New York? Chicago? Boston? Try Chaco Canyon, New Mexico, in the Four Corners region of the American Southwest. You'd be at Pueblo Bonito, the largest *Anasazi* village ever constructed, and the biggest apartment complex in what is now the United States, until a bigger one was built in New York City in the late 1900s!

The Anasazi, or Ancient Puebloans, are a people known for their elaborate villages; some, like Pueblo Bonito, were built on the desert floor and others, called cliff dwellings, like those found at Mesa Verde in southern Colorado, were constructed in the cliff sides above the deep canyons.

Cliff Palace, at Mesa Verde, Colorado, is the largest cliff dwelling in North America and was home to the Anasazi. It was inhabited around 1200 to 1300 C.E.

(© Corbis)

The Anasazi are the most geographically extensive culture in the arid desert West. Their culture evolved, beginning sometime about 100 B.C.E. and disappearing after 1300 C.E. No early Southwestern culture is better known than the Anasazi. They seemed to be particularly skilled in the use of precious desert water. They managed to farm perhaps some of the most inhospitable land imaginable, using subsurface irrigation, flooding, canal irrigation, and terracing.

Today, the descendants of the Anasazi live throughout Arizona and New Mexico and include the Hopi, Zuni, and other Rio Grande Pueblo peoples.

The Mound Builders

The mighty Mississippi River and its tributaries served as another major center of ancient culture. The Adena, Hopewell, and Mississippian people who lived in this region are best known for the hundreds of human-made mounds they left behind throughout the East.

The people who lived along the Mississippi River valley built mounds—hundreds and hundreds of mounds—burial mounds, temple mounds, and mounds shaped like animals.

The Effigy Mound Builders: Great Snakes Alive!

The first of these mound builders were the Adena and the Hopewellians. The Adena culture flourished between 1000 B.C.E. and 200 C.E., and the Hopewell culture existed from around 300 B.C.E. to 700 C.E. These early Natives radiated out from the Ohio

River Valley into what are now Kentucky, West Virginia, Indiana, Pennsylvania, and New York.

The Adena and Hopewell people were farmers. They cleared forests; prepared fields; and planted, cultivated, harvested, and stored at least seven different species of high-yield, high-nutrition seed crops like corn, squash, and beans.

Scholars believe they built and used their mounds for religious reasons, but their specific purposes are unclear. Some of these were burial mounds, thought to be the resting-places of priests or powerful Adena and Hopewell leaders, as common people were ordinarily cremated.

Code Talking

Effigy mounds were constructed to resemble an object, like a bird, bear, or snake.

One of the most famous of these mounds is the Great Serpent Mound in Adams County, Ohio, near Portsmouth. This *effigy mound* was made in the shape of a serpent swallowing an oval object, believed to represent the sun. The serpent is 1,254 feet long (four football fields in length!) and is 20 feet high in places. The meaning and symbolism of the Great Serpent Mound are still unknown.

Other than the artifacts they left behind, not much is known about Adena and Hopewell cultures. Based on the variety of objects, these people were evidently active traders. Copper from the Great Lakes, mica from the Carolinas, obsidian from Yellowstone Park, and shells from the Gulf of Mexico are common finds in burial mounds. These burial objects are seen as evidence of a highly complex and rich culture that was skilled in both representative and abstract artistry. Archaeologists have found ceramic figurines, copper headdresses, obsidian spearheads and knives, mica mirrors, incised pottery, and stone pipes shaped into animal and human figures. Historians believe that Adena and Hopewell societies were quite complex, because extensive cooperation and organization would have been needed to create such elaborate mounds.

No one knows what happened to the Adena and Hopewell peoples. Perhaps drought pushed them away, or invaders from other parts of the Americas forced them to abandon their villages. Perhaps they simply evolved into other peoples.

The Temple Mound Builders

The Mississippians replaced the Adena and Hopewell people. The Mississippians are often referred to as the *Temple Mound* builders because of the large, pyramidlike earthworks they built. The Mississippians inhabited the Missouri, Ohio, and Illinois River valleys.

The Mississippian culture lasted from about 700 to about 1700 C.E. and was active during early European exploration and settlement in the Americas. The culture had a highly organized social structure with leadership invested in a powerful chief. Perhaps more unique, the Mississippians had a ranked society with a complex religion that was sun-centered (that is, the sun was regarded as a deity or god). Some scholars have noted that the Mississippians might have been influenced by death rites of the Aztec, because some of the rituals appear to have involved human sacrifice.

Code Talking

Temple mounds are pyramid like mounds of earth with a flattened top upon which was erected a structure of worship.

Like the Adena and Hopewell people before them, Mississippi life was centered on agriculture, and their communities consisted of large walled towns and centers with civic-ceremonial mounds, as well as smaller villages. It appears that their earth pyramids served as burial places as well as temples, because some kind of religious structures were built on the flat tops of the mounds.

Tribal Truths

One Mississippian city, Cahokia, just east of St. Louis, Missouri, is thought to have had a population of about 20,000 to 30,000 at its peak in the early twelfth century.

Because the Mississippian culture existed into the eighteenth century, we know more about them than about many other ancient peoples. The French lived among the Natchez Indians, a Mississippian people who lived along the lower Mississippi River and recorded many of their ways of life firsthand. Their society, organized into what anthropologists call a chiefdom, was divided into two ranks: nobility and commoners. Membership in one rank or the other was determined by heredity through the female line, or by a system of matrilineal descent. The Natchez chief, called Great Sun, inherited his position of leadership from his mother's side of the family.

The Mississippian culture came to a close when, in 1729, the friendship between the French and Natchez soured. The French governor ordered the Natchez to evacuate their main village so that he could build a plantation on that site. Naturally, the Natchez resisted, and they killed the governor and some 200 of his men. The French struck back, killing many of the Natchez and enslaving the survivors, sending them to plantations on Santo Domingo in the Caribbean. With the demise of the Natchez culture, Mississippian culture came to an end.

Building on the Ruins of the Past

These old settlers left many artifacts and ruins behind. We can visit their remaining villages, houses, and temples. Unfortunately, scholars can only guess at what their beliefs were or how they lived their daily lives. No one today knows about their customs or has heard their languages. But there is no doubt that the tribes that live in the homelands of these ancient peoples built their cultures on their developments. Their gifts to agriculture alone allowed more recent tribes to survive. These ancient ones are the foundations upon which contemporary cultures were built.

The Least You Need to Know

◆ The Clovis and Folsom cultures were among the oldest in America.

◆ In the American Southwest, the Mogollons were among the earliest farmers, house builders, and potters.

◆ The Hohokams brought water to the desert Southwest via a vast network of canals, some of which are still in use today.

◆ The Anasazi, who are probably the ancestors of the Pueblo tribes, built the cliff dwellings and large apartment complexes in the Southwest.

◆ The Adena and Hopewell cultures built the effigy mounds thought to be representations of spirit beings and animals.

◆ The Mississippian cultures built temple mounds, large pyramidlike earth mounds upon which they erected religious buildings for worship.

Chapter 4

Where and How They Lived

In This Chapter

- ◆ What makes up a culture area
- ◆ The influence of geography
- ◆ The 10 culture areas

The political history of North America has dramatically (and negatively) impacted the culture of its original inhabitants. It's important to know what kind of culture existed before Euro-Americans arrived to get an idea of how contact with the non-Indian world affected Indian lives.

Native American culture is a *huge* subject, representing many aspects of life, including what foods people ate, the kinds of tools and objects they created, their religious beliefs, the language they spoke, their social organization, and the community's political structure—in other words, how they lived. No single book can adequately cover all aspects of Native ways of life. In this chapter, I will be able to sketch only a few details of these cultures for you.

To Each His and Her Own

As Native peoples spread out across the landscape, they settled in places they eventually called home. As these people adapted themselves to each new environment, they developed new ways of living. These ways include customs and traditions that reflected their beliefs, attitudes, and values.

Code Talking

In the study of Native Americans, it's easier to divide the Americas into geographic regions. Because environment determines many ways of life, tribes within each division share a significant number of cultural traits. The different geographic regions, therefore, define and delineate **culture areas**.

People didn't live in isolation, of course. Tribes were influenced not only by the cultures they brought with them, but also by the ways of life of their neighbors. Thus, cultures that shared the same environments, or *culture areas*, developed similar beliefs and customs. However, just because two tribes are found in the same culture area, it doesn't mean that their customs are going to be exactly the same!

There are 10 culture areas in North America: Arctic, Subarctic, Plateau, Northwest Coast, California, Great Basin, Southwest, Plains, Northeast, and Southeast. Each is unique and complex. To explore each culture area completely would take a lifetime of study, so we'll just hit the highlights.

Native North American culture areas.

(© Dale Martin)

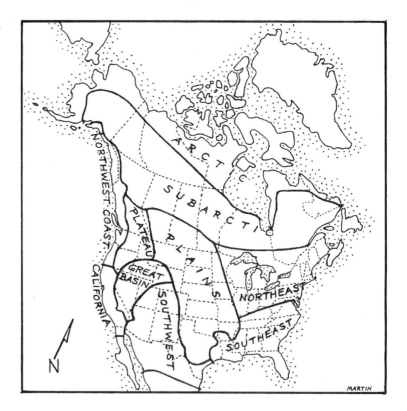

The Land of Ice and Snow: The Arctic

When people think of the Arctic, they typically imagine an empty, hostile landscape, home only to polar bears, reindeer, and Santa Claus. It's hard to picture people living in such a harsh environment. Perhaps not surprising, most folks know very little about the indigenous cultures of this frigid land.

A Desert of Cold

The Arctic culture area is the largest, spreading over 5,000 miles, from the Siberian side of the Bering Sea in the West to Greenland in the East.

It's a treeless land of ice and snow where it's dark for three or four months each year. It's a place where survival is always in question—the last place to expect people to live and thrive.

Surprisingly, there is little snowfall in the arctic. The snow that does fall is wind driven by winter gales and forms deep drifts. The dominant feature of the Arctic is the cold. In the interior, the winter temperatures seldom rise above 0° Fahrenheit and often stay at −50° Fahrenheit for days at a time.

Summer offers a little relief. The temperature does reach above freezing—but not long enough to thaw much ground. This is a land of permafrost, that permanently frozen layer of subsoil. The topsoil that does thaw in the summer turns into a muddy mire over the permafrost.

Tribal Truths _____

Have you ever heard the expression that something was as difficult as selling refrigerators to the Eskimos? That's supposed to represent selling the impossible, yet refrigerators in the Arctic and subarctic are essential—not to keep food cold, but to keep it from freezing!

Tribal Truths _____

Eskimo is an eastern Ojibwa or Algonquian word meaning "those who eat their meat raw." *Inuit* means "The People."

The Late Arrivals

The major peoples of the Arctic are the Eskimo (or Inuit and Yuit) and their relatives, the Aleut. As noted in Chapter 2, scientists believe they crossed the Bering Strait during the last migration about 4,000 to 6,000 years ago.

Language: Complexity and Simplicity

Despite the separation of great distances, the Inuit speak a language mutually intelligible from one end of the Arctic to the other. That doesn't mean that all Eskimo speak exactly the same language, but their languages are similar enough that they can understand each other. Inupik is spoken north of Nome, Alaska, and extending across Canada to Greenland, while Yupik is spoken south from Nome. Dialectic differences aside, for the most part, the Eskimo language remains vital and intact.

> **Tribal Truths** _____
>
> Do the Eskimo really have 57 different words for the single English word *snow*? Arctic legend holds that the Eskimo have to be able to communicate precise snow conditions for survival's sake. The Eskimo language does recognize differences for falling snow, drifting snow, snow on the ground, and so forth. But the list of different words doesn't approach 57. Conclusion? Maybe not 57, but certainly more than in English.

What's for Dinner?

The eastern Inuit subsisted primarily by hunting seals from kayaks, while the central Eskimo hunted seals out on the sea ice. The Inuit people of Alaska hunted whales, seals, and walrus. In the interior, the people herded reindeer.

Home and Family in the Arctic

While the Inuit people are often associated with the igloo or snowhouse, those in the central are most closely identified with its use. Even among those people, the snowhouse was a temporary winter dwelling. The people along the Alaskan coast lived in permanent villages in houses made of sod and wood. Each house was occupied by an extended family spanning three or four generations.

The basic social units were the nuclear family and the extended family, a husband and wife and their children and other relatives. A major trait of Inuit social organization was the partnership. A man might establish a partnership with another in a different area, providing opportunities for trade and cooperative hunting.

Befriending the Spirit World

The Inuit had a complex ceremonial system that recognized spirit forces that inhabited humans and other animals. Rites focused mainly on placating the animals spirits to ensure success in hunting.

Shamanism played an important part of Inuit life. *Shamans* (most often men) called upon spirit guides to control the weather, influence animal behavior, cure (and cause) illness, and see into the future. Because such medicine people, as they are sometimes called, were so powerful, they were greatly respected as well as feared.

Code Talking

A **shaman** is a person who is in direct contact with the spirit world, usually through a trance state. A shaman relies on the assistance of spirit helpers to carry out curing, divining, and bewitching.

Tribal Truths

Anthropologists have often characterized Eskimo shamans as mad—schizophrenics who use threats and the fear of the unknown to control people. They have suggested that some shamans suffer from a form of "arctic hysteria," madness induced by isolation and long winters. Real medicine people are the recipients of great gifts: knowledge, power, or extraordinary ability.

The World and Ways of the Aleuts

The Aleut people also make the Arctic their home. The Aleutian archipelago stretches some 1,000 miles south and west from Alaska's coast. The Aleutian chain consists of nearly 100 islands, some inhabited, but most not.

The Aleuts are related to the Eskimo, as evidenced by the similarities between their languages. Like many Eskimo groups, the Aleuts derived much of their subsistence from the sea, and their clothing, made from sea mammals, is similar to Eskimo clothing.

Unlike the Eskimo, however, the Aleuts lived in more permanent villages and had a society ranked by social class. Each island and village had a chief, a person of wealth and social status who owned many slaves (captured from nearby villages in intertribal raiding).

The Subarctic: A World Below and Above

The subarctic, which covers most of Canada and the interior of Alaska, is home to many different tribes belonging to two major language families. The Algonquian speakers, such as the Cree and Anishinabe (Ojibaw), live in the eastern subarctic (eastern Canada); and the Athabascans, such as the Kutchin, Slave, and Dogrib tribes, are associated with the western subarctic (western Canada and Alaska).

Living With the Caribou

The lives of most subarctic people revolved around the caribou, their most important food source. Men hunted the caribou using a surround method where they formed a ring of hunters around the herd, or they sometimes drove the animals into traps or enclosures. The women dried the meat to preserve it for future use.

The subarctic peoples were mobile, following the caribou and other migratory game. There were no permanent villages, nor did they build permanent housing structures, with the exception of some interior Alaskan tribes, who built permanent houses of logs or plants. The Naskapi in northern Quebec lived in tipis, some covered with caribou hides but others with birch bark.

There was no political structure outside the kin organization. An older man acted as group leader when decisions such as when and where to move needed to be made.

Cannibals, Monsters, and Curing

Subarctic beliefs and ceremonies were fairly simple. Their religious attitude reflected a belief in the existence of animal spirits. One prominent belief, particularly among Naskapi, Cree, and Anishinabe, involved the Windigo or cannibal monster. This being was thought to infect people with the desire to consume human flesh. It is possible that this belief originated from actual acts of cannibalism that took place during times of starvation.

Anishinabe religion had an organized association known as the Midewiwin or Great Medicine Society. It was a religious and curing organization open to men and women by initiation. Initiates would have visions and communicate with the supernatural, which then would guide their lives.

Reaching the Plateau

The Plateau is a highland area bordered in the west by the Cascade Mountains, with the Rocky Mountains serving as the eastern boundary. This area is a transition zone between the northwest coast to the west, the desert in the south, and the plains to the east. As such, peoples of the Plateau have much in common with their neighbors. Because of neighboring influences, Plateau culture is difficult to summarize.

The tribes of the Plateau include the Flathead, Kalispel, and Nez Perce in the East and the Klamath and Yakima in the West.

The Columbia and the Fraser river systems dominated the region and were integral for trade. Plateau traders, in dugout canoes, carried seashells to the Plains tribes and buffalo hides to coastal tribes.

Tribal Truths

Cultural influences inevitably accompanied trade to the Plateau. The Plateau tribes acquired the horse by trade and quickly took to horse raising. The Nez Perces became perhaps the most expert horse breeders of all Native peoples. The Cayuses, whose name was widely used to refer to all Indian ponies, were successful horse traders. The Palouse River Indians of the Plateau bred one of the best-known breeds of horse, the Appaloosa.

Basket Weaving 101

The Plateau was not known as an agricultural region. Most of the food production was centered on fishing (particularly salmon), hunting, and gathering. The Cayuse and Nez Perce women made cornhusk baskets, but these are more recent modifications from the root and grass twined bags of ancient times. Plateau tribes lived in independent village communities. These villages, rather than the tribe, were the main political units. Although hereditary leaders headed some tribes, a headman or chief who served so long as good fortune followed the village governed most communities.

Plateau religion was influenced most by the Plains tribes, and both shared the belief in spirit helpers provided by the supernatural. Like their neighbors, Plateau people sought spiritual guidance through *vision quests*.

Code Talking

The **vision quest** is not a manhood rite, although young men are encouraged to seek visions, some as early as nine years old. Men will seek visions throughout their lifetimes. Women do not deliberately seek visions, although they can receive spiritual guidance through dreams and during menstrual seclusion.

The Northwest Coast: A Bountiful Land

The Northwest Coast is an area of great abundance and wealth. Tribes who lived in this region enjoyed not only the salmon, but also halibut, trout, cod herring, smelt, and eulachon, or candlefish, so called because it was unusually rich in oil. The sea also provided whales, seals, sea otters, clams, mussels, and sea urchins. The mountains of the Northwest Coast were home to bears, deer, elk, mountain goats, wolves, and beaver. Not wanting for sources of food, the people of the Northwest Coast developed a rich social structure and elaborate rituals.

> ### Tribal Truths
>
> The people of the Northwest Coast, the Tlingit, Kwakiutls, Chinook, among others, believed that the salmon were a benevolent race of beings who lived in human form in the ocean. Once a year, the Salmon People transformed themselves into fish and offered themselves up to earth-dwelling people for food. If the human beings treated the Salmon People with gratitude, by proper ceremony and by respectfully returning their bones to the rivers to be carried back to the sea, the Salmon People would return again and again.

Acquiring Wealth to Give It Away

The Northwest Coastal people settled their villages along rivers or beachfronts that literally brought food, in the form of fish, right to their doorsteps. These villages were home to as many as 1,000 people who lived in large cedar-plank houses. These living quarters were impressive. They were built as multifamily dwellings, home to several generations of extended family members.

Rank and status heavily influenced Northwest Coastal society. A person's social position was a product of wealth, heredity, and his or her individual achievements. One was born into a clan and enjoyed the status of the clan. At times the people held *potlatches*, elaborate ceremonies sometimes lasting for days, to feast their guests and show off their wealth. Unlike their European counterparts and most societies today, status was earned by *sharing* wealth; the more one acquired, the more one had to give away. After a potlatch, the clan may have had no material wealth remaining, having given it all way, yet they gained status by their generosity.

> ### Code Talking
>
> **Potlatches** are ceremonial giveaways that were used to gain status. The term comes from the Chinook verb "to give." Potlatches were sometimes competitive, in which one clan put up its wealth against another, either giving away or destroying all their material possessions to demonstrate how wealthy they were. The focus wasn't on the possessions themselves; they were just measures of how generous one could be.

Tribal Truths

Totem poles serve many purposes. Some marked burial places for important chiefs. Others were portals or doors to the cedar-plank houses or to identify the clan. Figures on a totem pole included the Thunderbird, Sea Wolf, Bear, and Raven, each representing an important source of power and prestige. So there's nothing wrong with being the low man on the totem pole!

The Great Basin: A Tough Place to Make a Living

The Great Basin is that large area between the Sierra Nevada range in the West to the Rocky Mountains in the East and includes the present states of southern Oregon and southern Idaho, Nevada, Utah, and western Colorado. The region is home to a number of tribes, including the Washo, Paiute, Shoshone, Bannock, and Ute.

Life in the Great Basin was a constant challenge. The Natives lived in small family groups around lakes, streams, and springs. The camp usually consisted of one or two nuclear families, sometimes including grandparents. These family groups sometimes combined to form larger hunting units, but for the most part, Great Basin peoples lived in disbursed groups.

Tribal Truths

The Utes and Paiutes eked out a living hunting small game such as rabbits and lived in simple houses made from brush or reeds over a willow frame. They differ sharply from the Aztecs, who established a great civilization. Yet the Utes and Aztecs are related to one another and belong to the Uto-Aztecan language family. As the old saying goes, location, location, location.

They relied mostly on hunting and gathering, although some did practice agriculture. The women harvested cattail reeds, dug edible roots, and picked berries. The men fished and hunted ducks at the nearby lakes. Some groups organized communal hunts of rabbit or antelope but more typically practiced solitary hunting.

Pinon nuts (also called pine nuts, although they are really seeds) provided a major source of food for some Great Basin tribes. Several groups of related families gathered these tasty nuts in the fall. They could be eaten raw but were often cooked or ground into flour for making bread or mush.

Because so much energy was devoted to survival and because the social units were characteristically small, the Great Basin tribes didn't have a complex religious system. There were few ceremonies, and much of the religious activity was individual, consisting of seeking power though a spirit helper that appeared in a vision or dream. The Round Dance, a ceremony that celebrates the symbolic remaking of the world, took place around the harvesting of pinon nuts. The Round Dance was both religious and social in nature. The Utes performed a more elaborate 10-day ceremony called the Bear Dance, designed to ensure good fortune from the bears.

> **Tribal Truths**
>
> The Ghost Dance originated in the Great Basin. In the 1880s, a Paiute mystic named Wovoka (called Jack Wilson by non-Indians) had a vision that the world would renew itself, the buffalo would return, Indians would be reunited with their dead relatives, and the whites would go away, leaving North America as it was before they came.
>
> Wovoka taught the people the Ghost Dance, whereby followers danced until they fell into a trance and were reunited with their deceased kindred. The Ghost Dance spread to many western tribes but virtually ended when U.S. soldiers surrounded a Lakota band and then opened fire, killing many in an incident now known as the Massacre at Wounded Knee. After the Massacre, Natives became disillusioned because the Creator had seemingly forsaken his children and did not prevent their deaths (see Chapter 15 for more about the Ghost Dance).

California, Here We Come!

It seems that people have always been attracted to California. The climate is mild and there is plenty of food and water. That's probably why Native peoples who first came to this region at least 12,000 years ago settled there.

The California culture region is one of the most diverse in North America. It is home to more than 60 different tribal groups. Among the more familiar California tribes are the Shasta, Hupa, Yurok, Pomo, and Chumash.

Nuts to You!

The California culture region was richer in food resources than any other area in North America except the Northwest Coast. Agriculture, therefore, held no appeal to the California tribes—wild food was so readily available that farming would have required more labor than it was worth!

To some California tribes, acorns were a major food staple. The women gathered the nuts in the fall and stored them for later use. They often ground the nuts into a fine powder, leached the flour with water to eliminate the bitter flavor, then used it to make breads and mush.

The California tribes also ate grass seeds, roots, and berries as well as smaller game, such as deer and rabbits. Tribes in regions where elk and antelope were plentiful hunted larger game, while tribes along the coast ate seals, sea lions, shellfish, salmon, and other marine and freshwater fish. Because of the rich natural resources of the California region, the Natives established elaborate trade networks and utilized shell beads as money.

The social structure of the California tribes was strongly influenced by lineages, or lines of descent. Many tribes had a highly complex clan system with social rank established through heredity and wealth, and many groups maintained a class structure.

Jumping for Joy

Religion in the California culture region was centered around highly complex ceremonies. The White Deerskin Dance and the Jumping Dance were the principal ceremonies of the Hupas and Yuroks. Each ceremony lasted 10 days and was used to revitalize the world for the year ahead and to prevent illness and misfortune.

Tribes in southern California, like the Luiseno, held initiation ceremonies for young men that included the drinking of a potion made from jimsonweed. The concoction induced visions, from which a young man acquired his own personal guardian spirit.

Tribal Truths

In August 1911, a 54-year-old Indian stepped out of the brush in northern California and into history. Ishi, as he became known, was the last surviving member of the Yahi Indian tribe. Ishi (the Yahi word for "man") had been living the traditional way of life of the Yahi people long after the other California tribes adapted to the reservation system. Ishi lived at the Anthropology Museum of the University of California from 1911 until his death in 1916, sharing his knowledge about his language, culture, and beliefs with any who wished to learn.

The Southwest

The Southwest is the land of the Grand Canyon, Painted Desert, Rio Grande, and the Colorado River. This is a beautiful but harsh land, with boiling heat, bitter cold, and little rainfall. Yet here are the oldest continuously occupied settlements in North America. Here lived perhaps the oldest peoples of North America.

Peaceful Ones

The Hopi, whose name means "Peaceful Ones," have lived in the Southwest since time before memory. One of the main Hopi villages, Oraibi, Arizona, is nearly 1,000 years old. Here, the Hopi have followed their peaceful life of raising crops in the dry soil as an act of faith. When the Hopi were first given corn, they selected the smallest ear and accepted the challenge of bringing life out of the seemingly lifeless desert.

The Hopi believe that there were three worlds that were created and destroyed before this one. Humans in the previous worlds forgot the teachings of Creator, and fire, ice, and flood destroyed those worlds. The Hopi believe that they emerged from the World Below into this world through a hole symbolically built into their ceremonial and meeting chamber, called a kiva (see Chapter 3). This passage between the World Below and the earth is the *sipapu*.

Code Talking

The **sipapu** is a hole in the bottom of a kiva that represents the route taken when the ancient ones emerged from the prior world into this world.

The Hopi are not alone in Southwest. The Navajo, Apache, Pueblo, Pima, and Papago or Tohono O'odham, among others, share this desert homeland.

Planters and Herdsmen

The Southwest peoples are usually divided into two groups: Pueblo tribes and non-Pueblo people. The Pueblo peoples are sedentary farmers who lived in permanent towns (*pueblo* means "village" in Spanish). The non-Pueblo people include the Apache groups, the Navajo, the Pima, and Tohono O'odham.

Code Talking

The term **Pueblo** has many meanings. Coming from the Spanish word for "village," it means exactly that. When applied to a Native community, a pueblo refers to the 19 communities mainly in New Mexico such as Laguna, Isleta, Zuni, and Santa Clara. The Pueblos share a common tradition but are distinctive entities, or nations, unto themselves.

The Pueblo groups are generally divided into two major groups: Western and Eastern Pueblos. The Western Pueblos were to the west of the Rio Grande Valley and include the Hopi, Zuni, Acoma, and Laguna. The Western Pueblos share some cultural traits, including matrilineal clans and religious beliefs that focused on agriculture. Western Pueblo settlements tended to consist of multistoried, apartment-like complexes atop high mesas or hills.

The Eastern Pueblos are located along the Rio Grande in New Mexico. They tend not to have clans and have ceremonies centered on hunting and warfare. Eastern Pueblo villages tend to be single structures built around a central plaza. The Spanish destroyed many of the Eastern Pueblos, but many are still inhabited, including Jémez, Santa Domingo, Santa Ana, Taos, Isleta, San Illdefonso, Santa Clara, and others.

Newcomers to the Southwest

One of the latecomers to the Southwest is the Navajo or Diné ("The People"). It is believed that the Navajo did not arrive in their present homeland until around the late fifteenth century. As suggested by their language family, Athabaskan, the Navajo originated in the subarctic culture region and migrated southward.

Clan Mothers, Clan Fathers

The core of the Navajo social structure is the clan, of which there are approximately 60. Clan membership is established through the mother's side (matrilineal), and property and certain other rights are passed down through the female lines.

Unlike other Southwestern people, the Navajo avoided village life, preferring to settle in family units clustered several miles from their nearest neighbors. Unlike their Pueblo neighbors, the Navajos raised sheep rather than farmed.

Tribal Truths

When a Navajo man married, he moved into the home of his wife and became the overseer of her property. But he did not own this property, for, according to Navajo custom, the goods were handed down from mother to daughter in an unbroken line.

A World in Balance

Deeply religious, the Navajo based their beliefs on the concept of *hozho*, a word that translates roughly as "beauty," "balance," or "harmony." Hozho is that state of being by which all Navajo strive to live, that balance between good and evil. Illness is thought to be the product of an imbalance in one's life that must be corrected through ceremony. These ceremonies are elaborate and are meant to place the patient back into the state of "beauty" though the use of songs, rituals, and *sandpaintings*.

Code Talking

Sandpaintings are dry pictures painted with colored sand depicting images from Navajo mythology. A patient is placed upon the sandpainting in order to draw the power of the image, thereby facilitating the curing of illness. Following the ceremony, the paintings are destroyed.

Thriving Today

Today, there are approximately 125,000 Navajo, making them the second largest tribe in the United States (after the Cherokee). The Navajo live on the largest reservation in the United States, an area of 26,000 square miles in western New Mexico, southern Utah, and northern Arizona.

Warriors, Hunters, and Vision Seekers: The Plains

When one thinks of an American Indian, the first image that springs to mind is probably that of a mounted warrior wearing a feathered bonnet, dressed in buffalo- and deer-hide clothing, carrying a lance and shield. Certainly, this image doesn't represent all Native peoples of the Americas, but it does represent the Plains Indians. They have come to symbolize Indian people in the eyes of many. This is no doubt in part because the Plains Indians fought so resolutely to resist the advance of Euro-Americans during the nineteenth century.

The Plains is one of the largest and culturally diverse areas in North America. It extends from the Rocky Mountains in the West, to the Mississippi River in the East, and from central Manitoba in Canada south to the Panhandle region of Texas. The major characteristic of the Plains is the short grass—home to a wealth of game, most notably the bison.

But We're Here Now!

Culturally, the Plains Indians have varied origins. Some tribes entered the Plains from the Great Lakes region, while others moved onto the Plains from the Ohio Valley. Whatever the case, tribes who moved onto the Plains quickly adopted a new lifestyle, now characteristic of such tribes as the Blackfeet, Lakota (Sioux), Cheyenne, and Pawnee.

> **Tribal Truths**
>
> The American buffalo is not a true buffalo, like the Asian Water buffalo and the African Cape buffalo. Its scientific name is bison, and it belongs to the bovine family along with domestic cattle.

Although some tribes like the Mandan, Oto, Hidasta, and Caddo were primarily sedentary farmers, the majority of Plains tribes were mobile, following the vast bison herds. Even tribes who raised corn and squash supplemented their diets by hunting bison.

People on the Move

Their cultures were reflected in that mobile lifestyle. The principal dwelling, the *tipi*, was designed to be easily and quickly moved. Plains Indians tended to travel in bands or hunting units to take advantage of communal hunting techniques. Typically, the tribe separated into autonomous bands with a population of 300 to 500 people during the winter and reunited during the summer months for communal hunting and to hold religious ceremonies.

Code Talking

The word *tipi* is a Dakota word meaning "dwelling." It is a conical-shaped tent made from buffalo hides stretched around a pole frame. Tipis and ceremonial structures are always faced with the entrance to the east, the place of the rising sun. This is to welcome the spirit beings of the east to enter into one's home and bless it.

The tipi was an ideal home for the mobile Plains tribes. The women could put it up in about half an hour and take it down in 15 minutes.

(© Corbis)

Gazing at the Sun

The principal Plains ceremony is the sun dance. The ceremony does not recognize the sun as a deity; rather, the name comes from the Lakota phrase for the ceremony, *Wiwanyag Wacipi*, which means "gazing at the sun, they danced." The sun dance is a four-day ceremony during which participants fast, drink no water, and dance to fulfill vows they have made or to secure the blessings of the supernatural for the year to come.

While many Plains tribes practice a ceremony that is called a sun dance, each tribe tends to focus on some feature unique to that tribe. The Cheyenne call the ceremony the Medicine Lodge ceremony and focus on world renewal. The Crow used their sun dance to prepare for warfare. All tribes believe the sun dance is a powerful ceremony for healing.

The Plains Indians believe that the supernatural beings can bestow wondrous gifts on humankind. A person might actively seek this power by "questing," going off to an isolated place, usually on a mountaintop or butte to pray and fast. Should the supernatural take pity on the seeker, he or she will secure the blessings of deity.

The Northeast: Home of the Iroquois

The Northeast is sometimes referred to the Woodlands area because a vast deciduous forest of maple, birch, oak, hickory, elm, and willow dominates it. The boundaries of the Northeast are vague, but it begins east of the Mississippi River and includes what is now New England, the Atlantic states as far south as Virginia, the Ohio Valley, the Great Lakes, and Canadian territory about 100 miles north of Lake Erie and Ontario. It is a region with cold, snowy winters and hot summers.

Tribal Truths

The term *Iroquois* does not specifically refer to a tribe but rather to a language family and a confederation of tribes. If someone identifies him or herself as "Iroquois," you'd better ask "What tribe?"

The Northeast is home to several tribes, and the best known are the *Iroquois*, who lived in what is now northern New York State, notably the Seneca, Cayuga, Onondaga, Oneida, Mohawk (and later the Tuscarora) tribes. These tribes formed a confederacy known as the Iroquois League (see Chapter 7).

People of the Longhouse

The Northeastern tribes were primarily farmers and lived in quasi-permanent, often palisaded villages located near the growing fields. People lived in multifamily dwellings known as longhouses, large log homes up to 200 feet long. The interior was divided into a number of two-room sections, each with its own fireplace around which a single family resided. Up to 25 people might live in a longhouse, all members of a matrilineage.

A Woman's Place

Women had a great deal of power among those tribes. Clan mothers selected leaders, and women owned all property. Women decided on issues related to war and peace, and the clan mothers held great influence within their respected families.

Green Corn and False Faces

The Native peoples of the Northeast conducted many ceremonies, including those for curing, thanksgiving, and world renewal. One of the better known is the Green Corn Ceremony held at the beginning of the corn harvest to celebrate and give thanks for a bountiful year. Until this ceremony was completed, no corn could be eaten. Some Iroquois groups had masked ceremonies, the best known of which is the False Face Society. False Face clowns exorcise illness and evil during the spring and fall festivals.

The Southeast: The "Five Civilized Tribes"

The Southeast culture area extends from the Mississippi Valley to the Atlantic coast, and from the Ohio Valley south to the Gulf of Mexico. Perhaps this area is better thought of as the Old South, as it includes what are known as the southern states of the United States.

The major tribes of the Southeast include those best known as the "Five Civilized Tribes," specifically the Chactaw, Chickasaw, Cherokee, Creek, and Seminole. The "civilized tribes" appellation came into common use after these people were removed from the Southwest to what is now Oklahoma in the 1830s. The Cherokees and the others were "civilized" compared to tribes like the Cheyenne and Arapaho.

Almost all Southeastern people lived in towns along rivers and streams. As in the Northeast, these people were farmers. The division of labor was fairly strict. Men hunted and practiced warfare but assisted in clearing fields and harvesting crops, and women were the primary farmers, but these gender roles were considered complementary and not conflicting.

Tribal Truths

Some scholars don't divide the eastern part of the United States into separate culture regions, but there is certain logic to doing so. After all, the geography of the East is varied, as are the indigenous cultures.

Honored Women

Men didn't dominate or control women, and women had some influence over the political process. For example, each of the seven Cherokee clans was represented to the tribal council by an Honored Woman who spoke for the clan. These seven Honored Women sat in the tribal council and had many responsibilities. The Beloved Woman was the spokeswoman for the seven. The role of Beloved Woman, or Ghighua, was a prestigious title given to extraordinary women and the highest status to which a Cherokee woman could aspire.

Tribal Truths _____

In the Northeast and the Southeast, the role of women was decidedly more honored than non-Indian scholars tend to report. Here, women openly debated and lent their opinions on issues of the day. Women held important posts in religious and social institutions and generally were considered equal to men in nearly every way. In fact, Native women had rights in their societies that their non-Indian counterparts would not enjoy until well into the twentieth century.

Many People, Many Cultures

The point of this chapter is simple: The many tribes in the Americas have unique cultures and histories. Yes, there are similarities between the customs and traditions of tribes, but there are many, many differences as well. Even within the same tribe there are variations of beliefs and practices.

This point was often lost on Euro-Americans. The history of Native America is replete with examples where the U.S. government applied policies as if American Indians constituted a single tribe or culture. Now you know that's definitely not true!

The Least You Need to Know

- ◆ Native American tribes are grouped into geographic regions called culture areas.
- ◆ Culture is a complex set of values, beliefs, attitudes, mores, and traditions.
- ◆ There are 10 culture regions in North America.
- ◆ The U.S. government often treated all Native people as though they were one tribe.

Part 2

There Goes the Neighborhood

The first Europeans who came to the "New World" knew nothing about the original inhabitants of the land and so often misunderstood Native peoples and their culture. The Europeans stayed and established colonies, from which they extended their reach farther into the interior of the Americas.

Part 2 explores the tension created as Euro-Americans began to stake claims on land already occupied by Native peoples. As America grew, it reached farther West, exploring from one ocean to the other. And as its population grew, the demand for land caused conflict between the Natives and settlers and began a long and ugly pattern of Indian relocation.

Chapter

5

First Contacts: The Spanish and the French

In This Chapter

- ◆ Who Columbus "discovered"
- ◆ The Spanish leave a legacy of destruction
- ◆ The French establish alliances with the Indians

"In fourteen hundred ninety two, Columbus sailed the ocean blue." So begins the popular children's song about the so-called "discovery" of the New World by Christopher Columbus. As a result of this seemingly heroic deed, the United States celebrates the accomplishments of Columbus each October 12.

But from the Native point of view, Columbus began an invasion. Spain began the exploration, exploitation, and conquest of the so-called New World. France and Great Britain soon followed, until all of the Americas were claimed by European interlopers, driven by the search for wealth.

The Invasion and Conquest of the Americas

The history of the penetration of North America can be divided into two general stages. The sixteenth century might be called the Spanish stage, with Spain being most active in mounting expeditions in the West Indies, Central America, and South America, as well as incursions into the American Southeast and Southwest. The second stage, in the seventeenth century, begins with French explorations along the Atlantic coast, along the St. Lawrence, Ohio, and Mississippi Rivers, and into the Great Lakes.

The motive for these early explorers was the same: to claim lands and the riches of those lands for God and country.

The Natives Discover Columbus

At 2 P.M. on October 12, 1492, Rodrigo de Triana sighted land somewhere in the Bahama Islands. Shortly thereafter, the first white men of record stepped into the lives of Native peoples in the Americas.

When Columbus "discovered" the New World, he didn't happen onto an empty land. In 1492, there were more than 400 independent nations inhabiting territories on the North American continent. These nations, or tribes, had their own governments, cultures, and languages, as well as their own rich histories. The first act of Columbus, and a presumptuous one at that, was to label the natives "Los Indios," for he thought, incorrectly, that he had landed in the West Indies.

There's no conclusive evidence to determine just how many Native peoples lived in North America before Columbus. Some scholars have estimated a population of as few as 2 million, while others put the *pre-Columbian* population in excess of 18 million. The most widely accepted estimate is 7 million. Add to that the Natives of Mexico, Central America, and South America, where agriculture supported larger populations, and this gives a figure of approximately 75 to 100 million for the Western Hemisphere as a whole (compare this with around 70 million for Europe at the same time).

> **Tribal Truths**
>
> King Ferdinand and Queen Isabella promised a large reward to the first person to sight land. At around 10 P.M. on October 11, 1492, Columbus saw a faint light. Based on that observation, the admiral claimed the reward. The light couldn't have been land, however, because at that point, they were 35 miles from shore. Being in charge certainly has its privileges!

> **Code Talking**
>
> **Pre-Columbian** usually refers to that time before Native peoples had contact with Europeans. For the Arawak, a pre-Columbian time is before 1492. The Salish of Montana didn't have contact with Euro-Americans until they met Lewis and Clark; therefore, pre-Columbian time for them is before 1805. Because of the potential confusion of this term, I prefer "pre-contact," meaning before contact with Euro-Americans.

Columbus's first impressions of the so-called "New World" and its inhabitants suggest that he found paradise:

> So tractable, so peaceful are these people, that I swear to your Majesties there is no better nation on Earth. They love their neighbors as themselves, and their discourse is ever sweet and gentle, and accompanied with a smile, and though it is true that they are naked, yet their manners are decorous and praiseworthy.

"Send All the Slaves That Can Be Sold"

The intent of the Spanish was not to admire the New World, however, but to exploit it. Columbus pointed out to King Ferdinand and Queen Isabella, his Spanish sponsors, the commercial potential of his "discovery." The people of Hispaniola (the modern island of Haiti and the Dominican Republic) were trusting and docile, just the right qualities to make excellent slaves. "From (Hispaniola)," he opined, "in the name of the Blessed Trinity, we can send all the slaves that can be sold."

Tribal Truths

The people Columbus first encountered were the Arawak (sometimes mistakenly called the Taino) who lived on the chain of islands that constitute the Antilles and Bahamas. Although no longer living on most islands of the Caribbean, there is still a population of Arawak in Cuba.

 Native Voices

There was once a Lakota holy man, called Drinks Water, who dreamed what was to be; and this was long before the coming of the Wasichus [white men]. He dreamed that the four-leggeds were going back into the earth and that a strange race had woven a spider's web all around the Lakotas. And he said: "When this happens, you shall live in square gray houses, in a barren land, and beside those square gray houses you shall starve."

They say he went back to Mother Earth soon after he saw this vision, and it was sorrow that killed him.

—Black Elk, Oglala (Sioux)

For God and Gold, but Not Necessarily in That Order

The Spanish needed slaves to work the gold mines and the fields. Columbus established a colony on Hispaniola on his second voyage in 1494 and shipped a sizable amount of gold back to Spain. By 1515, there were 17 Spanish towns on the island.

Besides the mines, the Spanish established plantations to grow cotton, sugar cane, and grain, all by the labor of enslaved Indians.

The Caribbean Natives didn't take well to slavery. Contemporary scholars estimate that in 1492 there were between 2 and 4 million Natives on Hispaniola. By 1520, that number had fallen to just 20,000. This precipitous decline was caused by the extreme cruelty of the Spanish colonials as well as exposure to many unfamiliar diseases, against which the Natives had no resistance.

Souls for the Taking

The Spanish believed it was their right and duty to subdue the Natives. Spanish law required the conquistadors—Spanish explorers—to read to the Indians the *Requerimiento*. This document, written by theologians in 1513, required the Indians to "acknowledge the Church as the Ruler and Superior of the whole world," and recognize the pope to be high priest. Further, the Requerimiento established the Spanish king and queen as the lords of the land. The Spanish not only justified their conquests in the New World on this document, but also any accompanying atrocities as well.

Code Talking

The **Requerimiento** (the Requirement) was issued by Pope Innocent VII to Ferdinand and Isabella, allowing these monarchs to conquer Native peoples in the name of the Church in order to preserve the souls of their Native souls.

The interest in saving souls was nothing new to the Spanish. The spread of Christianity was one of the primary motivations that set Columbus off on his great quest. The challenge for the missionaries who accompanied the Spanish colonists was keeping the Natives alive long enough to convert them.

Cosmic Game of Finders Keepers

The morality of the Spanish actions in the New World in the early to mid-1500s was the subject of great debate. Bartolomé de Las Casas, the first Catholic priest to be ordained in the New World, went to Spain to intercede with the Spanish court on behalf of the Natives. He stated, "What we committed in the Indies stands out among the most unpardonable offenses committed against God and mankind." Las Casas's opponent, Juan de Sepulveda, a noted classical scholar, lawyer, and theologian who defended the efforts of the Spanish crown and its agents in the New World, justified such acts by saying that the Natives were naturally inferior and were meant to be slaves. According to Sepulveda, if the Indians refused to submit, then the Spanish were justified in using force against them. Sepulveda argued for the superiority of the Spaniard over the indigenous people, stating "In wisdom, skill, virtue and humanity, these people are as inferior to the Spaniards as children are to adults and women to men; there is a great difference between savagery and forbearance, between violence and moderation, almost—I am inclined to say—as between monkeys and men."

For the Native people whose souls were at risk, there was no question about their position. The were The People, The Original Ones, the Children of God.

Much of the debate turned on the issue of whether the Natives were human. In 1537, Pope Paul III ended the argument by issuing a Papal Bull (essentially, a decree) titled Siblimis Deus. In it, Natives were officially declared to be humans.

The arguments might seem silly now—of course Indians are humans!—but it was unquestionably consequential to the Spanish at the time. The Spanish government argued against Natives being human because if the land was vacant of any "human" occupation, then any nation could claim both land title and political jurisdiction, a rationale called *vacuum domicilium*. Spain and any other European nation could divide up the New World based on ownership by discovery.

> **Code Talking**
>
> Vacuum domicilium isn't something you clean your carpets with. It means "empty land," and it was the name of a doctrine saying that if there were no humans living on the continent, then it must be empty and, therefore, up for grabs.

The interests of the Natives were incidental to either side of the debate. Even those who came to the Natives' defense had ulterior motives. Las Casas, arguing that the Natives were "savage" but still human, was interested in the salvation of souls. After all, only humans have souls. (The Spanish were not the last to rationalize their actions on the assumption that "it was good for them.")

Las Casas won his debate, and new laws were passed in 1542 that forbade making Native Americans slaves and gave them the right to own cattle and raise crops.

Taking the New World by Storm

Of course, it's one thing to claim land, but it's quite another to control it. The Spanish set forth to explore the territories it claimed, primarily the Caribbean, Peru, and Mexico, and to conquer any Native people who might contest their presence.

Conquest of the Aztecs

In 1519, Hernán Cortés, with a force of 508 soldiers, landed near Vera Cruz in Mexico and began the conquest of the Aztecs. As noted previously, the Aztecs were a powerful people with a sophisticated society. Their capital city was Tenochtitlán (the site of present-day Mexico City), which had a population in excess of 200,000 people. The city was built on an island in Lake Texcoco with many gardens, pyramids, and canals. There was no doubt that they were a great civilization—even the Spanish marveled at the Aztec creations. One soldier described the marketplace as "so full of people and so well regulated and arranged, they had never been beheld before … I do not know how to describe it seeing things as we did that had never been heard of or seen before, not even dreamed about."

The Aztecs were conquerors, too, but as great as their civilization was, they quickly succumbed to the power of the conquistadors.

> **Tribal Truths**
>
> Legend has it that the Aztec emperor Moctezuma believed that Cortés was the Great White God, Quetzalcoatl. Accordingly, Montezuma made plans to greet Cortés with all the respect he owed to the White God whom his Aztec religion had taught him to expect. Precious gifts were brought to Cortés; the riches of the realm were opened to him. He was honored as a deity.
>
> Because the Aztecs believed Cortés to be a god, he gained access to the Aztec capital of Tenochtitlán, and using his advanced weaponry and the help of enemy tribes, laid siege to and conquered the capital of the greatest empire that had ever existed in the New World. Modern scholars now believe that disease and the assistance of the Spanish received from anti-Aztec tribes were the main cause for the conquest of the Aztec.

Florida and the Fountain of Youth

In 1513, Juan Ponce de León, best known for his quest for the Fountain of Youth, sailed east from Puerto Rico and found what he thought was an island that he consequently named "Florida." The Native peoples he found there—the Calusas, Timucuas, and Freshwater Indians—were hostile to him, having already heard about the Spanish, or the savage men "with houses on water." He was driven out of Florida but returned in 1521. He died in Cuba of a wound inflicted by the Calusas during his second expedition.

Conquest of the Inca Empire

The Spanish march across the Americas continued. In 1532, Francisco Pizarro conquered the Inca Empire with 168 men and 67 horses. On November 16, 1532, Pizarro met the Inca ruler Atahualpa at Cajamarca, in what is now Peru, and held him prisoner until the Inca delivered to the Spanish a storeroom filled with gold and silver. Rather than release the Inca ruler, Pizarro accused Atahualpa of plotting against him, and put him on trial for treason. The Spanish executed Atahualpa and brutally put down subsequent Inca uprisings. By 1535, the Inca society was completely overthrown.

Coronado and the Seven Cities of Cibola

Between 1539 and 1543, the Spanish invasion of what is now the United States became particularly vicious. As they moved inland, the Spanish plundered Native villages and enslaved their inhabitants. Some conquistadors, like Francisco Vasquez de Coronado, were searching for gold. To be precise, Coronado was in search of the legendary "Seven Cities of Cibola" or "Cities of Gold." Rumors of great cities of wealth in the New World had been circulating for years, and Coronado was determined to find them. In 1540, he and 1,000 soldiers traveled north from Mexico City in search of the golden cities. The trek took them through the present-day states of Arizona, New Mexico, Texas, Oklahoma, and parts of Kansas. Luck wasn't on his side, however, and Coronado returned to Mexico in 1542 having failed to find the gold he sought.

 Tribal Truths

The Seven Cities of Cibola are believed to be the towns of the Zuni and other Pueblo peoples in Arizona and New Mexico. Of course, none of these villages were paved with gold.

Dreams of Silver Blades and Crosses

Hernando de Soto arrived in the New World from Cuba in 1539. For more than 4 years, and with an army of 600 men, de Soto marched from Florida to Texas, leaving death and destruction in his wake. De Soto, too, was in search of the legendary Cities of Gold.

De Soto's expedition began in Florida, near what is now Tampa Bay. From there he made his way north through the country of the Creek (or Myskoke) Indians. When he encountered the Creek along the Savanna River, he was greeted by a woman chief who came to him bearing gifts. De Soto's mother must not have taught him his manners, for rather than returning this act of generosity, he took the woman prisoner and kept her as a hostage. She eventually escaped, and the Creek became a bitter enemy as a result.

This encounter set the tone for de Soto's conquest of the southern tribes. He battled the Choctaw, Chickasaws, Apalachee, Seminoles, and a tribe thought to be the Quapaws. De Soto was a particularly brutal conquistador; on one occasion, he and his men killed 11,000 Indians in a battle in present-day southern Alabama. The remains of more than 70 Indians (together with Spanish artifacts) were uncovered in a mound in Citrus County, Florida. Some of the bones had slash marks or sword cuts, indicating that these people suffered violent and bloody deaths.

De Soto died on May 21, 1542, on the banks of the Mississippi River. It's hard to imagine that any Natives mourned him.

Native Voices

I remember Desoto. He is buried somewhere in this river, his bones sunk like the golden treasure he traveled half the earth to find, came looking for gold cities, for shining streets of beaten gold to dance on with silk ladies He should have stayed home.

—Joy Harjo, Creek poet, from the poem "New Orleans," in the book *She Had Some Horses* (Thunder's Mouth Press, 1983)

"Men Like Us"

In 1542, Juan Rodriquez Cabrillo began an expedition up the California coastline. Upon entering San Diego harbor, he became the first European to step foot in present-day California, although he noted that the Natives there had already heard that "men like us … bearded, clothed and armed … [are] killing many native Indians." News travels fast.

By any measure, the treatment of the Natives by the Spanish was atrocious.

Oh, Kanata!: French Exploration of the New World

The Spanish weren't the only Europeans in search of adventure and riches in the New World. In 1534, Frenchman Jacques Cartier sailed up the St. Lawrence River, thereby laying claim as the discoverer of Canada. Like Columbus before him, Cartier made multiple voyages to the New World. And like Columbus, Cartier was in search of gold, spices, and a northwest route to Asia. With two ships, Cartier explored the St. Lawrence Bay and returned to France with two Natives as trophies for King Francis I.

Cartier's interests in Canada went beyond economics, however. Although he didn't bring priests with him on his initial journey, the idea of converting the Natives to Christianity must have crossed his mind. He observed that "they are a people who would be easy to convert."

 **Tribal Truths**

The generally accepted origin of the name Canada can be traced to the writings of Jacques Cartier in 1536. While sailing up the St. Lawrence River, Cartier noticed that the Indians referred to their settlements as *Kanata*, which, from its repetition, the French took to be the Native name of the entire country.

Ancient Tales

In 1562, Frenchman Jean Ribaut traveled up the east coast of Florida looking for a site to establish a colony. At the mouth of St. John's River, he met Natives who greeted him warmly and offered many gifts. When Ribaut prepared to leave, these Natives brought fish, oysters, crabs, lobsters, beans, and fresh water. Obviously, the Spanish hadn't reached this place. Ribaut sailed on to the southern tip of South Carolina to a place he named Port Royal. The Natives here were afraid of him, for the Spanish had preceded Ribaut. Yet the French explorer and his men were treated with courtesies he could hardly expect given the circumstances.

That seemed to be the pattern up and down the coastline of North America. The Spanish left a legacy of destruction among every tribe they encountered. The French, in contrast, were less interested in conquest than they were in acquiring the rich resources of the New World.

Champlain on Ice

Frenchman Samuel de Champlain made his first voyage to Canada in 1603 and explored the St. Lawrence River as far as present-day Montreal. In 1608, Champlain founded a settlement at Quebec and spent time with the Algonquin and Huron Indians. The Huron and the Iroquois were the two most powerful groups in the Northwest and were traditional enemies.

To prove his loyalty to his new allies, in 1609 Champlain launched an expedition against the Iroquois and engaged in a battle that resulted in the defeat of the Iroquois. Champlain himself killed two Iroquois leaders and mortally wounded another. This event would result in a century-long hatred between the French and the Iroquois confederation. The war, begun by the French and their allies against the Iroquois, continued sporadically until the French supremacy in Canada had ceased.

Native Voices

On our coming near the house, two mats were spread to sit upon and immediately some food was served in well-made bowls; two men were also dispatched at once with bows and arrows in quest of game, who soon after brought a pair of pigeons which they had shot .... The natives were good people, for when they saw I would not remain, they supposed I was afraid of their bows and arrows, and taking the arrows they broke them into pieces and threw them into the fire.

—Henry Hudson, upon meeting Natives on the Hudson River

Rolling Down the River

René Robert Cavelierde La Salle was a reluctant explorer. He had come to Canada from France in 1666 as an adventurer, having left the Society of Jesus, a Jesuit group, after finding himself unsuited for priestly life. La Salle began a business in the fur trade and taught himself several Indian languages.

Having heard of a great river system to the south (the Mississippi), La Salle undertook an exploration of the Ohio River in 1669. Although he ended up short of being the first European to discover the Mississippi River (that claim was made by the Joliet-Marquette expedition of 1673), La Salle later descended it, laying claim to all the lands drained by the river. He named the territory *La Louisiane* in honor of the French King, Louis XIV. It was this same Louisiana Territory the United States would acquire 120 years later.

Code Talking

Voyageurs were men employed by fur companies to transport goods to and from remote stations in the Canadian Northwest. The term is from the French word for "traveler."

Going Native

In spite of Champlain's attack on the Iroquois, the Indians truly liked the French. The French accepted the hospitality of their Native hosts with courtesy and consideration. The *voyageurs* learned their languages, married their women, and adopted their ways. The Jesuit priests traveled among the Natives and converted many without the severity typical of the Spanish Franciscans. More important, perhaps, there were too few French in Canada to push the Natives off their lands.

The Least You Need to Know

- ◆ Columbus didn't "discover" an empty land.

- ◆ The Spanish explorations in the Americas were motivated by the search for new sources of precious metals, namely gold and silver.

- ◆ The Spanish conquistadors were especially cruel, enslaving and killings tens of thousands of Native peoples.

- ◆ Commerce in furs determined French expansion into North America.

- ◆ The French, in comparison with the Spanish, were less brutal, treating Natives as allies in the fur trade as well as friends on a personal level.

Chapter 6

Colonization and Conflict

In This Chapter

- ◆ How Powhatan and Pocahontas aided Plymouth Colony
- ◆ A massacre in Virginia
- ◆ The Pequot War
- ◆ King Phillip's War
- ◆ The Pueblos revolt against the Spanish

The hostilities between the new settlers in the Americas and the Native Americans leaves a largely negative impression of Indians as an obstacle to Manifest Destiny, a threat to peaceful white development of a wild and untamed land, and the instigators of frontier brutality.

But when looked at from the perspective of Indian people, the conflicts with the English, Dutch, and Spanish colonists were acts of resistance. Natives acted to protect their people, culture, and land from invasion and exploitation from outsiders. Furthermore, although there certainly were hundreds of conflicts, in most early encounters explorers and colonists found the Natives they met to be peaceful, curious, and generous. Without the Indians' help, many more Europeans would have perished in the often-brutal environment.

The British Are Coming! The British Are Coming!

Compared to the French and the Spanish, the English were relative newcomers to North America. John Cabot explored what is now Maine and Nova Scotia in 1497 and 1498, but there were no return expeditions until the Pilgrims arrived in the 1600s. When the English did come to stay, their policy toward the Natives more closely resembled the Spanish than the French. The English wished to convert the natives to Christianity. They were also interested in "civilizing" them. And like the Spanish, they were not above kidnapping and enslaving unwilling potential converts.

The British Are Staying!

As every school child knows, the first permanent English colony was Jamestown, Virginia, founded in 1607. (An earlier attempt to establish a colony met with disaster when the 117 colonists on Roanoke Island, just off the North Carolina coast, vanished.)

Tribal Truths

A recent study of tree growth rings suggests that one of the worse droughts on record doomed the Roanoke colony. In all probability, the colonists were forced to abandon their homes or face starvation. The only clue to their disappearance was the word *CROATOAN* carved into a tree. Croatoan was a tribe south of Roanoke. The lost colony did not turn up among the Croatoan people, and so their disappearance remains a mystery. One prominent theory is that the colonists settled with a neighboring tribe. According to one scholar, the Roanoke survivors were assimilated into the Pembroke tribe of Indians of Robeson County, North Carolina. Other scholars believe that they assimilated into the Croatoan tribe.

The colonists of Jamestown struggled for survival. Jamestown wasn't a healthy place to live, and many colonists were soldiers of fortune, not skilled farmers. As a result, more than half the colonists died from diseases and hunger in the first year.

Learning to Live in a New Land

The whole colony might have perished had it not been for the aid of the neighboring tribes who provided food for the colonists. Squanto, a Patuxet Indian, was particularly helpful to the English, teaching them how to plant corn and fish.

Squanto had little reason to be so generous. In 1614, together with approximately 30 other Indians, Squanto was kidnapped and sold into slavery in Spain by Captain

Thomas Hunt, an associate of Captain John Smith, the governor of Jamestown. Ransomed by monks, he worked in a monastery for three years and then escaped to England. In 1619, Squanto returned to the site of his own village of Patuxet to find it deserted. Sadly, all the members of Squanto's tribe died of a plague, probably smallpox brought over on English ships, establishing another pattern: As the white settlement advanced, new diseases for which the Natives had no resistance devastated tribe after tribe.

Tribal Truths

The first Thanksgiving occurred sometime between September 21 or 22 and November 9, 1621. The English joined some 90 Wampanoag, led by Massasoit (or Ousimechan, meaning "Yellow Feather") in a three-day celebration. The menu included duck, geese, turkey, and deer. There is no evidence that the entertainment included watching the Lions and the Bears do battle.

Powhatan's Confederacy

Jamestown was located in the territory controlled by the Powhatan Confederacy, made up of some 30 Algonquin-speaking tribes. The Confederacy was under the leadership of Wahunsonacock, or Powhatan. He ruled about 12,000 people living in a 9,000-square-mile area. Powhatan inherited 6 tributary tribes from his mother and spent the next 30 years consolidating these tribes under his rule. It is possible that the aid given to the Jamestown colony was consistent with Powhatan's plan to incorporate the English colony into his realm. In other words, Powhatan may have been trying to colonize the colonizers!

One of the best-known stories in Jamestown history is when Powhatan's daughter, Pocahontas, then a child of 12 or 13, supposedly threw herself in front of Captain John Smith and saved him from being executed. Tribal history suggests that Smith was never in any real danger. Pocahontas was performing a ritual role so that Powhatan could adopt Smith and make him a sub-chief.

Tribal Truths

Although he is always called Powhatan, his real name was Wahunsona-cock. He was born in the Algonquan village of Powhatan, so that is what he was called by the English.

Speak for Yourself, John

In 1609, English ships arrived and unloaded 105 English colonists at the mouth of the James River, not just to trade, but to establish a colony. They called their settlement Jamestown, and soon their governor, Captain John Smith, went upriver to meet with Powhatan and other leaders of the confederacy.

Like the Spanish, the English at Jamestown demanded that the Indians provide them with corn and other foods. At first, this puzzled Powhatan, but this soon turned to anger. Fighting between the colonists and the Natives broke out after Smith left in 1609, and might have spelled disaster for Jamestown if Pocahontas had not served as a mediator between the Indians and the colonists. She was captured by the English and converted to Christianity. This bond was solidified when she married widower John Rolfe, one of her captors and teachers, in 1614.

> **Native Voices**
>
> What will it avail you to take that by force you may quickly have by love, or destroy them that provide you food?
>
> —Powhatan

> **Tribal Truths**
>
> In an attempt to gain concessions from Powhatan, a squad from Jamestown kidnapped Pocahontas. During her captivity, she was converted to Christianity and baptized as Rebecca. She and John Rolfe fell in love and were married. They traveled to England in 1616, and she died of some unknown disease in 1617 at the age of 22. She is buried in the church at Gravesend, England.

Virginia Massacre

By 1622, it was apparent to the Indians that the colonists intended to expand their holdings in Virginia. This physical expansion threatened the Indian way of life. Of even greater concern, perhaps, were the renewed colonial efforts to convert and educate the "savages." When the colonials tried to convert them, the Natives responded with silence. The English interpreted the silence as a sign of consent, until Opechancanough, Powhatan's brother, made their meaning all too clear. He attacked the English settlement as a demonstration of Indian power and in an attempt to drive off the English for good.

> **Native Voices**
>
> Had it been my fortune to capture the governor of the English, I would not have meanly exposed him as a show for my people.
>
> —Opechancanough

According to English accounts, Opechancanough planned to attack the Jamestown fort as well as the outlying settlements. But a young Indian boy who had been Christianized by the settlers forewarned the inhabitants. The news didn't spread fast enough, however, to save the English living in the settlements. This 1622 uprising was known as the

"Virginia Massacre" and resulted in the deaths of 347 colonists. In 1644, Opechan-canough was captured and put to death.

The Pequot War

The English negotiated with the Wampanoags in Massachusetts in 1621 for lands that would come to be called the Plymouth Colony. For more than 10 years after the founding of Plymouth Colony, there was peace between the colonists and the Natives of New England. However, the Pequots of the Connecticut River began to feel the pressure of the colonists' desire for more land. The Dutch had settled east and north from the Hudson River, and the English, west of Pequot homeland. This was in addition to the always-present tension that existed between the Pequot and their Narraganset neighbors.

The powder keg finally exploded when two coastal traders were killed at the hands of Indians. The English retaliated by attacking Indians on Block Island, during which the English killed every Indian male they could find, mostly Narragansets, and burned their communities. The English continued along the coast in search of Pequots, burning villages as they went. Some Narragansets in the more remote villages managed to survive.

The Pequot, led by Sassacus, then laid siege on Fort Saybrook at the mouth of the Connecticut River during the winter of 1636 and 1637. In the following spring, the Pequot attacked settlements up the Connecticut River.

Tribal Truths

Eventually, the Mashan-tucket Pequot were allowed to return to their old country and in 1666 were given a 2,500-acre reservation. By 1983, they were reduced to 214 acres and 55 tribal members. They filed suit to gain federal recognition and now own the largest gaming operation in the country.

The English gathered a force of 80 men under the command of Captain John Mason and, along with Mohegan allies, the Narragansets, and Niantics, headed to relieve the colonial settlements. On May 25, 1637, the English attacked a Pequot village and burned it to the ground. Estimates of the number of Pequot dead range from 600 to 1,000, many of them women and children. In July 1637, one colonial force trapped a large number of Pequots hiding out in a swamp in Long Island Sound. Sassacus managed to escape, seeking refuge among the Mohawks. Sassacus's luck had run out, though, and the Mohawks beheaded him as a gesture to the English that the Mohawks didn't support the Pequot.

The remnants of the Pequot that could be rounded up were sold into slavery in Bermuda or given to the Narragansets and Niantics in payment for their assistance. One group, the Mashantucket Pequot, went to live with the Uncas and Mohegans. The English forbid the use of the Pequot name and Pequot-named places had their names changed.

King Phillip's War

By the mid-1600s, a number of tribes had been wiped out or driven out of their homeland, and the English were intent on further extending their colonial boundaries.

Code Talking

A **sachem** is a leader or chief.

The powerful Wampanoag leader Massasoit, who had participated in the first Thanksgiving celebration, died in 1661, and his son, Alexander, succeeded him. Alexander died after a peace council with the governor of Massachusetts. Metacom, who became the new tribal leader or *sachem*, believed that Alexander had been poisoned.

Forced to acknowledge himself a subject of the English Crown and of the governor of New Plymouth, Metacom, who the English called King Phillip, promised not to dispose of any lands without authority of the governor and to pay 100 pounds a year in tribute. He also began to organize the Nipmucks, Sakonnets, Pocassets, Nausets, Pamets, and Narragansets for a general uprising.

Metacom had seen his father treat the colonists with great kindness and generosity, showing them how to plant corn, offering them land, and protecting them from other tribes. If the colonists were grateful, they had an odd way of showing it. They continued to demand more and more land and to take captured Natives and sell them into slavery. Metacom was understandably angered by his people's treatment at the hands of the English and their expansionist tactics, and he was justifiably distrustful of the English. The Plymouth authorities, sensing a new Wampanoag militancy, resorted to harassment in hopes of controlling the Natives.

Native Voices

But little remains of my ancestor's domain, I am resolved not to see the day when I have no country. The English are so eager to sell the Indians liquor that most of [them] spend all in drunkenness, and then raven upon the sober Indians.

—Metacom, a.k.a. King Phillip, Wampanoag leader

Metacom responded by uniting all the tribes in the area of the Hudson River. In the summer of 1675, the tribes gathered to plan an attack on the English towns and villages. Metacom and his allies, the Nipmuck and Narraganset, struck Connecticut, parts of Boston, and even parts of Plymouth. Only Rhode Island was spared, out of respect for the peaceful Quakers.

The English resorted to the age-old tactic of conquer and divide. They placed a bounty on Wampanoag scalps in hopes of gaining the support of the Narragansets. However, the Narragansets remained loyal to Metacom. Having failed in the art of persuasion, the colonists turned to the art of war. They attacked the Narraganset and, in a fierce battle in December 1675 called the Great Swamp Fight, killed an estimated 500 warriors and 599 women and children. The colonists suffered a loss of 207 militiamen.

Native Voices

Brothers, since these Englishmen have seized our country, they have cut down the grass with scythes, and the trees with axes. Their cows and horses eat up the grass, and their hogs spoil our bed of clams; and finally we shall starve to death.

—Miantunnomoh, Narraganset

During the summer of 1676, the English hunted down and defeated smaller bands of Natives. Metacom's wife and young son were captured, and many of his relatives killed. Although he was losing, Metacom wasn't ready to back down. One of his warriors proposed that they seek peace with the English; Metacom killed the man. Later, when surrounded, the brother of the dead warrior shot Metacom in revenge. With their leader dead and having suffered many losses, the Wampanoags and Naraganssets made peace with the colonists.

Tribal Truths

Two years after the founding of Jamestown, Henry Hudson, an Englishman in the employment of the Dutch East Indian Company, sailed down the river that now bears his name.

There he met several groups of Natives. On one occasion, in what is now New York, Hudson hosted several Indian leaders aboard his ship and treated them to brandy. One fell into a drunken stupor and remained onboard. When he awoke, he marveled at the occurrence, having never felt such an experience. The Natives thus called this place Mannahattanik, meaning "the place where we were all drunk." Later, in 1612, the Dutch established a trading post on what became known as Manhattan Island.

This first taste of alcohol would prove more significant than anyone might have imagined. The Europeans had, over centuries of use, developed a tolerance for alcohol. To the Natives, it was wholly ruinous. Here was a substance that they had no immunity to, and tribe after tribe succumbed to its devastating affects.

After the war, the captive Wampanoags, including Metacom's wife and child, were sold into slavery in Bermuda. It was plain that the English were firmly entrenched from Maine to the Carolinas. There would be no stopping the European invasion from soon engulfing the whole of the Americas.

War in the Southwest

While the tribes in the New England area were fighting to regain control over their lands, other tribes were fighting for their freedom. For the Pueblo tribes in the Southwest, Spanish colonization meant enslavement.

Pueblo Revolt

The Pueblos received some benefits from the Spanish—domestic animals, peach trees, and better farm implements. But they were under the spiritual control of the padres and the physical control of the local colonists. They were forced to pay a tribute of crops and animals to the governor. In addition, the Pueblos had to perform labor in his fields, and Pueblo women worked as domestic servants in his palace.

The Spanish were particularly cruel masters. While prevented by their home government from engaging in slave catching, prisoners of war could be enslaved legally, and it was always easy to start a war.

From Medicine Man to General

In 1680, 82 years after Spanish colonists settled in northern New Mexico, the Pueblo Indians revolted. Led by Popé from the San Juan Pueblo, the Indians attacked at dawn on August 10. Over the next several days, they killed 400 settlers.

> **Tribal Truths**
>
> Popé was a medicine man who was flogged and driven out of San Juan for practicing his traditional Native religion (the Spanish termed such practices "witchcraft"). He organized an uprising by sending messengers from Pueblo to Pueblo, using knotted cords to indicate the appointed day for the revolution.

On August 15, an army of 500 warriors converged on Santa Fe, where 1,000 colonists had crowded into the Palace of the Governors for protection. The Indians cut off their water supply, preparing for a long seige. The Spanish surprised the Indians with a counterattack that drove the Pueblos back. Still fearing for their lives, the Spanish finally abandoned Santa Fe on August 21, and the entire Spanish population, about 1,700 people, retreated to El Peso (now Juárez). By the end of the uprising, 400 Spanish had been killed, including 21 of 33 friars.

The Pueblos remained in control over their own territory under Popé's leadership for the next 12 years. They turned the public buildings in Santa Fe into a Pueblo village and transformed the Chapel of Our Lady of Light into a ceremonial kiva. They stopped speaking Spanish and refused to plant crops that were introduced by the Spanish.

Sadly, the Pueblos failed to thrive under Popé, who turned out to be a ruthless ruler. To make matters worse, a severe drought brought near-starvation conditions.

The Spanish soldiers returned in 1692, and the Pueblos agreed to accept Spanish rule once more. By 1693, the colonists returned, but by this time the Pueblos had changed their minds. Some Pueblos surrendered to the Spanish, while others fought them.

In the end, the Pueblos gave up and once more accepted Spanish rule. Although the Pueblos were not able to remain independent, the Pueblo Revolt is remembered as the most successful attempt by Indians to drive out European invaders in the history of the United States.

Fighting for Our Lives

The story of colonial America is much like the saga of Native people in general: the dispossession of cultures, the removal of tribes, the loss of land, and the pitting of one group or tribe against another. The wars in the colonial period of American history serve to remind us that Native Americans have, from the beginning of contact with Europeans, been in a fight for their lives.

The Least You Need to Know

- The Wampanoag at first helped Plymouth Colony survive.
- When Pocahontas "saved" Captain John Smith, it was probably part of a ritual to affirm Powhatan's relationship with the English.
- The Virginia Massacre was a result of English encroachment upon Indian lands and the colonists' attempts to "Christianize" the Natives.
- English desire for more land led to the Pequot War.
- King Phillip's War was caused by the expansion of the English into Native territory.
- In the Southwest, the Pueblos revolted against Spanish domination and temporarily drove the Spanish back into Mexico.

Chapter 7

Caught in the Power Struggle

- ◆ Native American involvement in European wars
- ◆ The establishment of the Iroquois Confederacy
- ◆ The Indians in the French and Indian War
- ◆ Pontiac's War
- ◆ The impact of the fur trade on Natives

Even though the Americas were claimed by rival European superpowers, European presence on the continent wasn't so secure. While the colonists resided along the coastlines and the rivers, Native people still controlled the interior. Initially, the colonists and the Indians tolerated each other, finding common ground in trade as each explored economic opportunities that North America offered.

However, the power struggle on the European continent soon extended to the New World, as the European nations sought to strengthen their footholds in the Americas. Here was a land of unimagined resources and riches. And in this rich land, the aboriginal inhabitants found themselves in the middle of an ugly power struggle between powerful European nations.

Pawns in an International Game

Colonial policy toward Indians varied with each nation. The English interest was to take over Native lands, requiring that the Indians abandon their homelands, to move along, so to speak. With Spain, the policy was to reduce the Indians to serfdom, slaves to care for the stock and crops and to work the mines. The French fraternized with the Natives, intermarrying in hopes to secure preference in the fur trade. The French design was, in the words of the great minister Coilbert, inducing the Indians "to come and settle in common with the French, to live with them and raise their children according to our manners and customs."

As different as each country's attitude and approach might sound, they all had the same goal: to use Native peoples as pawns in their international game. The Natives had come to rely on many of the items they acquired by trading with the Europeans, such as cloth, iron pots, beads, and bells, to say nothing of the rum or whiskey that lay to waste nation after nation.

But just as ruinous was the escalation of intertribal warfare that was a product of conflicts begun in far-off lands. Time after time, tribes allied themselves with European powers only to be used as weapons against foreign interests. The Indians killed and scalped each other and white colonists—all for the glory of some king across the ocean.

Tribal Truths

Scalping is believed to have been introduced by Europeans. The practice became widespread during this time as the French and English placed bounties on the lives of the other during conflicts. Scalps were accepted as evidence of having killed an enemy, and carrying a scalp was a lot easier than bringing in a body. Why did scalping continue even in the absence of a reward? Some scholars believe that Plains Indians, for example, collected the scalps of their enemies because they believed that hair contained power. Another explanation is that the Indians believed that a person went to the hereafter in the condition he or she was killed. What greater injury to inflict upon an enemy than to deprive the person of his or her hair in the afterlife?

A Lot of Little Wars

I've included the following list of wars that took place during the colonial period to give you a sense of how contentious a time it was and how fragile the brief periods of peace were.

Wars in America, 1689–1783

Dates	American Conflict	European Conflict
1689–1697	King William's War	War of the League of Augsburg
1702–1713	Queen Anne's War	War of the Spanish Succession
1712	Tuscarora War	
1715	Yamasee War	
1723–1727	Abenaki War	
1744–1748	King George's War	War of the Austrian Succession
1756–1763	French and Indian Wars	Seven Years' War
1759–1761	Cherokee War	
1763–1764	"Pontiac's War"	
1774	Lord Dunmore's War	
1775–1783	American Revolution	

Native people weren't drawn into every conflict, and some wars were brief and inconsequential. But the pattern remained the same: Native people fought and died next to and against their colonial neighbors.

King William's War, 1689 to 1697

After William of Orange became the king of England in 1689, the major European powers (England, the Netherlands, Spain, and Austria) allied to oppose the expansionism of French King Louis XIV. In America, hostilities broke out between the English and the French on Hudson Bay and between the Iroquois and the French in the area between the Mohawk and St. Lawrence Rivers. In general, the Iroquois tribes sided with the English; the Algonquian tribes with the French.

Despite French victories, the war ended in a stalemate. The Treaty of Ryswick, which ended the European counterpart of the war, restored all colonial possessions to their prewar status.

Tribal Truths

In 1710, four Mohawk leaders agreed to accompany English agents to London, where they had their portraits painted and met with Queen Anne. They were the first celebrity Indians in Europe.

Tuscarora War, 1712

The English colonists of South Carolina abused their relationship with the Tuscarora. English traders sold goods on credit in the fall, expecting to be paid back in the spring after hunting season. If the hunting season was bad and the debt was not paid, the trader seized the man's wife and children and sold them as slaves to the West Indies. Finally, the Tuscarora decided they had had enough. Led by Chief Hancock, the Tuscarora attacked colonists living near New Bern on September 22, 1711, killing more than 130 colonials.

English soldiers were dispatched to punish the Tuscarora and, with 500 Yamassee (Seminole) allies, the British army struck the Tuscarora on March 7, 1712. After a month-long campaign, the Tuscarora and the British reached an agreement of peace.

The British violated the peace when colonists crowded the Tuscaroras and made a regular business of kidnapping their children. The Tuscarora once more took up arms against the colonists, this time in North Carolina. South Carolina responded by assembling a new force to give aid to North Carolina. This force included 33 white men and nearly 900 Indians under the command of Colonel James Moore. Moore laid siege to the Tuscarora stronghold, and on March 20, 1713, crushed the resistance.

The victory was complete, forever ending the power of the Tuscarora nation. Several hundred Tuscaroras were killed and 400 more were sold into slavery. Survivors of the Tuscarora War retreated north and joined the Iroquois Confederacy as the Sixth Fire, or sixth tribe in the Iroquois Confederacy.

The Mighty Haudenosaunee

The Iroquois, or *Haudenosaunee*, were the most powerful Native group in colonial America. They made their home in upstate New York between the Adirondack Mountains and Niagara Falls. There were a number of tribes belonging to the Iroquoian-language family surrounded by Algonquin-speaking tribes. Although closely related linguistically and culturally, these tribes (the Onondagas, Mohawks, Oneidas, Senecas, and Cayugas) were in constant conflict with each other. Then, sometime between 1000 and 1500 C.E., a great visionary, Deganwidah, proposed that the warring tribes form a confederacy. Deganwidah, a Mohawk, was an imposing figure who commanded a great deal of respect. He was assisted by an Onondaga orator named Hiawatha. The two managed to persuade the various Iroquois tribes to form an alliance, the Great Peace (known to whites as the Iroquois League or Iroquois Confederacy).

Code Talking

The term **Haudenosaunee** is the word the Iroquois use to refer to themselves. The word means "People of the Longhouse."

The confederacy was founded on a number of noble principles: freedom, respect, tolerance, consensus, and brotherhood. These values contrasted dramatically from those that served as the foundation for European governments of that time.

Native Voices

Long, long ago, one of the Spirits of the Sky World came down and looked at the earth. As he traveled over it, he found it beautiful, and so he created people to live on it. Before returning to the sky, he gave them names, called the people all together, and spoke his parting words:

"To the Mohawks, I give corn," he said. "To the patient Oneidas, I give the nuts and the fruit of many trees. To the industrious Senecas, I give beans. To the friendly Cayugas, I give the roots of plants to be eaten. To the wise and eloquent Onondagas, I give grapes and squashes to eat and tobacco to smoke at the camp fires."

Many other things he told the new people. Then he wrapped himself in a bright cloud and went like a swift arrow to the Sun. There his return caused his Brother Sky Spirits to rejoice.

When Six Equals Five

Five nations—the Mohawk, Oneida, Onondaga, Cayuga, and Seneca (the five larger tribes in the area)—formed the original Great Peace Confederacy. The Tuscarora, the sixth nation, or symbolically the Sixth Fire, were forced out of the Carolinas by white encroachment and were admitted as a "junior" member sometime around 1722. The Tuscarora nation held no official position in the League.

Tribal Truths

A woman's place in ancient Indian culture was very different than in European cultures, at least among the Iroquois nations in the Northeastern United States. In the Iroquois nations the women owned the land they farmed. They also owned the houses and all the normal things of everyday life such as blankets, cooking utensils, and farming implements. Women had many responsibilities, but probably the most important one was having children to ensure the future of their tribe. Any children born into the family belonged to their mother's clan, not their father's, and were educated by their mother's relatives. Each of the dwellings they lived in were generally occupied by one clan, with the eldest and/or most respected woman of that clan ruling it as Clan Mother.

Holding Their Own

Ever since Samuel de Champlain made the mistake of attacking the Iroquois in 1609 in an effort to earn the trust of the Algonquin and Huron Indians, the Iroquois treated the French as enemies (see Chapter 5). The Iroquois fought the French throughout the establishment of the colony in Canada. The St. Lawrence Valley near Quebec wasn't safe for the Europeans and their allies, the people of the Huron tribe.

> **Tribal Truths** _____
>
> The Iroquois developed the game of lacrosse to train for warfare and as a way to resolve diplomatic tensions between tribes. It is called "little brother of war" in the Iroquoian language and is believed to have been given to them by the Creator sometime in ages past.

The better organized and more determined Iroquois were able to hold off French encroachment on their territory for quite some time. This Iroquois confederation turned five (later six) small Native American nations into a political and military power on the North American continent, holding a balance between French and English interests—that is, until they made the fatal mistake of siding with the British during the American Revolution, a decision that proved to be their downfall.

The Yamassee War

Poor treatment of Indians by English traders and settlers in South Carolina resulted in an Indian uprising led by the Yamassee that became known as the Yamassee War.

>
> **Code Talking** _____
>
> From the Creek word *simanoli* came the name of the Seminole tribe of Florida.

Approximately 100 settlers were killed, and Indian losses were far greater. When the militia defeated them, the Yamassee fled into northern Florida, where they were joined by Creeks and other tribes and by runaway slaves. From this amalgam, the Seminole tribe emerged, named for the Creek word *simanoli*, or "runaway." The Yamassees' former homeland became the new colony of Georgia.

The French and Indian War

By the mid-1700s, France and Great Britain were at war, vying for control of the Ohio Valley. The French, who claimed the entire watersheds of the Mississippi and St. Lawrence Rivers, which included the Great Lakes and the Ohio River Valley, became concerned about British encroachment into this area. The French established a number of forts on Lake Champlain and along the Wabash, Ohio, Mississippi, and Missouri Rivers. The British countered by building their own forts.

The British called the conflict the "French and Indian War," indicating that the Indians were allied with the French, but Indian participation was not so simple as the name implies. Although it's true that the French had many Indian partners as a result of their more cooperative trading practices, the British had the cooperation of the Iroquois, who, with English encouragement, made war on the Ohio Indians to break up their trade with the French.

The Northwest and Indian Country

Because of the earlier cooperation between the French and most Indian tribes (the major exception was the Iroquois), British relations with the Indians suffered until the expulsion of the French in 1763. Only through their victory in the French and Indian War did the British succeed in extending their territorial holdings into the Northwest and bringing the Indian population under their authority. After the Peace of Paris of September 1763, the British issued a proclamation officially delineating the "Indian Country" and setting paternalistic policies regarding trade and relations with the tribes. One continuing policy was the open trade in furs (for the British only), that allowed traders to introduce whiskey as a central commodity in the Indian trading system.

Carrying the Load

The actual engagements saw more Natives fighting than English or French. In the battle for Fort Duquesne in 1755, General Edward Braddock and the English were defeated by 72 Frenchmen, 1,436 Canadians, and 637 Indians.

William Johnson's In-laws

While the Caughnawaga tribe, an Iroquois-speaking people from Quebec, Canada, was allied with the French, Sir William Johnson kept their Iroquois brethren on the British side. He was a trader in the Mohawk Valley who earned a reputation of fairness among the Mohawk. He fathered eight children by a Mohawk woman named Molly Brant, his wife according to Native custom. Johnson led a combined force of Mohawk and English to victory—the only one in 1755—when they captured Lake George from the French.

If You Can't Join 'Em, Beat 'Em

Some tribes began the war as allies of one side but ended up switching alliances. The English induced the Cherokee to send a war party against the French-allied Shawnees in the Ohio Valley on the condition that the English would build forts to protect their families while the Cherokees were away. The Shawnee expedition wasn't a success and was made even less so when 24 Cherokees were murdered by English colonists as they returned home. The Cherokees, encouraged by the French, struck back hard against the English. They burned cabins and killed settlers on the frontier of Virginia and in the Carolinas and, in turn, had their settlements and fields destroyed by an English expedition.

Not all tribes got involved in the conflict. The Creek were courted by the English, as well as the French and Cherokees. Although a few young Creek men attacked English traders, the Creek remained unallied. The Creek's allies, the Choctaws and Chickasaws, also remained neutral.

> **Native Voices**
>
> The English are our friends and we love them, dearly—we desire that goods may continue amongst us and your friendship as formally. The Cherokees are what you called your greatest friends and we are sorry that you should be hurt by them. But [we] are resolved to have no hand in the war betwixt you—. It is our intent that our path shall not be spoiled, either to this place or to the Choctaws and Chickasaws. Some of the Cherokees may come to our towns; no doubt we shall have talks, if good, it's well, if bad, we shall give no ear to them. The day shall never come that the knot of friendship between us [i.e., the Creeks and the English] shall be loosed, it is not a slippery knot but tied very fast.
>
> —Creek Council to the English, 1759

Pontiac's War

By the middle of the 1700s, Britain emerged as the victorious colonial power in North America. Indian tribes, used to trading and allying themselves with the French, now had to deal with the English. The English regarded the Natives as a defeated race and saw no reason to try to remain on friendly terms with them.

When the French turned over the forts in the Great Lakes region to the British in 1760 at the end of the French and Indian War, the British acted as if the Indians on whose land the forts sat had become their servants, or as if the Indians didn't exist. Pontiac, the Ottawa chief, met with the British, who agreed to recognize the delineation of Indian land originally negotiated with the French, to uphold the trading practices previously in force, and to continue to supply the Indians with ammunition. Only after these agreements were reached did Pontiac agree to allow the British to occupy the former French forts. He warned the British that if they mistreated the Indians of the region, he would block their access to the interior.

Relations between the British and the Indians deteriorated almost at once. British traders cheated the Indians and plied them with whiskey. British soldiers abused Indians who came to the forts and refused to give out ammunition when requested. The British, it seems, didn't want allies; they wanted subjects.

As they grew increasingly unhappy with the British, the Seneca, Delaware, Potawatomi, Miami, Shawnees, Ottawa, and other tribes talked of throwing the British out. Pontiac emerged as their leader. Echoing the words of Neolin, the Delaware prophet, he announced that Wolf, the Master of Life, had said of the British, "Send them back to the country which I made for them! There let them remain."

Pontiac's Grand Plan

Pontiac planned to bring all tribes within a 200,000-square-mile area together to form an army to defeat the British and reclaim tribal lands. He formulated the plan at a grand council in April 1763. The plan was to be carried out in May 1763. Pontiac and 60 other chiefs would wage an attack simultaneously against Fort Detroit and other forts around the Great Lakes, including Green Bay, Mackinac, Sandusky, and St. Joseph.

In May 1763, the allied Indians began attacking forts throughout the Great Lakes area. Fort Sandusky, on the shore of Lake Erie, fell first; then a British fort among the Miami Indians, near present-day Fort Wayne, Indiana; then Forts Ouiatenon and Michilimackinac fell; while in Pennsylvania, two more forts fell.

All told, Pontiac and his allies attacked 12 forts, capturing 9 of them. The British abandoned a tenth.

Deadly Revenge

At Fort Pitt, the British resorted to biological warfare. Pretending to give the Indians gifts, they sent out blankets infected with smallpox, a disease that the Indians had no resistance to. Hundreds of Indians died from the terrible disease. Still, by the end of 1763, 8 out of 12 British posts had been captured and their garrisons wiped out.

Tribal Truths _____

In 1707, 1,400 Indians in a South Carolina colony were officially listed as slaves out of a total census of 9,580 free whites, white servants, black slaves, and Indian slaves. This continued a century-long pattern of formally enslaving Indians in the British colonies. There were three ways by which Indians became slaves: (1) as punishment, (2) as prisoners of war, or (3) as captives of other tribes.

Pontiac had been assured of help from the French, but France had relinquished all her lands along the Mississippi and could not support Pontiac's forces. His men were running out of ammunition and had no other sources for supplies.

In October 1766, Pontiac reluctantly agreed to peace, and the British agreed to prohibit colonists from moving into Indian Territory west of the Appalachians. Three years later, a peace treaty formally ended the rebellion.

Tribal Truths _____

Out west, the horse culture was beginning to thrive. Following the Pueblo Revolt in 1870, Plains tribes acquired the horse by trade and greatly enhanced their way of life. Instead of traveling only 5 miles a day, on horse the People could cover 15 miles. Using horses also allowed them to capture more game and thereby feed more people.

Impact of the Fur Trade

Reading the history of the conflicts between the Natives and Europeans, it seems that they were wholly occupied with making war on one another. However, when they weren't making war, they were engaged in an extensive trade in fur. The fur trade was a major component of the economy of the early period. Beaver pelts trapped in Canada and in the northern British colonies were especially valuable in Europe, where the climate and social prestige made wearing furs desirable. Even farther south, deerskins were shipped from Charleston to European markets.

Natives eagerly sought the goods they might receive in exchange for their furs. Trade items included steel knives, axe heads, firearms, mirrors, metal cooking pots, cloth, and beads. Competition for fur was stiff. In addition to the Americans, the Swedes, Dutch, French, British, Spanish, and Russians were all participants in the pelt trade.

In some colonies, the fur trade served as the major economic base. Cities such as Albany, New York; Montreal, Quebec; Detroit; and St. Louis, all started out as fur-trading centers. This lucrative trade fueled much of the early European exploration and financed the penetrations into the interior of the continent. Predictably, the great European explorers were fur traders.

Middlemen and Mixed-Bloods

While the Europeans supplied the financing, trade goods, and the equipment, the Indians provided the labor. Indian traders acted as middlemen, facilitating trade between distant tribes and European fur companies. By marrying white traders, Indian women played an important intermediary role, providing a method for white traders to develop partnerships within an Indian tribe. In Canada and the Great Lakes of the United States, Indian women and French and Scottish traders produced a new population, known as *Métis*. In some communities, these offspring carried their father's surnames. Last names among the Cherokee and Cree still bear the legacy of those early trading days. Scottish names like McIntosh, McDonald, and Ross give testimony to these partnerships.

Tribal Truths

A **Métis** is a person of mixed Native and non-Native heritage. During the period of the fur trade, Native women often married French and Scottish trappers and traders to form a unique blend of cultures and languages. The term is used in Canada to identify individuals of mixed descent that includes aboriginal ancestry. Estimates of the number of Métis in Canada vary widely, from 300,000 to 800,000. Métis account for more than 20 percent of the Aboriginal population.

After the American Revolution (discussed in Chapter 8) the newly established U.S. government took more control over the fur trade.

The government issued licenses to trade with Indians to any person who put up a bond. Trade with Indians was regulated based on rules prescribed by the president. A major difficulty, however, was that many unprincipled traders didn't bother getting licenses, and those who did had to resort to unscrupulous practices—mainly the use of alcohol—in order to stay competitive.

The Government Sets Up Trading Posts

The frontier businessmen involved in the trading industry with Native peoples were notoriously corrupt. Tribes grew increasingly more hostile as the traders, licensed and unlicensed, continued to cheat them, resulting in unrest among the tribes. President Washington, in his fourth Annual Address, stated his position:

> I cannot dismiss the subject of Indian affairs without again recommending to your consideration the expediency of more adequate provision for giving energy to the laws throughout our interior frontier and for restraining the commission of outrages upon the Indians, without which all pacific plans must prove nugatory.

To address this state of affairs, Washington submitted a plan of establishing government trading houses in Indian territories. Washington wanted to be sure that the Indians would not accuse the government of wrongdoings in trade, so he and his advisors settled on the idea of supplying trade goods directly through government personnel to ensure that the Natives were treated fairly.

The act providing for trading houses among Indian tribes was passed into law in 1796. The object of the law was to resolve frontier difficulties caused by corrupt traders. The government envisioned itself as the intermediary in a vast trade network referred to as the *factory system*. Tribes would then become dependent upon the federal government for their trade needs.

Code Talking

The **factory system** is a network of trading posts set up by the federal government in the late 1700s to trade with Native Americans.

In some cases, the trade goods were already necessities, replacing traditional items. Such was the case with metal knives and hatchets. After the white man supplied the Natives with this material, there was no need to fashion knives from stone, and the art of flint knapping was all but lost. Some trade goods were luxuries—nice things to have, but not critical. For example, Natives used mirrors and beads for decoration.

Other Objectives of Trading Houses

But this action had other results as well. By undertaking trade with the Natives, the United States ensured that these tribes would not establish a loyalty to European powers, still perceived to be a threat by the nascent country. The United States hoped for a trade monopoly with the Indian tribes.

The government trading posts were quasi-military in nature, creating a permanent settlement in the land and further expansion of the frontier. Some of the American cities that originated as trading posts were Des Moines, Chicago, Fort Wayne, and Green Bay. Some of these outposts were among the first non-Indian settlements in the Northwest.

Expansion and End of the Factory System

By 1811, 10 trading houses were strung along the southern and western boundaries of the United States. The economic returns of each house varied, some showing a profit while others lost revenue. Overall, however, the results represented a net gain of more than $12,000 between 1811 and 1815. Rarely does a government program show a profit!

The factory system came to an end in 1822, but not because they had been financially unsuccessful. Private traders lobbied Congress for the abandonment of the trading houses, citing unfair competition. After the factory system was shut down, Thomas L. McKenney, who was superintendent of Indian trade for many years, turned his attention to the reorganization of the subdivision charged with Indian affairs in the Department of War. McKenney became responsible for creating the structure of the Bureau of Indian Affairs (see Chapter 9).

Disease and Disappearing People

The trade industry took its toll on the Natives. Contagious diseases spread from tribe to tribe as Natives traded with Europeans and then with other tribes. The Blackfeet in northwest Montana and southern Alberta were severely decimated by smallpox first in 1781, long before they met Europeans. When Lewis and Clark first met the Mandan, on the Missouri River, they numbered some 1,250. In 1837, after an epidemic of smallpox and cholera, there were only 150 or so left.

> **Tribal Truths**
>
> Was smallpox introduced to Indians on purpose, as an early form of germ warfare? Certainly in colonial times, during the Pontiac War, this notion was discussed and, in one case, a British officer gave two chiefs blankets and a handkerchief out of a smallpox hospital. There is no evidence, however, that the U.S. government used the smallpox virus to conduct a systematic and intentional extermination of Native peoples.

Loss of Culture, Loss of Resources

The fur trade had a negative impact on the traditional Native economy. Trade had always been an element of tribal economic systems, but it was a secondary activity to hunting, fishing, or farming. With the coming of the fur trade, tribes began to divert their energy to trapping and trading. Additionally, in cultures where status was traditionally gained by exemplary actions such as war deeds, priorities began to shift. An enterprising man could accumulate great wealth and, therefore, status, by trade. Populations of beaver, otter, and muskrat were nearly wiped out by overhunting as men sought to acquire trade goods brought by the white man.

You Take One Barrel of Missouri River Water ...

Arguably, the biggest impact of the fur trade was the introduction of alcohol as a trade commodity. Traders quickly figured out that alcohol was a good way to attract Indians to trade. After the Indians were intoxicated, they were easy to take advantage of. Certainly, not all Indians drank, but for those who did, alcohol proved to have disastrous consequences.

Native Voices

You take one barrel of Missouri River water, and add two gallons of alcohol. Then you add two ounces of strychnine to make them crazy—because strychnine is the greatest stimulant in the world—and three plugs of tobacco to make them sick—because an Indian wouldn't figure it was whiskey unless it made him sick—and five bars of soap to give it a head, and half a pound of red pepper, and then you put in some sage brush and boil it until it's brown. Strain this into a barrel and you've got your Indian whiskey. One bottle calls for one buffalo robe, and when the Indian got drunk, it was two robes. And that's how some of the traders made their fortunes.

—Teddy Blue Abbott, fur trapper and trader

Finally, the fur trade led to the escalation of tribal warfare. European and American fur-trading companies often used tribes with which they had a trading relationship to harass rival companies and tribes. Prince Maximilian zu Wied, the German explorer and naturalist, witnessed an attack by Assiniboine and Cree warriors on a Piegan (Blackfeet) camp outside Fort McKenzie, an American Fur Company post.

The Colonies Move West

With the removal of the French, English colonists everywhere began to spill over the Indian boundaries. The Creeks were forced to cede a large tract of land to Georgia, and fortifications sprung up west of the Alleghenies. In Tennessee and in Kentucky, settlers like Daniel Boone were pushing westward and returning with news of green mountains and rich game. And so, the Europeans were continuing their advance upon the Natives from all sides. But more ominous, perhaps, there were clouds of war gathering as the American colonists began to grow more distant from the land of their nativity across the ocean.

The Least You Need to Know

- The tribes of the Northeast were sometimes unwilling pawns in the struggles between the French and the British for control in the Americas.

- The Iroquois is a confederacy of tribes, specifically the Onondagas, Mohawks, Oneidas, Senecas, and Cayugas (and later the Tuscarora).

- Although most tribes sided with the French during the French and Indian War, some Natives, like the Iroquois, fought with the British.

- Pontiac was able to lay siege to several English forts until a smallpox outbreak took its toll.

- The fur trade introduced alcohol and disease to the Native peoples.

Chapter 8

Native Americans and the Upstart States United

In This Chapter

- ◆ Native participation in the American Revolution
- ◆ The early Indian policies of the American government
- ◆ How the Northwest Ordinance dealt with Natives
- ◆ Treaties and American Indians

The experience of the French and Indian War convinced the English of the need for tighter control over their North American colonies. The colonists, on the other hand, gained confidence in their ability to control their own internal affairs. This situation resulted in a tension between the mother country and the colonies. The Native peoples of the Americas found themselves caught somewhere in the middle yet again.

Keeping the Hatchet Buried Deep

During the American Revolution, like in the French and Indian War, both sides worked hard to win the support of Indian tribes. While the British attempted to incite the Natives to attack the upstart Americans, the revolting colonies urged them to remain neutral, which in essence meant the Natives were siding with the colonies. In 1775, the Continental Congress sent a message to the Iroquois, informing them of the war and advising them that "this is a family quarrel between us and old England … we desire you to remain at home and not join on either side but keep the hatchet buried deep." Of the Iroquois League, only the Oneidas and the Tuscaroras remained neutral; the other tribes joined the British. So much for keeping the hatchet buried deep.

Joseph Brant, younger son of Molly Brant, the Indian woman married to William Johnson, became the leader of the Mohawks and supported the British from Canada. In the south, the British enlisted Indians into their army and sent ammunition and supplies to the Creeks and Cherokees. The Americans protested to the Creeks, advising them that this war was "like a dispute between a father and his child." The Creeks, unlike most of the Iroquois tribes, decided on neutrality.

Native Voices

We are now going to speak to our eldest brothers, the white people; we have heard all your talks to the red people and hope you will hear ours. We thought that all the English people were as one people but now we hear that they have a difference amongst themselves. It is our desire that they drop their disputes and not spoil one another; as all the red people are living in friendship with one another, we desire that the white people will do the same. It is the custom with the red people when they send such a talk and these tokens to prevent any of our warriors from going to war and we hope that the white people will do the same and agree to our talk—We send this wing and tobacco as a token of friendship and desire that the beloved men will smoke the tobacco and look at the wing and agree to each others' talk.

—Creek Council to the Americans, 1775

Treaty with the Delaware

In the Ohio Valley, the Delaware and Shawnees tribes found themselves pressured by British and American agents to join their side as allies. Led by the pro-American chief White Eyes, the Delaware, or Lenape, signed a treaty with the newly formed United States.

The treaty was signed at Fort Pitt, September 17, 1778, and was the first treaty ever made by the United States with an Indian tribe. The Delaware agreed to let American troops pass through their country to attack the British posts. They would sell the Americans corn and other supplies, and their warriors would enlist in the Army.

The Americans didn't keep their promises, however, beginning a pattern of treaty-making and treaty-breaking that would continue for another 100 years. The Americans didn't deliver the protection they promised in the treaty, and the American militia killed White Eyes as well as the Shawnee chief Cornstalk.

Tribal Truths

The Delaware tribe was first encountered by Europeans in 1620 living along the Delaware River in and around present-day Vernon, New Jersey, as well as in New York, Pennsylvania, and Delaware. In 1778, the Delaware were the first Indian tribe to sign a treaty with the newly established United States.

By the 1770s, the tribe had been forced westward and occupied the country between the Ohio and White Rivers in Indiana. Throughout the next 40 years, 13 treaties provided for the removal of the Delaware from Missouri to a reservation between Kansas and Missouri. Finding themselves in intolerable conditions, the tribe asked to be moved once again. Indian Territory was suggested, and in 1812, they settled in Oklahoma.

Indian Territory was established in the 1830s for the home of displaced tribes from the east, most notably the Five Civilized Tribes. The term *territory* is somewhat misleading; it never had a territorial government (see Chapter 11).

The Defeat of the Iroquois Confederacy

In July 1778, British colonel John Butler, with his Corps of Rangers, entered the Wyoming Valley in Pennsylvania with the objective of bringing British Loyalist refugees back to Fort Niagara. His troops consisted of 200 British soldiers, 200 Loyalists, and 700 Indians, primarily Senecas and Cayugas (both Iroquois). In a disparate battle with settlers, Butler's Rangers killed approximately 225 patriots, and many captives were tortured and later killed. A year later, General John Sullivan, of the Continental Army, in a retaliatory campaign, struck the Iroquois. He defeated the Iroquois and their Tory allies in the fiercely fought battle of Newtown, near Elmira, New York, then marched through Iroquois territory, burning their fields and destroying their villages. The revolution ended with the great Iroquois Confederacy forever broken.

The Last of the Mahicans?

In New England, the tribes generally supported their American neighbors. A number of Stockbridge and Mahican (or Mohican) Indians joined General Washington at the siege of Boston in 1775 and suffered great losses. They also fought alongside the Patriots at Bunker Hill and in numerous other engagements. Unfortunately, the Stockbridge paid a terrible price for their patriotism. The war cost them almost half their adult male population. To add further insult, upon their return, they found the Americans had taken over their lands while they were away.

> **Tribal Truths** _____
>
> James Fenimore Cooper made the Mohicans famous with his 1826 novel, *Last of the Mohicans*. Unfortunately, he also made them extinct in the minds of many readers. After the American Revolution, many Mahicans placed themselves under the protection of the Iroquois Confederacy. Those remaining in Massachusetts joined the Stockbridge; other Mahican descendants live in Connecticut and Wisconsin. So the Mohicans are still very much alive!

End of the Revolution

On September 3, 1783, at the Treaty of Paris, the British recognized the independence of the United States and acknowledged American sovereignty in all previously held British territories. The Native tribes who had allied with the British were not present at the signing of the peace treaty and now had to face the new power on the block. As it turns out, it didn't much matter who the Indian tribes sided with: They all suffered the same fate in the end.

The Utmost Good Faith: The Northwest Ordinance

In 1787, the first significant Indian policy established by the new U.S. government promised good relations with the Native Americans. The Northwest Ordinance, a group of laws passed by Congress, stated that Indians were to be treated with the "utmost good faith" and specifically that "their lands and property shall never be taken from them without their consent." However, the ordinance also provided for the settlement by whites of the Ohio country. These two goals—treating the Indians with utmost good faith, and settling the Ohio territory—clashed almost immediately.

It wasn't long before the United States violated that "utmost good faith" and took up its usual pattern: extinguishing Indian title to the land, surveying it into mile-section tracts, then selling it to settlers. Soon, settlers were extending farther into the Northwest Territory. By 1790, 4,300 whites were living in the Northwest Territory, many around the newly founded town of Cincinnati.

Considering the tension created by the advancing frontier and the demands by citizens for protection, the new U.S. government adopted a fairly humane Indian policy. President Washington and his secretary of war, Henry Knox, promoted a policy that they hoped would lead to the *assimilation* into Euro-American culture. Knox promoted giving the Natives farming implements and domestic animals, and advocated the establishment of missions among the Indians.

Washington unveiled his plans to Congress in 1791, announcing more orderly land purchases from the Natives, the promotion of commerce between Natives and settlers, training for Indians in economic pursuits, and the protection of the Natives against wrongdoings by whites. But first, he had to get the Natives' attention.

Code Talking

Assimilation is a concept and a policy directed at encouraging (and sometimes forcing) Indians to give up their cultural practices and adopt the lifestyle of the dominant Euro-American ways. For more on assimilation policies, see Chapter 13.

Little Turtle's Big Victory Against St. Clair

Washington sent three expeditions against tribes that were raiding settlements in the Northwest Territory. In 1790, the Miami, under the leadership of Little Turtle, routed the Americans led by General Josiah Harmar, and Washington ordered the governor of the Northwest Territory, General Arthur St. Clair, to assume personal command of future campaigns. St. Clair marched 100 miles from Cincinnati to meet Little Turtle and the Miami.

The governor should have stayed at home. On November 4, 1791, St. Clair and his men were badly defeated by Little Turtle in what is remembered as one of the worst routs in American military history. About 900 of St. Clair's men were killed or wounded, and the rest fled in panic. Fighting with the Miami was a young Shawnee man named Tecumseh, who distinguished himself admirably in the battle.

Tribal Truths

Little Turtle, or Michikinikwa, was the war chief of the Miami and was noted for his great speaking skills and intelligence. His forces inflicted the worse defeat ever suffered by the U.S. Army at the hands of Native peoples. St. Clair's forces consisted of a 1,300 men. Of these, 602 were killed and approximately 300 were wounded. Little Turtle's force consisted of about 1,000 warriors. Only 66 Indians were killed in this battle.

Washington was humiliated. He turned to negotiations, inviting the Iroquois leaders to Philadelphia (the U.S. capital at the time) to try to restore peace. The Iroquois ignored his invitation. He then sent three agents to confer with the Natives. Two were killed and the third barely escaped. Washington next turned to Joseph Brant, the Mohawk leader who had sided with the British during the Revolutionary War. Brant claimed later that Washington offered to double the pension he received from the British, plus add a significant bonus, if Brant were successful in making peace. Pleading illness, Brant refused to get involved.

Mad Anthony Wayne and the Battle of Fallen Timbers

Washington put Major General Anthony Wayne in command of the U.S. forces in the Ohio country. While Wayne was assembling and training his troops at Fort Jefferson, some 75 miles south of Cincinnati, the Ohio tribes, especially the Shawnees, were attempting to put together a coalition that would unite the tribes in the Midwest with the southern tribes. The Creeks, Cherokee, and the Shawnees endangered white settlements and threatened Nashville. Warriors under Tecumseh attacked travelers on the Cumberland Trail and raided Tennessee settlers. Soon the Shawnee chief, Blue Jacket, called on Tecumseh, who had acquainted himself well in warfare against St. Clair, to fight Wayne with him.

In the meantime, General Wayne marched his army of 3,000 men northward to just south of the present-day Toledo, Ohio. On August 20, 1794, Wayne defeated a force of about a 1,100 Indians fighting under Blue Jacket and Tecumseh. This confrontation took place in a part of the forest where a recent storm had knocked down many trees, hence the name the Battle of Fallen Timbers. Tecumseh and his Shawnee scouts fought hard but could not turn the battle. The Americans lost about 30 men, and probably 200 Indians were killed. Wayne pressed on, destroying every Indian village he could find. In the spring of 1795, he called a council of 12 tribes and dictated the terms of surrender, which included the cession of part of Indiana and nearly all of Ohio.

> **Native Voices**
>
> We were driven by the sharp end of the guns of the Long Knives. Our moccasins trickled with blood in the sand, and the water was red in the river.
>
> —Chief Kin-Jo-I-No, on the Battle of Fallen Timbers

In 1795, 1,100 chiefs, including Blue Jacket, of the eastern confederated tribes, signed the Treaty of Greenville. The seven-foot-long document was signed by the chiefs of the Shawnee, Delaware, Ottawa, Potawatomi, Wyandot, Miami, Chippewa, and Kickapoo, among others. Tecumseh refused to acknowledge the treaty and withdrew to present-day Indiana, where other Indians joined him. This wouldn't be the last time the United States would have to deal with this powerful Shawnee leader.

The Treaty of New York

Meanwhile, the tribes of the South—the Cherokee, Creeks, Choctaws, and the Chickasaws—were organized under the leadership of Alexander McGillivray, a mixed-blood Creek who had fought as a Tory during the Revolution and continued to hate Americans. In his efforts to resist the advance of American settlement in the lower Mississippi Valley, McGillivray had the support and encouragement of Spain.

Washington attempted to buy peace with the southern tribes by inviting McGillivray to New York and agreeing to pay him what amounted to a bribe to secure his signature on a treaty. A secret treaty, since known as the Treaty of New York, signed in 1790 by Washington and McGillivray, conferred upon McGillivray the rank of brigadier general with an annual salary of $1,200 and provided that six other leading chiefs should receive an annual stipend of $100. The treaty also promised peace between the Creeks and other tribes and ceded Creek land to the federal government. Despite the Treaty of New York, the Natives continued to raid American settlements along the border. At last, in the early 1790s, the Tennesseans invaded Indian country and attacked several tribes, putting an end to Native incursions.

> **Tribal Truths**
>
> Born Hoboi-Hilr-Miko in Alabama in 1759, Alexander McGillivray was the son of a Scot trapper and a half-French, half-Wind-Indian woman. McGillivray had led trade for the Panton, Leslie & Company in Florida and became the leading spokesperson for all the tribes along the Florida-Georgia frontier. He was a resident of Pensacola, Florida, at the time of his death in 1793.

Trick or Treaty!

By the late 1700s, *treaties* had become increasingly important for determining relations between the U.S. government and the Indian tribes. Because of the crucial role treaties have played in the history of Native Americans, let's take a closer look at them.

The Supreme Law of the Land ... or Not!

Treaties are the "supreme law of the land." This means that they are superior to state laws and constitutions and are equal in rank to laws passed by Congress. A treaty can be made on any subject, except that it may not deprive a citizen of a right guaranteed by the Constitution.

Until 1871, treaties were the accepted method by which the United States conducted its relations with Indian tribes. The United States has entered into more than 650 Indian treaties, and nearly every tribe has at least one treaty with the United States.

> **Code Talking**
>
> A **treaty** is a legally binding contract between two or more sovereign nations. The U.S. Constitution authorizes the president, with the consent of two thirds of the Senate, to make treaties on behalf of the United States. In treaties between the U.S. government and the Indians, tribes typically agreed to give up something, say land, to receive something in return from the U.S. government, such as medical care, education, and protection of their resources.

Before the War of 1812, the United States and Indian nations negotiated as relative equals. The new nation, weakened by years of war with England, would have been no match for the Indians. Consequently, the early Indian treaties were voluntary and mutually advantageous; the United States obtained land and assurances of non-aggression from the tribes, and the tribes received goods and services from the federal government.

After the War of 1812, in which the threat of British intervention in American internal affairs was finally ended, the federal government had less reason to maintain its friendship with the tribes. What the Americans wanted most was Indian land, which it systematically began to take by force. Indian treaties after 1812 were rarely voluntary.

End of Treaty-Making

In 1871, Congress pass a law (Title 25, Chapter 3, Subchapter 1, Section 71 of the U.S. Code, referred to as *Section 71*) abolishing the practice of making treaties with Indian tribes. This law declared that Indian tribes were not sovereign nations with whom the United States could make treaties. Since then, Congress has regulated Indian affairs through legislation, which is more convenient for Congress because laws, unlike Indian treaties, do not need the consent of the Indians before they come into effect.

> **Code Talking**
>
> **Section 71** of Title 25, Chapter 3, Subchapter 1, abolishes the policy of making treaties with Indian nations.

Congress passed Section 71 largely because the House of Representatives disliked its exclusion from Indian policy-making. Under the Constitution, treaties are made by the president and the Senate. Consequently, the House took no part in formulating Indian policy. The House pressured the Senate into passing Section 71 so that it would have a hand in regulating the government's relations with Indians.

The new law didn't affect existing treaties. Section 71 contains a provision that states "no obligation of any treaty … shall be hereby invalidated or impaired." Therefore, any Indian treaty made prior to 1871 was still valid.

This doesn't mean, though, that every Indian treaty is still valid today. To the contrary, most treaties have been "abrogated," that is, broken or breached by Congress. The Supreme Court held that Indian treaties have the same dignity as federal statutes, but no greater dignity. Therefore, a federal law can amend or even repeal an Indian treaty in the same way that it can amend or repeal a law.

Canons of Treaty Construction

Of course, many disagreements have arisen over the terms and provisions of Indian treaties. These disputes often involve interests in land, water, mineral rights, and hunting and fishing rights. Because of the frequency of these disputes, the Supreme Court has developed a set of rules that govern the interpretation of Indian treaties. These rules are known as the canons of treaty construction. There are three basic canons. First, uncertainties in treaties must be resolved in favor of the Indians. Second, Indian treaties must be interpreted as the Indians would have understood them. Finally, Indian treaties must be liberally construed in favor of the Indians.

These canons obviously benefit the treaty tribes. The Supreme Court meant for that to be the case. Tribes were at a significant disadvantage in the treaty-making process. For one thing, treaties were always negotiated and written in English and the tribes could never be sure what they were signing. Besides, most treaties were forced upon the tribes and were unfair to begin with. For these reasons, Indians should receive the benefit of the doubt when questions arise.

Native Americans and the Constitution

It's pretty clear that Native peoples were not included in the Constitution of the United States when it was adopted in 1787. That isn't to say that Indian people are not now covered by that landmark of democracy, but in the beginning of the republic, Natives were not citizens of the United States nor did the Founding Fathers ever believe they would be.

Native Americans are first referred to in Article 1, Section 2, which states, "Representatives and direct taxes shall be apportioned among the several states which may be included within this union, according to their respective numbers, which shall be determined by adding to the whole number of free persons, including those bound to service for a term of years, and excluding *Indians not taxed* [emphasis added], three fifths of all other Persons." The reference to "Indians not taxed" was due to the vaguely sovereign status the Indian tribes held at the time the Constitution was drafted. This clearly excludes Indians from participation in the constitutional process.

Code Talking

The **Commerce Clause** is Article 1, Section 8, Clause 3, which gives Congress the power to regulate commerce with Indian tribes.

The only other reference to Indians is Article 1, Section 8, Clause 3, which reads, "The Congress shall have power to … regulate Commerce with foreign nations, and among the several states, and with the Indian tribes." This is sometimes called the *Commerce Clause* and distinguishes Indian tribes from foreign nations and from states. The original Constitution does not address what tribes were, only what they weren't.

The Future's So Bright, Ya Gotta Wear Shades!

As the 1700s drew to a close, the American government was beginning to feel pretty secure. It had driven out the British (at least for the time being), secured the frontier from the Spanish, and had crafted a Constitution for all times. And the United States began a policy of making treaties with Indian tribes as a way to secure peace and to acquire Indian land. The United States now included not only the 13 original colonies but also lands that spread all the way to the Mississippi River. The Native tribes of the Old Northwest and the Old Southwest were pacified by the military might of the American government. For the first time in several decades, peace reigned over the new republic. But you get the feeling that peace won't last long.

The Least You Need to Know

- Native tribes generally supported the British during the American Revolution.

- The Delaware, or Lenape, were the first tribe to sign a treaty with the United States.

- Tribes who supported the Americans nonetheless suffered the loss of land.

- The Northwest Ordinance promised "the utmost good faith" toward Indian people.

- According to the U.S. Constitution, the relationship between American and Indian tribes was an economic one.

Chapter

Bossing Indians Around: A History of the BIA

In This Chapter

- Colonies organize agencies to deal with the Indians
- The newly formed United States creates the Indian Department
- Agents are given near-complete control
- The BIA is born

Many non-Indian people have heard of the *Bureau of Indian Affairs* (*BIA*), and it would probably be impossible to find an Indian person who has not. But unless you are a serious student of federal Indian policy, the bureau is some vague agency remembered for what it has done, or failed to do, for Indian people. At this point it might be helpful to describe what that agency is and tell a little of its history, which goes all the way back to the late 1700s.

The Indian Department of the Continental Congress

After the French and Indian War, the northern and southern colonies formed quasi-sovereign governmental units. Each established a superintendency of

Indian affairs to attempt to resolve the issues rising out of colonial settlement of tribal land.

When the Second Continental Congress was created, it assumed the powers of a national government and created three departments of Indian affairs to replace the two regional superintendents in the colonies. These three departments were known as the Northern Department, the Middle Department, and the Southern Department. Each was headed by a body of commissioners, and each reported to Congress. The duties of the departments were to preserve peace and friendship with the tribes and to prevent the tribes from taking up arms against the colonies.

> **Code Talking**
>
> The **Bureau of Indian Affairs (BIA)** is a branch of the Department of Interior charged with administering services to tribes under authority of treaties and agreements reached between Indian nations and the federal government.

> **Tribal Truths**
>
> Some Native peoples say the only thing they need to know about the Bureau of Indian Affairs is that BIA can also stand for "Boss Indians Around."

The three departments of Indian affairs existed until 1786. In August 7 of that year, the Congress of the Confederation, a legislative body that governed the United States from 1774 to 1789, modified the "Indian Department" into a southern district and a northern district. The southern district included all Indian nations south of the Ohio River, and the northern district extended to those tribes west of the Hudson River. Although called the Indian Department, this term was never an official title of the organization.

Superintendents of Indian Affairs

The Northwest Land Ordinance of August 1786 provided that a superintendent of Indian affairs be appointed by the Congress of the Confederation from each district. James White was the first person to serve as superintendent of the southern district; Arthur St. Clair, the governor of the Western Territory, also served as the superintendent of the northern district.

The duties of the superintendents were broad. As described by the Ordinance of 1786, "The said superintendents shall attempt the execution of such regulations as Congress shall from time to time establish, respecting Indian affairs …." Congress, however, didn't have many regulations, so the superintendents basically carried out directives formalized by the Northwest Ordinance of 1787.

The superintendents of Indian affairs reported to the secretary of war, and all directives were issued by the secretary. So at least initially, the regulation of Indian affairs was vested in the War Department. Wherever housed, this became the structure of what is now known as the Bureau of Indian Affairs.

The Best of Intentions

In the beginning, the Congress of the Confederation attempted to deal with tribes fairly. This attitude was incorporated into the Northwest Ordinance, which promised that …

> … The utmost good faith shall always be observed toward Indians; their lands and properties shall never be taken from them without their consent; and in their property, rights, and liberty, they shall never be invaded or disturbed, unless in just and lawful war authorized by Congress; but laws founded in justice and humanity shall from time to time be made, for preventing wrongs done to them, and for preserving peace and friendship with them …

Under the directives of Congress, the superintendents of Indian affairs set about to negotiate with Indian nations. White and St. Clair both traveled to Indian territories to negotiate treaties on behalf of the united former colonies.

Indian Affairs "Enjoined on, or Entrusted to Him"

Because the War Department was part of the Executive Branch, Indian affairs were ultimately left up to the president to deal with, and the secretary of war was entrusted to carry out those duties as assigned by the chief executive.

The first Congress never abolished the southern and northern districts nor did it change the relationship between Indian tribes and the federal government. Indian affairs, at that early juncture of American history, were the responsibility of the president!

Governors, Indian Agents, and Subagents

The northern and southern districts of Indian affairs ceased functioning in 1790, when territorial governors were charged with the oversight of Indian affairs in their respective territories. Their positions were "ex-officio superintendent of Indian affairs." This became standard procedure up to 1867.

The difficulty with this procedure was that often the position of superintendent of Indian affairs conflicted with duties as governor. The governors were responsible for the development of the territory, with the goal of eventually achieving statehood.

Certainly, Congress didn't look favorably toward governors who couldn't control their territories' "Indian problem." As a consequence, governors often pursued policies that eliminated the Indians as a way of solving the "problem."

Superintendents were not the only personnel involved in the administration of Indian affairs. Because of the growing complexity of the relationship between Native tribes and the federal government, the Indian office was expanded in 1800 to include the appointment of persons living among Native peoples. Many treaties specified that a representative of the federal government was required to reside in proximity to the tribe with which the government had a treaty. In fact, an early treaty with the Delaware, signed in 1778, provided for "... a well-regulated trade, under the conduct of an intelligent, candid agent, with an adequate salary, one more influenced by the love of his country ..."

Native Voices

Generally, our Great Father sends big men. They come up—find condition on Indians. Make many papers for benefit of Indians ... when they go back papers never come up.

—Chippewa leader

As reservations were located for western tribes, agencies were established as the more-or-less permanent presence of the federal government. The agent oversaw the distribution of treaty annuities and served as the temporary dispensers of authority of the United States.

In 1822, the Indian Department employed 3 superintendents of Indian affairs, 17 agents, and 25 subagents. These constituted the whole of the administrative personnel in the agency (not counting interpreters and blacksmiths). There was, however, no official delineation of the duties for agents or their powers. Thus, individual agents and subagents wielded a great deal of authority not specifically granted to them.

A political appointee, the Indian agent clothed and fed "his" Indians and implemented whatever policy was popular back east. Because of the isolation of the agencies, the agent wielded absolute power. Tribes became dependent upon their agents, because without the agents' good graces they would starve to death.

Native Voices

The Indian agent they have sent us is so mean that he carries around in his pocket a linen rag into which he blows his nose, for fear he will blow away something of value.

—Plains Chief

The situation was ripe for skullduggery. Politicians and bureaucrats bought and sold agent positions like so much candy. These positions could be quite lucrative. Agents received kickbacks from cattle dealers and sold off reservation resources such as timber and mineral rights. Goods intended for Indians were stolen outright or replaced with inferior substitutes. In one scheme on a Montana agency, the flour mill triple-bagged flour, and the agent issued payment for three "bags" of flour when the Indians only received one bag.

Indian Peace Commissioners? An Oxymoron?

When the federal government negotiated a treaty with an Indian tribe, the president appointed commissioners to represent the interests of the United States in the treaty. These appointees were termed *Indian peace commissioners* and were authorized to reach an agreement with the tribes. What was never made clear to many tribes was that the peace commissioners were not the final authority on treaty negotiations—all treaties must be ratified by the U.S. Senate. Sometimes Congress changes the terms negotiated in the field by the peace commissioners before ratifying them. When Congress ceased negotiating with tribes in 1871, the need for peace commissioners to negotiate treaties became unnecessary.

Code Talking

Indian peace commissioners were appointed by the president of the United States to negotiate treaties on behalf of the federal government.

Establishment of the Bureau of Indian Affairs

In 1824, Secretary of War John C. Calhoun created the Bureau of Indian Affairs, and Thomas L. McKenny, formerly superintendent of Indian trade (see Chapter 7), became its first head. The duties of the office included approving all vouchers for expenditures, administering the funds appropriated to "civilize" the Indians, deciding on claims arising between Indians and whites under the trade and intercourse acts, and handling correspondence dealing with Indian affairs.

Tribal Truths

Even though Thomas McKenny was appointed head of the Bureau of Indian Affairs in 1824, it wasn't until 1826 that he had a title. By an act of Congress, the head of the bureau became the commissioner of Indian Affairs.

The bureau, although still in the War Department, often dealt with issues wholly unrelated to war or the military. Recognizing this, Congress passed an act in 1832, creating the Office of Indian Affairs and transferring the authority over financial transactions from the secretary of war to the commissioner of Indian Affairs.

Enter the Department of Inferior, Er, Interior

In 1789, there were only three executive departments: the State, Treasury, and War. Domestic affairs were spread among the three. The idea of establishing a separate department for domestic matters was proposed on a number of occasions, but it wasn't until 1849 that a department of the Interior was established.

In the three years between 1845 and 1848, the United States added more than a million square miles of territory in the West, reaching from Mexico to Canada, much of it via treaties with Indian nations. Along with its acquisition came the problem of managing it.

Land management fell to the General Land Office, under the Department of the Treasury, and Secretary of the Treasury Robert J. Walker, foresaw a staggering work-load as lobbyists and land speculators descended on his office. Walker maintained in his 1848 annual report that the Land Office had little to do with other Treasury functions, nor did the Patent Office in the State Department or the Indian Affairs Office in the War Department have much to do with their responsibilities. He proposed that they all should be brought together under a new "Department of the Interior."

History was ripe for Walker's idea by 1849. A law creating the Department of the Interior passed the House of Representatives on February 15, 1849, and reached the Senate floor, where it passed, on the last day of the thirtieth Congress—31 to 25. By this narrow margin, the Department of the Interior was created on March 3, 1849.

> **Tribal Truths** _____
>
> If you look at the Department of the Interior, you will find, among others, the Fish and Wildlife Service, the National Park Service, Bureau of Reclamation, Bureau of Land Management, and the Bureau of Indian Affairs. What do all these agencies have in common? The administration of land. The Bureau of Indian Affairs is charged with the preservation of American Indian land just as the National Park Service is dedicated to the preservation of national parks.

Military and Civil Policies Toward Indians

From the 1850s through the 1880s, there existed an almost contradictory situation in American policies toward Indian tribes. The military interest was to totally defeat the western enemies—tribes that stood in the way of westward expansion. The U.S. Army gave no quarter and expected none in return.

Yet in the office of the commissioner of Indian Affairs, the policy was to promote policies for the best welfare and improvement of Native peoples. The civil policy was a *peace policy*. Not all white people supported this approach, however. Many western-ers blamed Indian uprisings on the laxity of the military and overprotection by "Indian lovers." They agreed with the War Department that only a policy of force would keep the troublesome Natives in their place.

During the period of the Indian wars, some advocated that Indian affairs be returned to the War Department. Certainly there was some logic to that proposal. The relationship between the western tribes and the federal gov-ernment was rooted in hostility, as tribes tried to resist the invasion of their territories.

The resolution came with the defeat of the western tribes and the establishment of reser-vations. By this time, the policies of the fed-eral government could be carried out by the Bureau of Indian Affairs without military assistance.

During the reservation period, until fairly recently, the Bureau of the Indian Affairs acted as the guardian to the Indian ward. The BIA developed a pattern of paternalism as the bureau fed, clothed, educated, and converted the American Indian, most often without the consent of Native peoples.

Code Talking

The **peace policy** was the guiding principle of President Ulysses S. Grant, who attempted to reform the Bureau of Indian Affairs. Under this plan, civilians recommended by religious organ-izations were appointed Indian agents.

Tribal Truths

Because religious institu-tions were still active in Indian affairs after the Civil War, President Ulysses Grant turned many Indian agencies over to superintendents who were nominated by reli-gious agencies. By 1871, 67 of the 74 Indian agencies were headed by such nominees. This remained practice until the 1880s.

The Least You Need to Know

♦ Colonies established three agencies to deal with Indians.

♦ The early Indian Department was under the supervision of the secretary of war and the president of the United States.

♦ Indian agents ruled over many aspects of Indian people's lives.

♦ The BIA became part of the Department of the Interior when it was created.

♦ The BIA has a history of paternalism toward Native peoples.

Chapter **10**

Exploring the Interior

In This Chapter

- ◆ The Louisiana Purchase
- ◆ Lewis and Clark's Expedition
- ◆ How the expedition affected Native peoples

Every school child has heard of the Lewis and Clark Expedition. Most understand that its purpose was to explore this undiscovered and unknown part of the West known as the Louisiana Territory—the vast area stretching from the Gulf Coast to the present Canadian boarder in the North and from the Mississippi River to the Rocky Mountains in the West. Yet the story isn't as simple as the history books would have you believe. The territory wasn't unknown, nor was it empty. There were thousands of Native peoples living there, unaware of national and international politics that would make a dramatic impact on their lives.

The United States Expands Its Territory

France claimed the Louisiana Territory by virtue of the explorations of LaSalle, Cartier, and Champlain. These claims of ownership seem rather presumptuous when one considers that these lands claimed by European powers were not empty but, rather, were home to perhaps millions of Native peoples.

With their victory in the French and Indian War in 1763, Great Britain had effectively driven the French out of North America for the time being. Before going, however, France ceded "Louisiana" to Spain, not wishing Great Britain to have it.

Code Talking

The **right of deposit** allowed American traders to offload their barges into warehouses in New Orleans, where their cargo would await transfer to larger seagoing vessels.

The young upstart Americans began to spread out over North America in greater numbers than ever. Toward the end of the seventeenth century, the United States had reached the Ohio Valley and was nearing the Mississippi River. There seemed no doubt that soon the Americans would cross the Mississippi, not stopping them until they reached the Pacific Ocean. In 1800, Spain, perhaps seeing the handwriting on the wall, by virtue of the secret Treaty of San Ildefonso, retroceded Louisiana back to France.

When the treaty became public, it caught the attention of President Thomas Jefferson. He had been long interested in the Mississippi, seeing its potential for commerce. However, as long as Spain held Louisiana, or more specifically the port of New Orleans, America's interests were protected. Spain had granted the United States the *right of deposit* at the port of New Orleans, giving American merchants easy access to the interior of the Mississippi. While Spain was willing to accommodate American presence in New Orleans, France's position was uncertain.

A Bargain at Any Price

An official transfer of Louisiana to French ownership had not yet taken place in 1802, so the Spanish still retained the administrative control over New Orleans. Spain, believing that Americans were using the right of deposit to avoid paying a duty on goods, revoked their right of deposit and charged the Americans with smuggling.

Code Talking

The **Louisiana Territory** was a region first claimed by France by virtue of its explorations of the Mississippi and Missouri Rivers. Louisiana Territory began at New Orleans and encompassed what is known today as the Great Plains.

Jefferson directed Robert Livingston, U.S. minister to France, to begin negotiations for the purchase of New Orleans, or at least to reinstitute the right of deposit that Spain had formally granted.

French emperor Napoleon's willingness to listen to the American proposal was not an act of altruism. At one time, France had hoped that New Orleans would be a staging point for expansion into the West Indies. Mosquitoes brought yellow fever to French troops in Santo Domingo and relief forces were unable to reach the islands to reinforce Napoleon's armies.

Napoleon abandoned any further designs in the Americas and sold not only New Orleans to the Americans but the rest of Louisiana as well. The agreed-upon sale price was 60 million francs, or approximately $23 million, which comes to about 4¢ an acre for roughly 909,000 square miles of land. The Louisiana Territory, in a sense, was sold by a country that didn't particularly want to sell it to a country that didn't particularly want to buy it (America's interest was primarily in acquiring New Orleans).

Lewis and Clark Go on a Trip

Thomas Jefferson planned an expedition that was to cross the continent and, on the way, gather information about the territory that had fallen into American hands. He named as leader of the expedition his private secretary and Virginia neighbor, 32-year-old Meriwether Lewis. Lewis chose as a colleague 28-year-old William Clark, an experienced frontiersman.

Purposes of the Expedition

In a lengthy letter to Meriwether Lewis, Jefferson outlined in some detail his expectations for the proposed expedition. One objective was to search for a water route that would link the Missouri River with the Pacific Ocean, thereby giving the Americans a direct course to the fur country in the Pacific Northwest. This *Northwest Passage* would prove not to exist.

A second purpose of the expedition was to learn as much about the Indian nations of the Louisiana country as possible. Jefferson hoped to learn about their languages, food, clothing, laws, customs, and "occupations." Quite a tall order!

Code Talking

The **Northwest Passage** is a mythical water route from the eastern part of the North American continent to the Pacific Ocean.

Jefferson's motivation for getting to know the Natives of Louisiana was simple. He wished to initiate conversations with local tribes to secure an advantage in the fur trade from the French and British, who still occupied some of the continent, though they had lost much of their power. He ordered Lewis and Clark to treat the Natives with respect in order to achieve this advantage: "In all your intercourse with the natives, treat them in the most friendly and conciliatory manner which their own conduct will admit."

To That Undiscovered Country

On March 10, 1804, the United States took formal possession of Louisiana, and later that month, the Corps of Discovery, as the Lewis and Clark Expedition was officially called, started up the Missouri River. In August, near present-day Omaha, Nebraska, the expedition made council for the first time with a western tribe. Here they met representatives of the Oto and Missouri tribes. Over the next several years, the expedition would encounter nearly 50 Native tribes.

Almost Over Before It Starts

Not even a month into their journey, in September 1804, the party had an encounter that almost ended the trek. Near what is now Pierre, South Dakota, the Teton Sioux (the Lakota) claimed one of the party's boats as a toll for moving upriver. A fight nearly ensued, but was defused by the diplomacy of a chief named Black Buffalo. For three more uneasy days, the expedition stayed with the tribe.

Tribal Truths

Over the course of the expedition, Lewis and Clark developed a ritual they used when meeting a tribe for the first time. The captains would explain to the tribal leaders that the their land now belonged to the United States, and that a man far in the east—President Thomas Jefferson—was their new "great father." They would also give the Indians a peace medal with Jefferson on one side and two hands clasping on the other, as well as some form of presents (often trade goods).

It is not recorded how tribes reacted to the news that their land was no longer theirs and that they had a new father.

The Corps of Discovery reached the villages of the Mandans and the Hidatsas north of what is now Bismarck, North Dakota, in November and spent the winter of 1804 and 1805 there.

The Mandans and Hidatsas numbered some 4,500 people and were one of the most influential tribes on the Northern Plains. They were farmers who lived in earthlodges but enjoyed the fruits of the plains as well. The Mandans and Hidatsas were important cultural mediators in the region. Tribes on the plains traded for corn and other crops, and white traders came to the Mandan villages, bringing beads, cloth, and other trade goods.

Native Voices

History hasn't been kind to us. There's a belief that the Mandans are extinct. Probably the Hidatsas even more so. I want to say that we are alive and well, living here on the Fort Berthold Indian Reservation and we are contributing members of society. A lot of our people have become doctors and lawyers and business people, and educators. And we are looking very positively towards the future of our people, to make a better life for ourselves and our children.

—Calvin Grinnell, a member of the Three Affiliated Tribes, the Mandan, Hidatsa, and Arikara, and a member of the Fort Berthold Lewis and Clark Bicentennial Committee

While at the Mandan villages, the expedition collected robes, pipe bags, tipi liners, and shirts, as well as samples of animals and plants from the Upper Missouri. They also observed and recorded Mandan customs and ceremonies. The party witnessed a "buffalo calling" ceremony and seemed to be the only ones surprised when bison showed up near the village the next day. The observations of the expedition are important because these records are the earliest accounts of Mandan culture.

The Path Ahead

At Fort Mandan, the captains hired Toussaint Charbonneau, a French Canadian fur trader living among the Hidatsas, as an interpreter. He had a young wife of about 16, Sacagawea, who had been captured by the Hidatsas (or Minnetaree) approximately 5 years earlier. Charbonneau supposedly won Sacagawea in a game of chance shortly before the corp reached the Mandan villages. The captains learned that Sacagawea's homeland was near the headwaters of the Missouri and believed she might be helpful when they reached that point.

With three new members that included two unpaid civilians (Sacagawea and her newborn son Jean Baptiste) the corps left the Mandan villages on April 6, 1805. Captain Lewis wrote, "We are now about to penetrate a country at least 2,000 miles in width on which the foot of civilized man had never trodden." We can safely assume that the people living in the territory at the time would have heartily disagreed with Lewis's statement!

Tribal Truths

Is it "Sacagawea" or "Sacajawea"? We know her name means "Bird Woman," as Clark notes as much in his journals (*sacaga* means "bird" and *wea* "woman"). In the Hidatsa language, the name would be pronounced with a hard g. So repeat after me. Sacagawea, G not J.

> **Tribal Truths**
>
> Reading the journals of the expedition can be challenging. Captain Clark was a creative speller. He managed 15 different ways to write "Charbonneau," all incorrect, as well as 27 spellings of "Sioux." He enjoyed "water millions" from Oto gardens and swatted pesky "musteetors" along the Missouri. He even managed to misspell the last name of his co-leader, rendering it "Lewers." Apparently the ability to spell is not a measure of "civilized man."

On April 25, 1805, the first white man of record set foot in what is now Montana, beginning a series of firsts for Euro-Americans in this region. Shortly after passing the confluence of the Yellowstone and Missouri Rivers, the party killed an enormous bear that they referred to as a white bear. In truth, this was the first white contact with the grizzly bear. At first, Lewis didn't believe the Native accounts of the ferocity of the white bear, but after being chased across the Plains on numerous occasions by grizzlies, he stated that the "curiosity of our party is pretty well satisfied with respect to this animal."

> **Tribal Truths**
>
> The Lewis and Clark Expedition noted large herds of bison and elk along the Missouri River, and the sighting of grizzly bears became commonplace en route. The Crow Indians called the Yellowstone River "Elk Creek" because of the vast numbers of elk and other hoofed animals there. Ironic, perhaps, the elk and the grizzly bear can now only be found in the most remote mountainous regions while the bison were nearly hunted to extinction by Euro-Americans. Another measure of "civilized man"?

From the Great Falls to the Headwaters

In the weeks that followed, the expedition slowly made its way up the Missouri. It reached the Great Falls of the Missouri on June 13, 1805, and here they spent a month resting and portaging around the 16 miles of rapids that make up the Great Fall. Then they trekked on to Three Forks of the Missouri River.

Sacagawea's Return Home

Under Sacagawea's guidance, the group found themselves in the heart of Indian country, but they had yet to encounter a single Indian since leaving Fort Mandan with Sacagawea four months earlier! Lewis, anxious to meet Indians, marched ahead of the main party with two men. Now following a game trail on foot, the small company crossed from Montana into what is now Idaho, and on August 11, 1805, they spotted a lone rider—an Indian—some distance ahead.

Lewis was in the lead, followed by his two men. Lewis gestured to the Indian to come forward but was unable to convince the man to do so. He shouted, "*Ta-ba-bone!*" the word the Shoshoni used to refer to whites. Unknown to Lewis, there was no exact word for white man, and he had been taught a word that means "stranger." To make matters worse, Ta-ba-bone also means "enemy" because all strangers to the Shoshoni are enemies until proven otherwise. So Lewis was shouting, "I'm the enemy! I'm the enemy!" It's no surprise the horsemen turned and rode away.

Code Talking

Ta-ba-bone is the Shoshoni word for "stranger."

Several days later, however, Captain Lewis did finally meet a group of Shoshoni face to face. As luck would have it, their leader was Sacagawea's brother, Cameahwait. The Shoshoni gave the expedition horses (the water route was now at an end) and, perhaps more important, vital information about the trail ahead.

Tribal Truths

Imagine trying to communicate with 50 different tribes! The corps used sign language, but that had limitations. Sacagawea proved most valuable during the party's council with the Shoshoni. Lewis and Clark spoke only English. François LaBiche, one of the party, spoke English and French. Charbonneau spoke French and Hidatsa, but not English. Sacagawea spoke Shoshoni (her mother tongue) and Hidatsa. So just to say "Hi!" to the Shoshoni, the captains had to go through LaBiche, Charbonneau, and Sacagawea. It's a wonder they communicated at all!

Meeting the Flathead

On September 4, 1805, at Ross' Hole in the upper Bitterroot valley of present-day Montana, the corps met the Flathead or Salish. There were 33 lodges, 80 men, and a total of 400 people in this village.

The Flathead were unlike any tribe the party had yet encountered. The others spoke languages belonging to language families that they had at least heard and were, therefore, familiar. The Flathead language is a part of the Salish language family. One member of the expedition observed, "These natives have the strangest language of any we have yet seen. They appear to us as though they had an impediment in their speech or brogue on their tongue. We think perhaps they are the Welch Indians."

> **Native Voices**
>
> According to a European legend, the Welsh prince, Madoc (or Madog), sailed west and disappeared. Some believe he reached North America 300 years before Columbus and his descendents adopted the lifestyle of Natives. At one time, the Mandan were thought to be the Welsh Indians because many had fair features. To Lewis and Clark, the Salish tongue sounded foreign and, therefore, perhaps Welsh.

Poor Cold Lost Strangers

To the Flathead, this strange party was likewise odd. These were the first white men they had ever seen. Being good hosts, the first thing the Flathead did was to bring these strangers buffalo robes because their skin seemed so pale from the cold.

In the eyes of the Flathead, the expedition seemed to be peaceful. No war party traveled with a woman and with infants. But among the men, one was painted black, which, according to Flathead beliefs, meant that he had either been to war or was coming back from war. This "warrior" was Captain Clark's slave, York.

> **Tribal Truths**
>
> York was the subject of much interest whenever the corps met any Indian tribe. Even those who were familiar with white men had never seen a black "white" man. Natives were constantly trying to wipe what they believed was paint from York's body. At Fort Clatsop, men brought their wives to lay with York in hopes of having offspring from him. Lewis and Clark reported that the Natives around Fort Clatsop lacked morals because of this kind of behavior. In reality, these Natives perceived York as somehow sacred, because of his difference from the rest of the party. By bringing their women to York, they hoped to gain some of his power.

The expedition spent four days with the Salish. They then traveled north, heading to a place known as Travelers' Rest near Missoula, Montana.

It took them 53 days to reach Traveler's Rest. While camped there, the expedition learned of the "Road to the Buffalo," east of present-day Missoula, Montana. This Indian road led to the buffalo country east of the Front Range of the Rockies. From this point, they were only four days overland to the Great Falls. From Great Falls they went farther west, reaching the country of the Nez Perce on September 20, 1805.

Meeting the Nez Perce

The *Nez Perce* were not frightened of the white men and treated them to a filling meal of buffalo, dried salmon, and camas bread. They told Clark about the route ahead. Their leader was Twisted Hair, a chief who Clark described as "a cheerful man with apparent sincerity."

The corps remained among the Nez Perce for several days preparing for the rest of their journey. Twisted Hair and two of his sons helped Clark find good timber for making canoes, and the captains traded goods for horses, which they temporarily left in the Indians' care intending to reclaim the horses on the return journey.

Code Talking

Nez Perce is a misidentification given the tribe by the interpreter of the Lewis and Clark Expedition in 1805. The French translate it as "pierced nose." Even though the Nez Perce didn't pierce their noses, they kept the name and today pronounce it *nezz purse*. Their own name for themselves is Ni Mii Pu (*Ni-MEE-Poo*), meaning "The People."

Tribal Truths

The expedition received assistance from many Natives along the route. One who proved extremely helpful was a Shoshoni named Old Toby, hired to provide information and guidance through western Montana. Old Toby's knowledge and direction brought the expedition through the Bitterroot, Lolo, Missoula, and Blackfoot valleys. After pointing the way, Toby presumably went back to his people, leaving without accepting any compensation.

On to the Pacific

Riding in their newly constructed canoes and with the current pushing them, the expedition quickly descended the Clearwater and then the Snake rivers, and at last they reached the Columbia. The river was teeming with salmon (Clark estimated 10,000 pounds of salmon drying in one village), but the men wanted meat to eat, so they bought dogs from the Indians.

On October 18, Clark sighted Mount Hood in the distance, a landmark they expected to see (Mount Hood was named by a British sea captain in 1792). Soon they passed through the raging falls of the Columbia and into the Gorge to the Pacific Ocean, their western destination.

The Trail Home

After wintering in Oregon, on March 23—now 1806—the expedition set off for home. In May, the expedition arrived back with the Nez Perce but had to wait for the snows to melt on the Bitterroots before moving on. The Nez Perce once again provided the explorers with food. Lewis termed them "the most hospitable, honest, and sincere people that we have met with in our voyage."

The expedition split on July 3, 1806, with Meriwether Lewis heading back to the Great Falls to explore the Marias River and Clark across to the Yellowstone Valley.

Exploring the Yellowstone

Captain Clark, with 23 men (plus Sacagawea and her baby Jean Baptiste) returned to Ross' Hole, bypassed the Shoshoni, and arrived back at the three forks of the Missouri in early July. At the three forks, Sargent Ordway, a member of the corps, departed down the Missouri with 9 men; Clark and the remaining party, along with 49 horses, headed up the Gallatin River to the present site of Bozeman, Montana.

Tribal Truths

Raiding horses was a pastime enjoyed by many Plains men. They gained status by entering into the villages of their enemies and appropriating their horses.

Native Voices

The Crow did not count the capturing of the horses from Clark and Pryor as a coup because the white men slept too much.

—Howard Boggess, Crow tribal member and historian

Here, Sacagawea pointed out a mountain crossing used by her people, and on July 15, 1806, Clark and his party entered into the Yellowstone Valley near Livingstone.

The plan was to build canoes, but they found that the trees were not large enough. They were forced to travel by horseback along the cobbled riverbed. This proved to be difficult traveling and the horses quickly went lame. The situation worsened when one of the men drove a snag into his thigh, necessitating another attempt to build canoes. The group managed to construct two 28-foot cottonwood boats.

The party spent several days constructing their crafts, but they were not alone. During the night, Crow warriors managed to steal away half the group's horses. One corps member was entrusted with the rest of the horses while the rest of the party took to the water. On the second night out, the watchman was relieved of any further responsibility when the Crows came back for the rest of the horses.

Pompy's Tower

On the second river day, Captain Clark climbed to a massive gray rock by the side of the Yellowstone, dubbed it "Pompy's Tower" after Sacagawea's young son, and carved his name and the date July 25, 1806, on its side. This remains, to date, the only conclusive physical evidence of the Lewis and Clark Expedition that survives to this day.

Lewis Meets the Blackfeet

Meanwhile, Meriwether Lewis and a party of nine traveled overland back to the Missouri River. From here Lewis, with three men—George Drouillard, Ruben Field, and Joseph Field—followed the Marias River north. They reached a point near Cut Bank, Montana, that marks the farthest north the expedition reached. This they dubbed Camp Disappointment, largely because they experienced several days of rain and gloom but partly because Lewis realized that the Marias was not a viable candidate as the Northwest Passage.

On July 26, 1806, the four men headed back. They met a party of eight Blackfeet warriors where Badger Creek enters the Two Medicine River. The Blackfeet insisted that the white men camp with them for the night, a prospect that made Lewis nervous. He wrote in his journal, "I was convinced they would attempt to rob us." Despite these misgivings, Lewis nonetheless presented gifts to the Blackfeet and they all settled in for the night.

In the early morning hours of July 27, Lewis was awakened by a cry from Drouillard who shouted, "Damn you, let go my gun." Drouillard was wrestling with a Blackfeet warrior over control of a rifle. Ruben Field chased another warrior some 50 paces from the camp and stabbed the man in the heart. Lewis recovered the rifle and chased another warrior 300 paces and shot the man in the belly. The party quickly gathered up their horses, pausing to place a peace medal around a dead man's neck. The explorers galloped away, riding for 24 straight hours, met up with the group with the canoes on the Missouri, and paddled off toward the rendezvous with Clark.

This incident marks the only violent confrontation between a Native group and the expedition. The Blackfeet remember this incident as the "Two Medicine Fight" where the Americans killed He-That-Looks-at-the-Calf and one other. This event poisoned Blackfeet

> **Tribal Truths**
>
> Is it Blackfeet or Blackfoot? There is no clear preference. The general rule of thumb is that it's Blackfeet in the United States and Blackfoot in Canada. No one knows why.

and American relations for the next 30 years. The Americans were never able to establish a fur-trading post among the Blackfeet because of it.

Home at Last

In August, the now recombined party arrived back at the Mandan villages. Here Lewis and Clark bid farewell to Charbonneau, Sacagawea, and her baby Jean Baptiste. Here John Colter, later to become one of the first "mountain men," was given permission to leave the expedition and return to the Yellowstone to trap beaver.

The rest of the trip was uneventful. They reached St. Louis on September 23, 1806, 28 months after they left, having traveled more than 8,000 miles!

Impact of the Lewis and Clark Expedition

The Lewis and Clark Expedition forever changed history. Whether the change was positive or negative depends largely on whether you are a Native person or not.

The expedition changed the landscape in a way that may seem relatively unimportant. As they traveled across the land, they gave names to the mountains, rivers, and streams. Clark named the Judith River after Judith (Julia) Hancock, a girl he later married. Lewis honored Maria Wood, his cousin, by naming the Marias River for her. The three forks of the Missouri are now recognizable as the Madison, Jefferson, and the Gallatin. Even the little Milk River bares a name bestowed by the expedition (named because it appeared the color of tea with a tablespoon of milk added to it). No longer is the Yellowstone called "Elk Creek" or the Milk "the river that scolds the other," as Native peoples in the area had been calling them since the dawn of time.

Tribal Truths

Whatever happened to Sacagawea? One Shoshoni legend holds that she returned to her people and lived to be an old lady who died in 1884. She is said to be buried in the Fort Washakie cemetery (Wyoming), next to her sons Jean Baptiste (baby Pompy) and Basil. This story is not likely true, because Jean Baptiste is known to be buried in Oregon and her second child was a girl.

Another, more likely story is that she died shortly after the expedition ended. On December 20, 1812, a clerk at Fort Manuel wrote, "This evening the wife of Charbonneau, a Snake [Shoshoni], died of a putrid fever. She was good and the best woman of the fort."

More important, though, the Louisiana Territory was no longer "that undiscovered country from whose borne no man returns." It now truly belonged to America (at least in their minds).

From Sea to Shining Sea

The United States doubled its territory with the Louisiana Purchase. The extent of her power and authority now extended from one ocean to the other in North America. But what of the people who came with the sale? What of the Native tribes who called this land their home, no matter who believed they owned it? By whose right did this land belong to the Great White Father?

The Least You Need to Know

- ◆ The United States "purchased" the Louisiana Territory from the French in 1803.

- ◆ One of the purposes of the Lewis and Clark Expedition was to seek the Northwest Passage, a northern sea route between the Atlantic and the Pacific oceans.

- ◆ Thomas Jefferson wanted to learn as much as possible about the Natives of the Louisiana Territory in order to establish a trade relationship later on.

- ◆ The Lewis and Clark Expedition came into contact with nearly 50 tribes, most of whom were helpful.

- ◆ The only violent encounter between Natives and the company was with a party of Blackfeet.

- ◆ The Lewis and Clark Expedition took 28 months, covered nearly 8,000 miles, and forever changed the lives of Native Americans.

Chapter 11

Expansion and Removal

In This Chapter

- ◆ Tecumseh takes a stand
- ◆ Tribal participation in the War of 1812
- ◆ The Seminole Wars
- ◆ The "Five Civilized Tribes"
- ◆ Establishing a new Cherokee homeland
- ◆ Crying a Trail of Tears

At the turn of the nineteenth century, the tribes east of the Mississippi River were clearly unable to withstand the settlement of Americans into tribal lands. While there were several attempts to unify tribal efforts to resist white expansion, American policy in those early years was directed at solving the so-called "Indian problem" by forcibly removing Native peoples from areas that white settlers wished to claim.

This has been a pattern from the beginning. When settlers want more Native land or resources, the situation is always described as the Indian's problem. Of course, the real problem was that the Indians had the land and non-Indians wanted it. By eliminating the Indians, you eliminate the problem. So throughout American Indian history, the Indian problem was resolved by pushing the Indian farther and farther from their homeland or reducing that homeland. This idea is grounded in the idea of "Manifest Destiny," the belief that it is the providence of America to extend itself from sea to shining sea.

Tecumseh Fights for His Homeland

The knowledge brought back by William Clark and Meriwether Lewis provided President Thomas Jefferson with a new solution to the pesky Indian problem. If the Natives refused to assimilate into mainstream society, and were seen as an impediment to westward expansion, why not remove them to those "empty" lands west of the Mississippi? Tribes in the Great Lakes and the Ohio Valley were much too disorganized to resist.

Tribal Truths

Tecumseh was a statesman, orator, patriot, warrior, and an honorable man. He is regarded as one of the greatest Native leaders to ever live.

Native Voices

Americans grew from the scum of the great water, when it was troubled by an evil spirit and the froth was driven into the woods by a strong east wind. They are numerous, but I hate them. They are unjust; they have taken away your lands, which were not made for them.

—Tenskwatawa, the Prophet in a sermon to his followers at Prophet's Town

With the establishment of the Territory of Indiana in 1800, westward movement had extended beyond the Ohio Valley. As governor of the territory, William Henry Harrison's prime task was to obtain title to Indian lands so that settlers could continue to push westward. When the Indians retaliated, Harrison was responsible for defending the settlements.

Living the Old Ways

In 1808, Tecumseh and his brother, Tenskwatawa, known as the Prophet, established "Prophet's Town" on Tippecanoe Creek in Indiana Territory where their people lived according to the old ways. Followers of the Prophet, who was a great mystic and religious leader, believed that if they cast off all elements of Euro-American society, including alcohol, firearms, and trade goods, they could live a better life. Tecumseh and the Prophet began visiting tribes of the Old Northwest to form an alliance as a means of protecting lands held by Indians. They met with some success among the Southern tribes, but others, like the Iroquois, rejected their attempts.

In 1809, a number of chiefs signed the Treaty of Fort Wayne, Indiana, and with it ceded 3 million acres of Indian lands to William Henry Harrison, the governor of the territory for approximately 8¢ an acre. Angered by this move, Tecumseh protested to

Harrison, contending that the chiefs had been given whiskey and besides had no authority to sign agreements for lands they did not own. Tecumseh's objections fell on deaf ears.

In August 1810, Tecumseh paid a return visit to Governor Harrison, accompanied by 300 warriors. As you might imagine, the meeting was contentious. At one point, it seemed that it might come to blows. Neither side budged, and nothing was resolved.

In an attempt to keep the Americans from encroaching on Native lands, Tecumseh forged an alliance with the Creek, Choctaw, and Chickasaw. The Creek were a powerful ally. They could call up 6,000 warriors and had important alliances with England, Spain, and France.

Tecumseh traveled to the Northwest hoping to gain support from the British, believing that war was inevitable. Harrison, meanwhile, was looking for an excuse to attack Prophet's Town.

Tribal Truths

Tecumseh came from the Shawnee village of Chillicothe on the Little Miami River. His father, a Shawnee chief, was killed fighting settlers in the Ohio Valley. Two older brothers had been killed fighting the Americans under the Miami chief Little Turtle.

Native Voices

Sell a country! Why not sell the air, the clouds, and the great sea, as well as the earth? Did not the Great Spirit make them all for the use of his children?

—Tecumseh, Shawnee leader

The Battle of Tippecanoe

In 1811, having given up on diplomacy, Harrison made plans to attack.

While Tecumseh was away seeking more allies, Harrison led about 1,000 men toward Prophet's Town. But before Harrison could attack, the Indians sprung on his camp on Tippecanoe River. After heavy fighting, Harrison repulsed them, but 61 of his soldiers were killed and 127 were wounded. Harrison declared victory, burned all the Shawnee log buildings and food stores, and forced the Shawnee into a treaty ceding vast amounts of land. The Battle of Tippecanoe, upon which Harrison's fame was to rest, disrupted Tecumseh's confederacy.

The tribes whose warriors had been killed began to fall on nearby non-Indian settlements. Many settlers were killed and farms abandoned.

None of this was in Tecumseh's plans. He had always sought peaceful solutions.

The War of 1812

Meanwhile, on June 18, the United States declared war on Great Britain in what came to be known as the War of 1812. Once again, Indians were caught in the middle, as both the United States and Britain sought Indian alliances. At a council at Fort Wayne, in Indiana Territory, Brigadier General William Hull called upon Indian leaders to join the United States. Several Indian leaders were eager to serve the Americans. Tecumseh argued passionately against it. He gathered a large war party and marched off to join the British.

> **Native Voices**
>
> Here is a chance ... such as will never occur again—for us Indians of North America to form ourselves into one great combination.
>
> —Tecumseh, Shawnee leader, on the beginning of the War of 1812

Tecumseh and his forces fought several skirmishes against the American general Hull and helped the British capture Hull's army and the city of Detroit. Tecumseh, who had formed his army from a number of tribes, had difficulty keeping some of his soldiers in check.

Keeping the Red Sticks in Line

In the fall of 1812, Tecumseh visited the Creeks, who were part of his alliance. The Creeks gave him a bundle of red sticks, each denoting a day until they would join in a concerted attack on the Americans. However, the Creeks, elected not to wait for the appointed hour and attacked settlers near Mobile, Alabama, killing a great number. This assemblage of Creeks became denominate as *Red Sticks*.

> **Code Talking**
>
> The **Red Sticks** were Tecumseh's Creek allies during the War of 1812. The name comes from a bundle of red sticks that the Creek gave Tecumseh to represent the number of days until the Creek launched an attack on the Americans.

On August 30, 1813, the rogue Red Sticks struck again, this time attacking Fort Mims near the Florida panhandle and killing hundreds of men, women, and children. The Americans called for revenge.

Their time soon came.

The Great Leader Dies

On October 5, 1813, in what was called the Battle of the Thames, Governor William Henry Harrison defeated combined British and Indian forces. The English, under the leadership of Major-General Henry Proctor, numbered 800 regulars, with Tecumseh leading an alliance of 1,200 warriors. After the initial clash of forces, Proctor withdrew from the field, leaving Tecumseh and his warriors to fight on. After several hours of intense fighting, Tecumseh was killed. The Indians scattered, and the Americans soon regained control of the Northwest.

Then, in March 1814, Jackson's army of some 3,000 men, which included approximately 600 Cherokee and Creek allies, arrived at the bend of the Tallapoosa River, where the Red Sticks were encamped. While the main army, led by Jackson, was having difficulty destroying a barricade with two cannons, the Indian allies were invading the Red Sticks' camp from across the river. The distraction of the rear attack allowed Jackson's army to charge the barricade. By the end of the day, some 800 of the approximately 1,000 Red Sticks lay dead.

The defeat devastated the Red Sticks. Although the partisan Creeks remained in a state of war for several months, by August 1814 they surrendered and signed the Treaty of Fort Jackson. The treaty required the Creeks to cede some 20 million acres of land—more than half their ancestral homeland—to the United States. Jackson pushed on, and with his Choctaw allies he captured Pensacola and won a great victory in the defense of New Orleans.

Although the battle took place after the War of 1812 was technically over and peace negotiations were under way, it was a highly publicized fight in which Jackson defeated the British with the help of a number of Choctaw warriors.

The War of 1812 was over. Those tribes that sided with the British paid with their lives and their land. Ultimately, the Creeks, Cherokees, and Seminoles, no matter which side they fought on, were separated from their homelands.

Settlers flocked to the region, followed by Indian land cessions. Indiana became a state in 1816 and Illinois in 1818.

Seminole Wars

The Seminole Wars is the name given to three conflicts between the United States and the Seminole Indians of Florida (1817–1818, 1835–1842, 1855–1858). Each war was fought for the same reason: to resist the opening of Seminole land for white exploitation and settlement.

Round One to Andrew Jackson

The First Seminole War (1817–1818) began over attempts by U.S. authorities to recapture runaway black slaves living among Seminole bands. Under General Andrew

Jackson, U.S. military forces invaded the area, scattering the villagers, burning their villages, and seizing Spanish-held Pensacola and St. Marks.

As a result, in 1819, Spain was forced to cede its Florida territory under the terms of a treaty.

> **Tribal Truths**
>
> *Seminole* means "runaway" or "wild" in the Creek language. Although Creeks who escaped from the U.S. military campaigns against them make up the majority of Seminole stock, it includes an amalgam of people, all of whom were refugees from their traditional homelands. These include the Hitchiti, Apalachee, Mikisùkî, Yamassee, Yuchi, Tequesta, Appalachicola, Choctaw, and Oconee people as well. Africans who had escaped from slavery also joined the group and were accepted as part of the tribe.

Round Two to Osceola—Sort Of

The Second Seminole War (1835–1842) followed the refusal of most Seminoles to abandon the reservation that had been specifically established for them north of Lake Okeechobee and to relocate west of the Mississippi River. Whites desired this land and sought to drive out the Seminoles under the Indian Removal Act (discussed later in this chapter). Led by their powerful war leader Osceola, the Seminole warriors hid their families in the Everglades and used guerrilla tactics to defend their homeland. The Seminoles hid during the day and raided at night. The U.S. Army pursued them through malarial swamps in a long, frustrating war. As many as 2,000 U.S. soldiers were killed in this protracted fighting. Only after Osceola's capture, while negotiating under a flag of truce, did Indian resistance weaken. Most but not all Seminoles agreed to move peacefully to lands west of the Mississippi River, in what would be known as Indian Territory.

> **Tribal Truths**
>
> Osceola was not a chief but came to be acknowledged as a leader of Seminole resistance. He successfully led the Seminole warriors against the United States during the fighting in the Everglades. In October 1837, Osceola and several chiefs went to St. Augustine, Florida, under a flag of truce to attend council with the government. While there, Indians were seized and imprisoned. Osceola was removed to Fort Moultrie at Charleston, South Carolina, where he died.

Round Three? Surrender at a Price

In 1841, Congress appropriated more than $1 million to capture by bribe or bullet the surviving Seminole Indians. The Seminole Council, headed by Holatta-Micco (Billy Bowlegs) was determined to defend their holdings. The military began to criss-cross the swamps with the intent of destroying crops that might help the Seminoles who remained in hiding. By 1842, 230 Indians were captured by this strategy.

The government also offered white bounty hunters rewards of $500 for Seminole men, $250 for Seminole women, and $100 for Seminole children. Indians could receive the same rewards for giving themselves up. The Seminoles rejected the financial compensation and began their guerrilla warfare.

Billy Bowlegs rejected government bribes totaling $5,000 plus a $100 per Indian if he turned over his own men, but when his granddaughter was seized, he surrendered to save her life. On May 4, 1858, the last of the famous Seminole warriors met the soldiers at Billy's Creek and were sent forever from Florida. A handful of Seminoles remained in the Everglades, but the fighting was over and the U.S. government was clearly the victor. For those Seminole who remained deep in the Everglades, they prided themselves at having never surrendered to the United States.

Black Hawk's War

Black Hawk, whose name in his Sauk language was Ma-ka-tai-me-she-kia-kiak, was the leader of the Thunder clan of the Sauk Indians in Illinois. In an effort to halt the settlers' westward expansion, he sided with the British against the Americans in the War of 1812. As white men continued taking over the Indians' cornfields and lodges, dissident Sauk and Fox Indians looked to Black Hawk for leadership.

In 1832, Black Hawk, who had been driven into Iowa the year before, led his people back across the Mississippi to the disputed Illinois area to plant crops and to resist further white encroachments. Because the band of 1,000 included old men, women, and children, the move was clearly not warlike. But Governor John Reynolds called out the Illinois militia, and the U.S. government dispatched troops.

Black Hawk's Betrayal

Upon learning that they were being pursued, Black Hawk's band attacked, catching the Illinois militia unaware and inflicted a stinging defeat on them. But the Indians' strength soon waned. They sought aid from other tribes, but it did not materialize; food supplies were quickly exhausted; and desertions, malnutrition, and illness finally took their toll. Black Hawk retreated northward through the Rock River Valley, and in the final battle, or massacre, at the Bad Axe River in Wisconsin, most of the Indians were slaughtered. Black Hawk escaped, but he was soon captured and taken, first to Jefferson Barracks, Missouri, and then to Fortress Monroe in Virginia. In 1833, he was returned as a hostage to the charge of a rival leader, a final blow to his pride from which he never recovered.

Native Voices

The sun rose dim on us in the morning, and at night it sunk in a dark cloud, and looked like a ball of fire. That was the last sun that shone on Black Hawk. His heart is dead, and no longer beats quick in his bosom. He is now a prisoner of the white man; they will do with him as they wish ... Farewell, my nation! Black Hawk tried to save you, and avenge your wrongs ... He can do no more. He is near his end. His sun is setting, and he will rise no more.

—Black Hawk, Sauk and Fox

As a condition of peace, the United States dispossessed the Sauk and Fox of their land in Illinois and eastern Iowa, and the Winnebago of theirs in southern Wisconsin. The ruthlessness of the Black Hawk War so affected the Indians that by 1837 all surrounding tribes had fled to the far West, leaving most of the Northwest Territory to the white settlers.

Indian Removal

When Andrew Jackson was elected president in 1828, it was clear that his solution to the "Indian problem" was to remove those Indians of the East and South to the West by force. Southern states began that process even before his inauguration by passing laws extending their jurisdiction over Indians within state boundaries, completely overstepping the bounds set by the U.S. Constitution. The tone of this legislation was definitely anti-Indian in sentiment; for example, Georgia and Alabama made it illegal for a Native person to testify against a white man in a court of law. This kind of narrow-mindedness became official government policy when Congress passed the *Indian Removal Act* on May 28, 1830.

Code Talking

The **Indian Removal Act** authorized the president to grant Indian tribes unsettled western prairie land in exchange for their desirable territories within state borders (especially in the South), from which the tribes would be removed.

Some tribes from the Old Northeast had already been relocated to western lands. The major resistance came from the tribes in the South, specifically the Chickasaw, Cherokee, Choctaw, Creek, and Seminole (the so-called Five Civilized Tribes). The Choctaws fell first.

Indian Territory

The idea of a separate "Indian Country" was first discussed after the French and Indian War. Thomas Jefferson suggested removal to the western lands in the first decades of the nineteenth century. But it wasn't until the removal policies of the 1830s that the United States acted upon this idea. *Indian Territory*, in U.S. history, applied to the country set aside for Native Americans by the Indian Intercourse Act (1834). The Indian Territory included present-day Oklahoma north and east of the Red River, as well as Kansas and Nebraska. Several tribes were moved there, but each tribe maintained its own government.

Code Talking

Indian Territory was located in present-day Oklahoma, Kansas, and Nebraska. It was set aside by the Indian Intercourse Act of 1834 as the homeland for those tribes removed from the northeast and southeast United States. It would turn out to be their last homeland.

Resistance Is Futile

In 1830, the state of Mississippi abolished the Choctaw government, and the Chocktow agreed to cede their homeland and be removed to Indian Territory. The Creeks were the next to yield. In 1829, they agreed to accept Alabama jurisdiction. Later, when the Creeks complained about white squatters, the federal government's response was to remove them. Thousands were rounded up and removed to Indian Territory.

Tribal Truths

The term "Five Civilized Tribes" was given to the Cherokee, Choctaw, Creek, Chickasaw, and Seminole after they were removed to Indian Territory. They were more "civilized," by comparison, to some of the other tribes that were removed from the Northeast. Some Cherokees, for example, owned slaves. Civilization is apparently a relative concept.

Cherokee vs. the State of Georgia

The Cherokees were the next victims. They fought removal by turning to the only weapon they had left: the law. They pressed their case in the courts, hoping that the state of Georgia would be forced to back down from their threats on Cherokee sovereignty.

Tribal Truths

The Cherokee were among the most progressive Native peoples of their time. Many were educated as teachers, doctors, and lawyers. Most Cherokees could read and write their own language at a time when most of their white neighbors were illiterate. The Cherokee linguist, Sequoyah, developed a syllabary (a phonetic system, where each sound in speech is represented by a symbol) in 1809. In 1828, the Cherokee Phoenix, the oldest Indian newspaper in the country, began publication, using the Cherokee syllabary.

Unfortunately for the Cherokee, gold was discovered on their lands, making it all the more valuable to the state of Georgia. Georgia passed a series of laws that violated the autonomy of the Cherokee Nation, attempting to gain control over the gold fields. They forbade the Cherokee government and courts from meeting and made it illegal for the Natives to mine their own gold!

The state ordered a survey of Cherokee lands in preparation for white settlement. Even white missionaries working on the Cherokee Nation suffered at the hands of the state when they were required to pledge allegiance to the state of Georgia. Suffering under the oppressive actions of the state of Georgia, the Cherokees sought relief from the U.S. Supreme Court.

In order for the Supreme Court to have jurisdiction of the dispute between the Indians and the state of Georgia, the Indians couldn't be considered citizens of the state of Georgia. All disputes between a state and its citizens are under the jurisdiction of that state. However, if the Cherokee Nation were considered a foreign state (as they had been in previous treaties), then they would fall under federal jurisdiction and the Supreme Court could intervene on their behalf. The court, however, ruled that it *did not* have jurisdiction over this case. This decision proved to be one of the most important cases impacting tribal sovereignty.

Domestic Dependent Nations, Whatever *That* Means

The court, under Chief Justice John Marshall, ruled that the Cherokee Nation was not a foreign state and, therefore, the Supreme Court held no jurisdiction on the matter. Marshall's court went on to define what Indian nations were. Marshall, writing for the majority, described the Cherokee as "a distinct political society … capable of managing its own affairs and governing itself"; and such societies were "domestic dependent nations," whose "relation to the United States resembles that of a ward to his guardian."

The implication of the Marshall decision is that, from the constitutional point of view, tribes were no longer considered to be sovereign nations. Further, the Court described the relationship between Indian nations and the federal government as one where Indian tribes are dependent on the United States as a child is dependent upon a parent. This decision established the paternalistic pattern of interaction between tribes and the federal government that exists even today.

Worcester vs. the State of Georgia

The Cherokees may not have had any recourse in the courts, but private citizens did. Two missionaries, Samuel Worcester and Elizur Butler, were arrested by Georgia for refusing to take an oath of allegiance. Worcester sued, claiming that the state did not have jurisdiction over him while he was in Cherokee Nation, as the Nation was not a part of the state of Georgia. There was no question of the Supreme Court's jurisdiction, and, in February 1832, it rendered a decision that favored the Cherokee. The court stated that the "Cherokee Nation, then, is a distinct community, occupying its own territory, with boundaries accurately described, and which the citizens of Georgia have no right to enter."

The Cherokees' joy at winning this case was short-lived. President Jackson is supposed to have said, "John Marshall has made his decision; now let him enforce it." Jackson ignored the court ruling and advised the Georgia officials to continue their persecution of the Cherokees.

Trail of Tears

Georgia moved to secure Cherokee lands by holding a lottery. Cherokee landowners were evicted and displaced. Accepting the inevitable, some Cherokee moved west to Oklahoma on their own. Others remained hopeful that they would be able to negotiate the settlement issue.

The U.S. Government used the Treaty of New Echota in 1835 to justify the removal. The treaty, signed by about a 100 Cherokees known as the *Treaty Party*, relinquished all lands east of the Mississippi River in exchange for land in Indian Territory and the promise of money, livestock, and various provisions and tools.

Code Talking

The **Treaty Party** were those Cherokees who signed the Treaty of New Echota in 1835, which was used by the United States as the authority to remove thousands of Cherokees from their homeland.

Under orders from President Jackson, the U.S. Army began enforcement of the Removal Act. General Winfield Scott was sent with 7,000 soldiers to remove the Cherokees by force.

Native Voices

When we look into the history of our race, we see some green spots that are pleasing to us. We also find many things to make the heart sad.

—John Ross, Cherokee chief

In the winter of 1838 and 1839, 14,000 Cherokees were marched 1,200 miles through Tennessee, Kentucky, Illinois, Missouri, and Arkansas into rugged Indian Territory. An estimated 4,000 of them died from hunger, exposure, and disease!

Some 100,000 Creek, Cherokee, and others were forced to march westward under U.S. military coercion in the 1830s; up to 25 percent of the Indians, many in manacles, perished en route. Today, to the Cherokees, it is remembered as the Trail of Tears.

Native Voices

I saw the helpless Cherokees arrested and dragged from their homes, and driven by bayonet into the stockades. And in the chill of a drizzling rain on an October morning I saw them loaded like cattle or sheep into wagons and started toward the west. Chief Ross led in prayer and when the bugle sounded and the wagons started rolling many of the children ... waved their little hands goodbye to their mountain homes.

—An Army private

Problem Solved?

And so, the federal government accomplished what it had set out to do. Because the Native Americans refused to assimilate into non-Indian culture, there was but one solution to the "Indian problem": removal of all Indians from the east.

The lands west of the Mississippi River had long been considered a vast wasteland, uninhabitable except for a few nomadic "savages." The explorer Zebulon Pike saw only one advantage of the region for the United States. He wrote of the region that ...

> [O]ur citizens being so prone to rambling and extending themselves on the frontiers will, through necessity, be constrained to limit their extend on the west to the borders of the Missouri and Mississippi, while they leave the prairies

incapable of cultivation to the wandering and uncivilized aborigines of the country.

Indian Territory was to be a buffer zone, a place in the empty interior where Indian peoples would live out their lives. Perhaps some good would come from the Natives' isolation. Some, like the Cherokee, demonstrated that they were capable of "civilized" life. Perhaps there would become a time when Indian Territory would become an Indian state.

At last, a solution to the Indian problem.

Native Voices

It affords me sincere pleasure to be able to appraise you of the entire removal of the Cherokee Nation to their new homes west of the Mississippi .... Their removal has been principally under the conduct of their own chiefs, and they have emigrated without any apparent reluctance.

—President Martin Van Buren, 1838

The Least You Need to Know

◆ Tecumseh united a number of Natives to fight with the British against the Americans during the War of 1812.

◆ The Seminole fought three wars against the United States to prevent their removal from their homelands.

◆ Black Hawk fought the United States when the Americans tried to force the Sauk off their land.

◆ The Five Civilized Tribes were removed from their homes so that white squatters could resettle their lands.

◆ Despite a favorable ruling by the Supreme Court, the Cherokees were forcibly removed from their homelands to Indian Territory in what is known as the Trail of Tears.

◆ Indian Territory, which includes what is now the state of Oklahoma, was to be the final home of many Indian nations.

Part 3

Reservations and Resistance

Ah, the Old West! You can almost hear the bugle calls of the Seventh Cavalry and taste the grit. Most of us grew up on John Wayne's version of the West—yipping warriors killing innocent settlers traveling out West to seek their fortunes.

Part 3 offers a different picture of the West. The conflict in the West came when Native warriors attempted to protect their families from the soldiers and buffalo hunters trying to eliminate the bison and the people. And the Indian wars were between one people trying to survive in their homeland and another people invading that land to seek gold and a hundred acres.

Sadly, Part 3 is also about the eventual loss of most of the land those people were trying to protect. Tribes, now placed on reservations, had to learn a new way of survival.

Chapter 12

The War Out West

In This Chapter

♦ The origins of the Oregon Trail

♦ The Flatheads seek the Black Robes

♦ A reservation system is created

♦ The American Civil War draws in Native peoples

♦ The Great Sioux Uprising

In the first half of the nineteenth century, the policy of the federal government was to solve "the Indian problem" by removing the American Indian from the eastern part of the United States to the West. This was obviously only a temporary solution.

Most American politicians never imagined that Americans would settle west of the Mississippi River. But the demand for land to accommodate the expansion westward once again placed Native Americans in contact with settlers. Predictably, this contact resulted in conflict as tribes resisted the western movement. Finally, they were forced to accept the reservation system—living on small islands of land far removed from the expanding American frontier.

The Great American Desert

When the earliest non-Indian pioneers first encountered the Great Plains, they saw a strange and even alien landscape, completely different from the fertile lands they had left behind in the Ohio Valley. The physical character of the Plains was stark and dramatic. The Plains is treeless, semi-arid, and a seemingly empty land. Early explorers dubbed this region the *Great American Desert*, and in the 1840s, settlers rushed across it on their way to Oregon and California.

Code Talking

The **Great American Desert** was a term used in the early nineteenth century to describe the Plains region west of the Mississippi River.

This perception delayed any direct conflict between Native peoples of the Plains and Euro-Americans for the time being. No settlers wanted to stake their fortunes on the vast Plains when gold awaited them in California. No settlers wanted to build a home in the wilderness when Oregon offered so much more.

Tribal Truths

The common misperception is that Native Americans were the emigrants' biggest problem along the Oregon Trail. Most Native tribes were in fact quite helpful to the whites journeying across their lands. The real adversaries of the pioneers were disease and accidental gunshots.

Oregon Trail

The Oregon Trail was much more than a pathway to the state of Oregon. It was the only avenue to the entire western United States. The states of Washington, Oregon, California, Nevada, Idaho, and Utah trace their beginnings as a part of the United States to the Oregon Trail because the trail was the only feasible way for settlers to get across the mountains.

Seeking the Black Robes

Some of these early emigrants initially weren't bound for Oregon. They were missionaries who were interested in saving the souls of Flathead Indians in what is now Montana.

In the early 1800s, Iroquois Indians came west with the fur trade and spoke to the resident western tribes about Catholicism. Jesuit priests, whom the Natives called "*Black Robes*," had converted the Iroquois. From the Iroquois the Flathead learned about the great miracles performed by saints and prophets who seemingly possessed great power. The Flathead were outnumbered and outgunned by their traditional enemies, the Blackfeet, so they sent out delegations to try to find the Black Robes to get them to bring the "Great Book."

In 1831, four Flatheads journeyed to St. Louis in search of the Black Robes and their book, but three died on the way. William Clark, who was then the superintendent of Indian Affairs at St. Louis, escorted the lone emissary to a number of churches. He traveled from church to church, seeking missionaries to come to the Flathead. A speech attributed to the Flathead was published in the local newspaper and was reprinted in the eastern press, inspiring several missionaries to travel to Montana to set up missions. In 1835, the American Board of Foreign Missions, representing several Protestant churches, sent the Reverend Samuel Parker and Dr. Marcus Whitman to Oregon to set up a mission. Dr. Whitman and his wife, Narcissa, were the first emigrants who made the trip west in a covered wagon in 1836.

Code Talking

Black Robes was the name the Native peoples gave to the Jesuit priests who came to preach among the Hurons and Iroquois in the seventeenth century.

The Flatheads didn't welcome the missionaries because they were not the Black Robes (Jesuits) but Protestants, who were rather boring by comparison. Having already traveled this far, the rejected missionaries continued west, where they eventually found a home among the Nez Perce and tribes in Oregon and Washington.

Native Voices

My people sent me to get the "White Man's Book of Heaven." You took me to where you allow your women to dance as we do not ours, and the Book was not there. You took me to where they worship the Great Spirit with candles, and the Book was not there. You showed me images of the good spirits and the picture of the good land beyond, but the Book was not among them to tell us the way.

—From a speech attributed to a Flathead delegate but that was actually made up to solicit funds for missionary activities

End of the Trail

But the big wave of western migration didn't start until 1843, when about 1,000 pioneers made the journey. The 1843 wagon train, dubbed "the great migration," kicked off a massive move west on the Oregon Trail.

The glory years of the Oregon Trail finally ended in 1869, when the transcontinental railroad was completed. In all, more than a half a million people went west on the trail.

There's Gold in Them Thar Hills!

Missionary zeal wasn't the cause of the westward migration. On January 24, 1848, James Marshall found a tiny piece of gold in a stream near John Sutter's sawmill in northern California. News of the discovery inspired the great Gold Rush of 1849.

Hearing the news, thousands of miners went west to seek their fortunes, many traveling the Oregon Trail and then splitting off in southern Idaho and traveling through Reno, Nevada, before reaching the California gold fields.

The Beginnings of a Reservation System

The gold fields of California were in the homelands of a number of Native tribes, including the Wiyot, Yurok, Karuk, and Wintu. In the early years of the gold rush era, 100,000 Euro-Americans came to the area, causing devastation for the California tribes. Miners and settlers demanded land, and non-Indians perpetuated a policy of terrorism against Native peoples, through murder and sexual assault, to rid the area of a Native presence. It is estimated that two thirds of the Native population of California, or approximately 100,000 people, died in the first several years following the discovery of gold.

> ## Native Voices
>
> It seemed they had one thing in mind. And that was to get into the gold fields. And they did, and it didn't make any difference. How they got in and what was in the road or anything. They just went rushing right through the whole thing, tore [Indian houses] down, tore up villages.
>
> —Axel Roderick Lindgren Jr., an elder of the Yurok tribe

> ## Code Talking
>
> A **reservation** is land that has been set aside by the federal government for the use, possession, and benefit of an Indian tribe or group of Indians. Reservations were established by acts of Congress, treaties, and executive orders.

The solution to the problem for California was to remove those surviving Natives from areas demanded by whites to areas that whites didn't want. Such lands were "reserved" for the tribes to separate the Indians from the frontier communities. This evolved into the *reservation* system whereby tribes were placed on isolated lands entirely surrounded by other lands controlled by the states or territories, the United States, or non-Indian landowners.

After the 1850s, reservations were successfully established throughout California, and from this early experiment the program was extended to other areas west of the Mississippi River. Previously, whites tended to live in the established states and territories in the East, and Natives predominately in the unorganized Indian country in the West. Thus, the removal of Indians from inhabited areas and their concentration in an "Indian Country" gradually gave way to their placement on reserved "islands" of land, usually within the larger areas they once possessed. Reservations are thus not lands given to Indians by the federal government, but rather lands they were allowed to hold onto—tiny remnants of their once vast homelands.

The Road to War Is Paved in Gold

The gold fields of Colorado and Montana were in mountainous areas that were not typically occupied by the Plains tribes. Therefore, the discovery of gold itself in most cases didn't create much conflict with the Plains Indians. The major source of conflict was the wagon trains crossing Native lands, loaded with miners and settlers.

As traffic along the Oregon and California trails increased, the hostility between Plains tribes and pioneers increased as well. The Natives blamed the pioneers for the spread of diseases among the tribes and for the disruption of the migration patterns of the large herds of bison that the Plains Indians so depended upon for their livelihood.

For as long as the Natives could remember, Bison made migrations north and south on a predictable cycle. The hunters of the Plains counted on the bison crossing through known passes or traveling over an area at certain times of the year. The traffic on the Oregon Trail disrupted these patterns. As thousands of pioneers traveled the trail, their animals foraged farther afield from the main trail until a swath of bare ground, sometimes as wide as two miles, was cut across the plains. Bison, not seeing feed immediately before them, would turn away from the trail. The hunters correctly blamed the wagon trains for this disruption and escalated their attacks on the settlers in response.

The First Fort Laramie Treaty

The federal government's response to this increased hostility was to negotiate a treaty with the western tribes to resolve any differences between the tribes and the Americans. On September 17, 1851, the Sioux (Lakota), Cheyenne, Arapaho, Crow, Assiniboine, Gros-Ventre, Mandan, and Arickara signed a treaty, called the First Fort Laramie Treaty, with the federal government. It permitted travel along the Oregon Trail and protected the tribes "against the commission of all depredations by the people of the said United States." In this treaty, the government agreed to pay restitution to the tribes if any non-Indians caused any harm to the Natives.

Tribal Truths

When the First Fort Laramie Treaty was signed by all the tribal representatives, they were to receive "the sum of $50,000 per annum for the term of 50 years, with the right to continue the same at the discretion of the President of the United States for a period not exceeding 5 years thereafter, in provisions merchandise, domestic animals, and agricultural implements." Congress, without the knowledge or consent of the tribes, reduced that to a term of 10 years. So much for having a contract.

Usually the government negotiated treaties with individual tribes. However, negotiations for this treaty brought nearly all the northern tribes together at a location near Fort Laramie, Wyoming. Imagine 8,000 to 12,000 Indians camped together! The Sioux were there in all their glory, as were the Cheyenne and Arapaho from the central plains, and the Crow from the Yellowstone Valley. Many of these tribes had never met before except in battle. And in this treaty, they agreed to maintain peace not only with the whites, but with each other as well.

Native Voices

I will go home satisfied. I will sleep sound, and not have to watch my horses in the night, or be afraid for my women and children. We have to live on these streams and in the hills, and I would be glad if the whites would pick out a place for themselves and not come into our grounds.

—Cut Nose, Arapaho, after signing the First Fort Laramie Treaty

This was not the first treaty with western tribes, nor would it be the last. This treaty ceded no land. Its importance is that in Article 5 of the agreement, each tribe agreed to recognize a defined tract of land as their respective territory. Defining tribal territories was the first step toward forcing tribes to cede this land in future treaty sessions.

The Great Treaty-Making Period

The First Fort Laramie Treaty was only one treaty signed between 1853 and 1856. In that period, 52 treaties were negotiated, more than any at any other time in history. Approximately 174,000,000 acres of land were acquired from the tribes by the United States as a result of these treaties. To put it another way, tribes lost land equivalent to the area of the state of Texas, or 7.4 percent of the total area of the United States.

The White Man's Civil War in Indian Territory

Natives weren't the only "problem" facing the U.S. government at this time. The southern states were becoming increasingly dissatisfied with what they felt were unfair taxes and slave policies. In 1861, the South seceded from the Union, and the North and the South declared war on one another. The Civil War brought new sorrows upon the Native peoples. For some, their involvement meant choosing a side and fighting with and against the white man. Some tribes tried to remain neutral, believing that this was not their fight. For yet other tribes, the Civil War meant that fewer white soldiers guarded the forts that invaded their lands.

The Lesser of Two Evils?

Everything Native peoples saw convinced them that the United States never intended to honor the treaties and agreements that the government signed with Indian tribes. So, when the War Between the States broke out, Native American sympathies were generally with the South. In the case of some tribes, they had much in common with the southern cause. A few of the leading men among the so-called civilized tribes owned plantations worked by African American slaves and ardently supported the South, but, in general, most tribes allied themselves with the Confederacy because it was the only chance they saw for survival.

Generally, support for the Secessionist southerners depended upon the locations of the tribes. The Choctaws in the Southeast joined the South as did the Chickasaws, although their support wasn't unanimous. The Creeks and Seminoles to the West, along with the Cherokee, had divided loyalties. The Cherokee tried to remain neutral and attempted to convince other tribes to follow the same course.

> **Native Voices**
>
> Our duty is to stand by our rights, allow no interference in our internal affairs from any source, comply with all our engagements, and rely upon [the] Union for justice and protection.
>
> —Chief John Ross, Cherokee

In 1831, Albert Pike of Arkansas was commissioned by the Confederacy to rally support among the tribes in Indian Territory. He negotiated treaties among the Creeks, Choctaws, and Chickasaws that were more favorable to the tribes than those ever made with the U.S. government. These treaties compelled the Confederacy to assume the obligations of existing federal treaties and offered tribes the privilege of sending delegates to Congress. Other tribes, both "civilized" and otherwise, joined in their support of the southern cause, although many tribes remained uncommitted.

Stand Watie and the First Cherokee Mounted Rifles

In addition to support for their cause, the South needed soldiers. The Osage committed 500 warriors to the Confederate army. There was a Choctaw-Chickasaw regiment (later three), a Creek regiment, and a Creek-Seminole battalion. The Cherokee, however, were split with a minority, under Stand Watie, in favor of furnishing troops to the Confederacy. The majority of Cherokee, under John Ross, wished to avoid direct involvement in the war. Watie organized a company, and then a regiment, known as the First Cherokee Mounted Rifles that fought in the Confederate victory over the Union forces at Wilson's Creek in southwest Missouri on August 10, 1861.

During the war, the regiment fought in numerous smaller fights and skirmishes along the border of Indian Territory. On June 23, 1865, Stand Watie surrendered and signed a treaty of peace at Doaksville, Indian Territory. He was the last Confederate general to lay down arms.

In all, Confederate Indian troops from Indian Territory numbered 6,435 men.

Grant's Indian

Even though Natives, for the most part, threw their support behind the southerners, some Indians strongly supported the northern cause. Just under 3,600 Native Americans served in the Union army during the war. Perhaps the best known was Colonel Ely Samuel Parker, a Seneca from New York. Parker was well educated in the white ways. He studied law and engineering and became a captain of engineers in the New York State Militia in 1853.

The Iroquois were initially denied entry into the Union army. In March 1862, Parker wrote to the commissioner of Indian affairs about the matter, and the next month, Iroquois recruits were permitted to enlist. Parker was commissioned a captain in May 1863 and was a division engineer before he was assigned to General Ulysses S. Grant's personal military staff as a military secretary in September 1863. He became known as "Grant's Indian." He served with Grant from Chattanooga to Appomattox, where he wrote in duplicate the terms of General Robert E. Lee's surrender. He later received a promotion to brigadier.

Tribal Truths

After the war, Parker continued to serve on Grant's staff until 1869, when President Grant assigned him to the post of commissioner of Indian affairs. Investigated for allegations of corruption, Parker was eventually acquitted of the charges, but in June 1871, he resigned his post and retired to private business in Connecticut. When Parker married Minnie Sackett in 1867, Ulysses S. Grant was his best man.

Reconstruction in Indian Territory

In 1865, the Cherokees, Choctaws, and Chickasaws surrendered to Union representatives. How each tribe fared largely depended on the particular bargaining strength of the tribe. The Choctaws and Chickasaws received the best terms, ironic because they were among the most ardent supporters of the Confederacy. The Cherokees were treated better because of the negotiating skills of their chief, John Ross. The Creeks and Seminoles, loyal to the Union, were nonetheless required to subscribe to a confession of war guilt.

Specifically, the tribes in Indian Territory were forced to cede half their land as a home for other Indians. The Seminoles were relocated and were required to agree to the construction of two railroads across their country. The Cherokees, Creeks, and Seminoles were required to grant their freed slaves citizenship and property rights, while the Choctaws and Chickasaws were given the choice of adopting their freed men.

Massacre in Minnesota

While the Civil War was raging, tribes in the West were finding the absence of a military presence on the Plains refreshing. They were free to travel and hunt without the usual interference from the government, who preferred Indians to stay put. But for some reservation Indians, the war meant that the government was paying less attention to its obligations.

Let Them Eat Grass

In 1862, the Santee Sioux in Minnesota held a deep and smoldering resentment as a result of having been swindled out of their land and annuities. By the great council at Traverse des Sioux on the Minnesota River in 1851, the Sioux signed away more than 30,000,000 acres in Iowa, Dakota Territory, and Minnesota and were left with a reservation extending 10 miles on either side of the Minnesota River. In 1858, this reservation was halved, leaving the Santee with a narrow strip of land 150 miles long but only 10 miles wide.

Each year, the Natives were supposed to receive an annuity payment in cash and goods in compensation for the millions of acres they ceded to the government. Non-Indian settlers and unscrupulous traders, who allowed the Santee to run up large debts, surrounded them on all sides. When annuity payment day arrived and the pay tables were set up, the traders were on hand. As each Indian stepped up to receive his or her payment, the trader was there to make his claim. No accounting was demanded, and the Indians often found themselves with nothing left.

The Santee objected to this arrangement and requested that the government bar the traders from the pay tables. As a result, the traders cut off the credit they had once so freely extended. The Santee were then facing starvation. One of the traders, Andrew Myrick, expressed what was no doubt the opinion of most traders when he retorted, "So far as I'm concerned, if they are hungry, let them eat grass."

Massacre on the Prairie

On August 15, 1862, Myrick's words came back to haunt him. A group of Sioux were out hunting some distance from the reservation. (The lack of game meant that the Santee had to venture farther and farther from their home for food.) And on this day, they were both unsuccessful and in bad humor.

One member of the hunting party taunted the others, telling them that here they starved while the white farmers, who were living on former Sioux lands, were prospering. As the badgering went on, one of the hunters told the others that they were afraid to kill a white man. Unfortunately, they were near the farm of Howard Baker and his family. The four Sioux went to the farm where they innocently challenged Mr. Baker and several neighbors who were visiting to a shooting match. After the white men fired their rifles at the targets, the four Sioux turned their weapons on the men and killed them, along with three women and a child.

 Native Voices _____

We are only little herds of buffalo left scattered; the great herds that once covered the prairies are no more. See! The white men are like the locusts when they fly so thick that the whole sky is a snowstorm. You may kill one—two—ten; yes, as many as the leaves in the forest yonder, and their brothers will not miss them. Kill one, kill two, kill ten, and ten times ten will come to kill you. Count your fingers all day long and white men with guns in their hands will come faster than you can count.

Little Crow is not a coward. He will die with you.

—Little Crow, Santee Sioux leader

When the Indians arrived back at their village, they immediately told their chief, Shakopee, what they had done. He was no lover of the white man and advised the young men to go and tell Little Crow, the most influential Sioux leader, the news.

On Monday, August 18, 1862, the four men and Shakopee told Little Crow about the murder of the five whites and how a full-blown war should be started. Little Crow was reluctant, because he was trying to keep peace with the whites. However, he could not hold back those who saw this as an opportunity to pay back the whites for the years of mistreatment they suffered.

The Killing Begins

Afraid that he would lose his prestige, Little Crow reluctantly consented to the raids. At dawn, the Indians attacked houses and stores in the village of Lower Agency. Any white man found there—traders, physicians, interpreters, teamsters—were killed outright. The women and children were taken captive. Among the first killed was Andrew Myrick. He tried to escape by running out into the prairie but was cut down by a bullet. The Sioux pulled a handful of prairie grass and stuffed it into the mouth of his corpse.

Over the next 40 days, the army attempted to put down the uprising, but the Sioux continued to attack settlements and settlers up and down the Minnesota River. Twelve hundred refugees flooded into the small town of New Ulm. The Dakota laid siege to the tiny town but were driven back by a small band of militiamen. In the end, the town was nearly burned out, but somehow survived. Finally, Colonel Sibley, with several thousand men, many veterans from the 3rd Minnesota who had been taken prisoner by the Confederacy and had been paroled back to Minnesota, defeated the Sioux at the Battle of Wood Lake, effectively ending the uprising. In the end, on September 24, Little Crow and his followers scattered, some going into Canada, while others escaped to the West.

It is not known how many white civilians died, but thousands of people abandoned their homesteads and sought safety elsewhere. Many lived on isolated farms, miles from any neighbors. It is estimated that more than 500 civilians and soldiers died and more than 60 Dakota Sioux were killed.

Not all Sioux took part in the uprising. Many went out into the countryside to warn settlers of the fighting, and others protected families from the marauding bands. Chief Wabasha moved his tipis next to the nearly 200 white and mixed-blood captives, preventing them from being massacred.

Tribal Truths

John Other Day was dubbed one of "the faithful Indians" who aided in the Sioux uprising. Other Day turned "civilized" four years before the uprising started. He heard of the Sioux's planned attack on New Ulm and went to the agency to warn the people. Other Day stood guard all night outside a warehouse to protect the 67 people inside. The next day, he led the group on a three-day journey to safety. Later, Congress rewarded Other Day for his efforts in rescuing the 67 people from New Ulm. He was given $2,500 for his efforts. Although the country considered what he did a heroic act, the Sioux saw him as a traitor. They burned his home and ruined his fields. He used the money from the government to buy farmland in Hutchinson, Minnesota, where he and his wife could "start over."

The Trial of the Century

When peace was finally restored, Sibley rounded up as many Sioux as he could find, eventually bringing in about 2,000. He whittled this down to about 400. They were tried over a period of months at Lower Agency. When the last verdict was in, of the almost 400 men who had been tried, 306 were sentenced to be hung for murder, rape, or, in most cases, simply for taking part in a battle.

For most Minnesotans, hanging 400 Santee Sioux was an act of justice. In the East, there were voices of protest, but few in Minnesota much cared what folks elsewhere thought. One Minnesotan, the Right Reverend Henry Whipple, Episcopal Bishop of the Missionary District of Minnesota, went to President Lincoln himself to plead the Indians' cause. Whipple argued that the actions of the Sioux were the result of years of broken promises and being brazenly cheated and victimized. Lincoln agreed and decreed that the Minnesota Sioux had been fighting a war and, therefore, most of those under the death penalty should be treated as prisoners of war. Under the new criterion, the list of condemned men was reduced to 40. One of that number was later pardoned and one other died before the execution of the sentence. The remaining 38 Santee were hanged in Mankato on December 26, 1862. This marked the largest mass execution in American history.

Those Santee Sioux who weren't executed were still technically prisoners of war and were taken to a prison camp for Confederate soldiers in Rock Island, Illinois, where they were interned for three years. Upon their release, the prisoners returned to find that their reservation was no more and that their families had been deported to Dakota Territory. Minnesota's "Indian problem" was resolved, as Minnesota had got rid of almost all its Sioux.

Tribal Truths

The bodies of the executed Santee Sioux were buried in a mass grave, but they didn't rest long. The bodies were dug up by a number of doctors who wanted the skeletons for office reference, as medical books were few and expensive. One of the doctors was William W. Mayo, who taught his sons, William and Charles, anatomy using one of the Mankato skeletons. The Mayos, father and sons, went on to establish the now world-famous Mayo Clinic in Rochester, Minnesota.

There Were No Winners

During the American Civil War, tribes fought for and against the North or the South. Ultimately, it didn't matter who they fought for or if that side won or lost. The tribes in the South that supported the Confederacy were made to suffer far more than the states that had seceded from the Union, and those who supported the Union were mistreated simply because they were Natives. In the end, Native peoples were the real losers of the "white man's war."

The Least You Need to Know

- The Oregon Trail caused a disruption in the migration pattern of the bison, creating unrest among the Plains tribes.

- Tribes in the Pacific Northwest were generally peaceable and helpful to the earliest settlers on their lands.

- Reservations are not lands given to Indians by the white man but lands that Indians were allowed to retain.

- Native peoples were as divided by the American Civil War as were many Americans.

- Stand Watie, a Cherokee brigadier general in the Confederate army, was the last officer to surrender.

- President Lincoln declared that the Santee Sioux who participated in the Great Sioux uprising in 1862 were prisoners of war, not criminals.

Chapter **13**

More Gold and Blood

In This Chapter

- ◆ The Sand Creek Massacre in 1864
- ◆ The Sioux and Cheyenne make war against the United States
- ◆ Baker's Massacre

The Great Plains was largely ignored by settlers heading west. Miners and settlers were lured by the new opportunities in California, Oregon, and Washington. But when gold was discovered in Colorado and Montana, miners flooded lands that once teemed with game and caused tribes to react against this threat to their very existence. In Colorado and Montana, the U.S. military was called in an attempt to keep miners out, but in the end were instead used to subdue tribal efforts to retain their lands. Sadly, some of the military campaigns became one-sided. Indians paid with their blood for the western settlers' gold.

The Sand Creek Massacre

The discovery of gold in 1858 and 1859 on the South Platte River in what is now Colorado led to a massive influx of white fortune-seekers into the buffalo hunting grounds of the plains tribes. The trail through Kansas and into Colorado, along the Smokey Hill River, ran directly through Cheyenne and Arapaho territory. The buffalo avoided the long line of miners (almost a 100,000 in 1859) and, as had been the case with the Oregon Trail in the 1840s, the Indians found it difficult to find enough game.

The Indians refused to relocate to reservations in 1861, but Southern Cheyenne chiefs such as Black Kettle and White Antelope continued to work for peace, traveling to Washington that year to plead their case to President Lincoln. The president gave Black Kettle a large American flag and White Antelope a peace medal but little else.

The increased traffic across the plains led to an increase in hostilities between the Southern Cheyenne and Arapaho and the white miners and settlers who were flooding the area. On April 11, 1864, a rancher named Ripley, who lived northeast of Denver, claimed that Indians had driven off his horses. Lieutenant Dunn was dispatched from Camp Sanborn to find and return the stolen stock. The Indians were located and willingly offered to return the horses. When several warriors rode forward to shake the soldiers' hands, the latter began to snatch their weapons from them. A skirmish broke out, and the Indians killed several soldiers.

As tensions rose in 1864, Black Kettle and other Cheyenne and Arapaho chiefs traveled to Denver to meet Governor John Evans and military commander Colonel John Chivington of Colorado. The purpose of the meeting, for the Cheyenne and Arapaho, was to reassure the governor that the Indians did not want war. Governor Evans maintained that he supported peace, yet, unknown to Black Kettle, Evans was planning for war.

Native Voices

All we ask is that we have peace with the whites. We want to hold you by the hand. You are our father. We have been traveling through a cloud. The sky has been dark ever since the war began. These braves who are with me are willing to do what I say. We want to take good tidings home to our people that they may sleep in peace. I want you to give all these chiefs of the soldiers here to understand that we are for peace, and that we have made peace, that we may not be mistaken by them for enemies. I have not come here with a little wolf bark, but have come to talk plain with you.

—Motavato (Black Kettle) speaking to Governor Evans, Colonel Chivington, Major Wynkoop, and others in Denver, autumn 1864

Evans was an advocate for war with the Plains tribes as a way to rid Colorado of what he believed was a hindrance toward the settlement of his state. To make matters worse, on the day of the "peace talks," Chivington received a telegram from General Samuel Curtis (his superior officer) informing him that "I want no peace till the Indians suffer more …. No peace must be made without my directions."

Unaware of Curtis's telegram, Black Kettle and the others, believing that they had made their peace with Evans and Chivington, traveled south to set up camp on Sand Creek under the promised protection of Fort Lyon, while those who remained opposed to the agreement headed north to join the Sioux.

Tribal Truths

John Chivington was an elder of the Methodist Church. During the Civil War, he was offered a chaplain's commission in the First Colorado Volunteer Regiment but he refused it requesting instead for a fighting commission. Chivington, it is believed, had political ambitions, and candidates who were military heroes tended to get more votes than those who sought a peaceful settlement of the "Indian problem."

Killing the Nits and the Lice

Chivington, believing "the Cheyenne will have to be soundly whipped before they will be quiet," made plans for war. On the dawn of November 29, 1864, Chivington's Colorado volunteers and regular troops from Fort Lyon, under orders to take no prisoners, descended on Sand Creek. His directions were simple: "Kill and scalp all, big and little; nits make lice."

Black Kettle, believing there was no danger, ran up President Lincoln's American flag and a white flag of truce on a large lodge pole in front of his tipi to reassure his people. The troops responded by opening fire.

The main body of Indians fled toward the dry creek bed and began to frantically dig pits in its sandy banks for protection. Those warriors who had been able to grab their weapons engaged in a desperate rear-guard action, killing 8 and wounding 38 of their attackers. White Antelope died in front of his tipi wearing Lincoln's peace medal, his arms folded, singing his death song, "Nothing lives long, except the earth and the mountains."

Black Kettle and his wife followed the others up the stream bed. His wife was shot in the back and left for dead. The troops kept up their indiscriminate assault for most of the day and committed many atrocities. One lieutenant killed and scalped three women and five children who had surrendered and were screaming for mercy. Finally breaking off their attack, they returned to the camp, killing all the wounded they could find before mutilating and scalping the dead, including pregnant women, children, and babies. They then plundered the tipis and divided up the Indians' horse herd before leaving.

Native Voices _____

But what do we want to live for? The white man has taken our country, killed all of our game; was not satisfied with that, but killed our wives and children.

—Southern Cheyenne Council

More than 150 Indians, including 8 leading chiefs, were slain (some sources put the figure as high as 500). The vast majority of victims were women and children. Black Kettle's wife, although shot nine times, somehow managed to survive the attack. The survivors, more than half of whom were wounded, sought refuge in the camp of the Cheyenne Dog Warriors (who had remained opposed to the "peace" treaty) at Smokey Hill River.

The Colorado volunteers, exhibiting their scalps, returned to a hero's welcome in Denver. The Denver *News* reported that "all acquitted themselves well. Colorado soldiers have again covered themselves with glory." However, as details of the massacre became public, mostly from soldiers who were revolted by the actions of their comrades, support for the soldiers, particularly back east, began to waver.

A congressional investigation subsequently determined the so-called battle to be a "sedulously and carefully planned massacre," but no one was ever brought to justice for it. Both Chivington and Evans failed to realize their political ambitions in Colorado. Chivington returned to his native Ohio, where he ran for minor offices with little apparent success.

John Bozeman's War

After the Sand Creek massacre, the Southern Cheyenne and the Southern Arapaho went south away from the military conflict, and a tenuous peace settled upon the Southern Plains. The Civil War was about to end and the armies were to be demobilized. For the whites out west, this meant that a professional army could replace the militias that had been hastily established and ill trained. For the tribes of the Plains, this meant that the *long knives* would be returning.

Code Talking _____

The Plains tribes called the soldiers **long knives** because of the swords the officers carried.

Deserters and veterans, Confederate and Union, came out west, many to start over. Others wanted to strike it rich mining for gold that they imagined lay on the ground ready to be picked up. Many of these men followed the gold strikes from one community to the next, following a dream of sudden wealth and prosperity.

Montana Territory, Grasshopper Creek, and Last Chance Gulch

On July 28, 1862, the first major gold discovery in what is now Montana occurred at Grasshopper Creek, and the mining camp of Bannack was established. The strike set off a massive gold rush that swelled Bannack's population to more than 3,000 by 1863.

An even larger strike was made by six men camped in a gulch by a creek lined with alders. They were only looking for enough gold to buy tobacco, but they found the world's biggest surface field of gold at Alder Gulch, about 60 miles to the East of Bannack, as the crow flies. Only three weeks later, Virginia City became a thriving town. By fall, between 7,000 and 10,000 people were living in and around Virginia City.

Tribal Truths

In May 1863, six men from Bannack were on their way to look for gold in the Yellowstone gold fields when a band from the Crow tribe captured them. One of the six men, William Fairweather, put a rattlesnake in his shirt. His bravery impressed the Crow so much they agreed to release the men. The Crow made them promise not to continue on to the Yellowstone, so they started back for Bannack. These same men discovered gold in Alder Gulch, leading to widespread settlement of the area.

In July 1864, a group known as the "Four Georgians" stumbled upon gold in what is now the main street of Helena, Montana. The claim was staked and named "Last Chance Gulch." In August 1864, gold was discovered on the banks of the Yellowstone River, near what is now Yellowstone National Park. Thus, in two years following the first major gold strike, the population in what is now Montana became numerous enough that citizens proposed territorial status, which was granted in 1864.

Red Cloud's War

Like so many men of the Civil War era, John Bozeman was struck with gold fever and headed west in 1858, abandoning his wife and three children. And like so many miners, John Bozeman arrived at the Montana gold fields too late. After his quest for gold failed to pan out, Bozeman realized it would be more profitable to "mine the miners" than to mine gold. In 1863, he and John Jacobs blazed the Bozeman Trail (also known as the Montana Trail), a cutoff route from the Oregon Trail, and guided miners to Virginia City through the Gallatin Valley.

There were a number of routes to the gold fields, but they were either too indirect or too expensive. A miner with a lot of money could travel up the Missouri River by riverboat to Fort Benton, Montana Territory, and then overland to Virginia City. Most miners, however, followed the Oregon Trail to the Snake River in southeastern Idaho and then went straight north to Montana.

John Bozeman's route was 1,500 miles shorter than other routes and had the advantage of passing on the western side of the Big Horn Mountains of what is now the state of Wyoming. There was plenty of water and forage and the travel was easier, with fewer mountain passes. There was only one drawback: Bozeman's route passed through the heart of unceded Indian Territory and the choicest of all the hunting lands of the Sioux nation and their Cheyenne allies.

On July 6, 1863, Bozeman and Jacobs started up the trail, guiding 46 wagons and 89 passengers. They had traveled only 140 miles north of their departure point on the Oregon Trail when a large party of Northern Cheyenne and some Sioux confronted them. The train was turned around, but once out of sight of the Indians, Bozeman doubled back and made it through to the mining country by traveling mostly during the night.

The Bloody Bozeman

The Bozeman Trail became a lighting rod for Sioux and Cheyenne hostilities from the moment it was opened. The tribes feared that the trail would disrupt the movement of the game herds, as the Oregon Trail had done (see Chapter 12) and the settlers and miners would bring disease and death to the Indians. Bozeman demanded that the military be brought in to protect travelers.

The government wanted to avoid open hostilities between travelers and the Sioux. It had been customary to call upon western tribes to resolve such differences by negotiation. This had been the case with the First Fort Laramie Treaty, which resulted in a period of peace, albeit short lived.

Red Cloud, leader of the Sioux, was wary of the motives of the white men. At a meeting at Fort Laramie he asked if the Army had any designs for a permanent presence along the trail. The commissioner assured Red Cloud that all that was sought was the safe passage for settlers. As luck would have it, at that same time, Colonel Henry Carrington showed up at the post with enough material to build several forts. Red Cloud stormed out of the meeting; those Lakota leaders who remained behind signed an agreement consenting to the road, but they said they could not guarantee safe passage.

Native Voices _____

When the Great Father at Washington sent us his chief soldier to ask for a path through our hunting grounds, a way for his iron horse to the mountains and the western sea, we were told that they merely wished to pass through our country, not to tarry among us, but to seek for gold in the far west. Our old chiefs thought to show their friendship and goodwill, when they allowed this dangerous snake in our midst. They promised to protect the wayfarers.

Yet, before the ashes of the council fire was cold, the Great Father is building his forts among us. His presence here is an insult and a threat. It is an insult to the spirits of my ancestors. Are we then to give up their sacred graves to be plowed for corn? Dakotas, I am for war!

—Red Cloud, Lakota Sioux leader

The Sioux had a just complaint. At issue was the status of John Bozeman's road. According to the First Fort Laramie Treaty of 1851, the tribes of the Northern Plains agreed to "recognize the right of the United States Government to establish roads, military, and other posts, within their respective territories." The Bozeman Trail, however, was not a military road but a commercial road, the product of private enterprise.

The Army went ahead with plans to build three forts along the Bozeman Trail—Fort Reno (near Kaycee, Wyoming) in 1865 and forts Phil Kearny (on Piney Creek, near present Sheridan, Wyoming) and C. F. Smith, on the Bighorn River at the mouth of Bighorn Canyon in 1866. The forts, however, guarded no travelers as the soldiers themselves were in a constant state of siege.

Give Me Eighty Men

At Fort Phil Kearny, on December 21, 1866, a party of Sioux made one of its many attacks on a party from the post out cutting wood. Colonel Carrington's policy to this point had been to relieve the wood-cutting party but not to pursue the Indians. Carrington had under his command a brash officer, Captain William J. Fetterman, who grew impatient, believing he could take care of the Sioux if given the chance. He had once bragged, "Give me 80 men and I'll ride through the entire Sioux Nation." Fetterman prepared to set out with 78 soldiers to once more chase off the Sioux and Cheyenne. At the last minute, two civilians joined Fetterman. Half of his wish was fulfilled: He now had his 80 men.

Carrington's orders were specific: "Support the wood train. Relieve it and report to me. Do not engage or pursue Indians at its expense. Under no circumstances pursue over Lodge Trail Ridge."

The Sioux and Cheyenne warriors slowly lured Fetterman and his men farther away from the fort by stopping to dismount every so often to fire their weapons at the soldiers but still keeping just out of reach. Fetterman disappeared over what is now known as Ambush Hill, where he met more than 1,000 warriors. The fighting was quickly over and resulted in one of the most decisive Indian victories during the Indian wars.

Hayfield Fight and the Wagon Box Fight

Because of their isolation, the Army didn't hear from their far-flung posts along the Bozeman Trail during the winter of 1866 and 1867. So when spring came and the forts were still intact, there was some hope that the Indians might cease their hostilities. But two incidents the following summer convinced the federal government that the Bozeman Trail was not worth the lives it cost to keep it open.

On August 1, 1867, a party from Fort C. F. Smith was out cutting hay when Cheyenne warriors attacked them. Three whites were killed in what is called the Hayfield Fight. The next day at Fort Phil Kearny, the Sioux attacked a wood camp and six individuals in an incident known as the Wagon Box Fight.

> **Tribal Truths** _____
>
> Ironically, John Bozeman met an untimely death on the Bozeman Trail at the hands of so-called renegade Blackfeet in April 1867. Local lore tells another story, however. Thomas Coover, who managed to survive the Indian attack, accompanied Bozeman that faithful day. When Coover led authorities back to the site of the supposed attack, investigators noted that the tracks indicated that the Blackfeet horses were shod, not a very likely circumstances at that time. Further, John Bozeman, so the story goes, was quite a lady's man. One rumor suggests that the amorous Bozeman had wronged Coover and he used the opportunity of being alone with Bozeman to settle the score.

While the Hayfield and Wagon Box fights were relatively bloodless from the Army's perspective, the attacks on two forts separated by several hundred miles convinced the military that the Sioux and Cheyenne were not going to allow the Bozeman Trail to remain open. After these bloody engagements, which included the Fetterman Massacre, the Wagon Box Fight, and the Hayfield Fight, an exasperated U.S.

government finally sued for peace. The road was closed, and the three forts along its route were abandoned and then burned by the victorious tribes while the evacuating troops were still in sight of them. By that time, 154 soldiers and civilians lost their lives along the trail that earned the nickname "The Bloody Bozeman."

In 1868, by the Second Fort Laramie Treaty, Red Cloud agreed to accept life on a reservation, and the government abandoned the Bozeman Trail. Red Cloud went down in history as the only Native American leader on the Plains to defeat the United States military. However, he also consented to life on the reservation. The Second Fort Laramie Treaty provided that the reservation was to be surveyed and land allotted to individuals. The treaty offered farm implements, livestock, and the services of a doctor and teacher. The obvious intent of the treaty was to push the Lakota down the road to civilization.

The Piegan War of 1870

At the height of their power, the Blackfeet numbered between 30,000 and 40,000 strong. But smallpox took its toll, again and again, on the tribe. In 1781, both the Shoshoni and Blackfeet suffered great losses due to the disease. In 1836, half of the Blackfeet died of the "white scabs" disease, and subsequent outbreaks in 1845 and in 1857 reduced the Blackfeet to a piteous few. In 1868, smallpox was introduced by the arrival of a Missouri River steamboat, once more hitting the Blackfeet. Because they attributed the spread of the great sickness to the increasingly numerous white settlers who were invading Blackfeet territory, hostilities between the whites and the Blackfeet escalated. After all, the Blackfeet thought they were in a fight for their lives.

In late August 1869, in revenge for the murder of two innocent Blackfeet by the citizens of Fort Benton, Montana Territory, the Indians entered the Prickly Pear Valley (near Helena, Montana) and killed Malcolm Clark, one of Montana Territory's most prominent citizens.

Tribal Truths

The Blackfeet are actually a confederacy of three Algonquian-speaking tribes, composed of the Blood (or Kainah), the Piegan or Pikuni, and the Blackfeet proper, or Siksika. No one is certain how the name Blackfeet originated; some believe it derived from an incident when this tribe crossed over a stretch of the plains that had been blackened by a prairie fire, while another theory suggests they got their name because they blackened the soles of their moccasins. Another mystery is why in the United States they are called "Blackfeet" and in Canada they are referred to as "Blackfoot."

On January 1, 1870, General Alfred Sully, Montana superintendent for Indian Affairs, and U.S. Marshall W. F. Wheeler went to the Blackfeet Agency with warrants for the arrests of Clark's murderers. They gave the Blackfeet two weeks to turn in the responsible men. The Blackfeet leaders agreed to try to bring the men back but were unable to comply because Clark's killers had escaped into Canada.

I Want Them Struck and Struck Hard

After two weeks, Major Eugene Baker of Fort Ellis (near present-day Bozeman, Montana) was dispatched in sub-zero weather to look for the village of Mountain Chief, who was thought to be harboring the murderers. On January 23, 1870, Baker attacked a camp on the Marias River. Tragically, this village was not Mountain Chief's but rather the camp of Heavy Runner, whose followers were mainly friendly to the whites.

> **Tribal Truths**
>
> Ironically, Baker's Massacre occurred a few short miles from where Captain Meriwether Lewis killed He-Who-Looks-at-the-Calf, a Blackfeet warrior, on July 26, 1806 (see Chapter 10).

Chief Heavy Runner came out of his lodge waving a paper that certified that he was of good character and friendly to the whites. He ran toward the soldiers, shouting to them to cease firing and entreating them to save the women and children, but fell with several bullet holes in his body.

The First Great Lesson in Good Manners

Baker maintained that he defeated 120 "vigorous warriors," and a Montana history text later described the massacre as "the first great lesson in good manners taught the Red Man in Montana." Subsequent investigation, however, revealed that Baker did not attack a well-guarded village. Lieutenant William Pease, the Piegan Indian agent, reported that Baker and his men killed 140 women and children, 18 old men, and only 15 men of fighting age.

Baker's Massacre achieved the goal of the Piegan War of 1870. After this attack, the Blackfeet would never again be much trouble for the settlers who moved onto their lands. After 100 years of disease, starvation, and near-annihilation, the Blackfeet settled on the reservation, never to regain their status as "Raiders of the Northern Plains."

Nothing Lasts Forever but the Rocks

As 1870 drew to a close on the northern and southern plains, the settlers and the tribes settled into an uneasy peace. For the Blackfeet, the Southern Arapaho, and the Southern Cheyenne, peace had come at a high cost. Each tribe suffered a great defeat and had nearly been annihilated. In the case of the Northern Cheyenne and the Lakota, peace came only after they drove the soldiers out of their homeland and regained control over their own destinies. This tranquility turned out to be as lasting as a summer snowstorm in the Rockies.

The Least You Need to Know

◆ The Sand Creek Massacre resulted in the death of more than 150 peaceful Cheyenne.

◆ Red Cloud was the only Indian leader to defeat the U.S. military in warfare.

◆ Baker's Massacre resulted in the death of 173 Blackfeet, including Heavy Runner, a Piegan leader who was friendly with the whites.

Chapter 14

The Road to the Little Bighorn

In This Chapter

◆ Reservation life becomes unbearable

◆ The battle for the Black Hills and its gold

◆ Custer's bluster and blunders

◆ Natives pay dearly for Custer's death

Although there are more films about the Battle of the Little Bighorn—the famous battle where General Custer made his Last Stand—than any other engagement fought in world history, the general public has only been told the *what* of the story—not the *why*.

Much of the mystique of the battle focuses on General George Armstrong Custer, portrayed as either the egomaniacal villain who disobeyed orders and deserved to die, or the sainted hero who fought to his death against insurmountable odds. Neither image is correct, of course, but that doesn't diminish people's interest in the boy general.

For Native peoples, the Battle of the Little Bighorn represented the last best chance to resist the invasion of the non-Indian onto their lands. They fought to their deaths to protect their families and their way of life. Their victory at the Battle of the Little Bighorn is a symbol of resistance—something Indians can take pride in amid so much defeat. The clash during which Custer made his last stand was the climax of a series of clashes between Natives and the U.S. military.

One Good American Cow and a Pair of Oxen

Following the closure of the Bozeman Trail and the military posts along it in 1868, the Lakota Sioux believed that their troubles with the white soldiers had ended. After all, many of them had given up much of their land and their freedom by agreeing to accept life on the Great Sioux Reservation.

Native Voices

God made me an Indian. He did not make me a reservation Indian.

—Sitting Bull, Hunkpapa Sioux

Life for the nearly 200,000 reservation Indians was anything but pleasant. The buffalo had nearly disappeared from the Northern Plains (the result of non-Native "hide hunters" who left the meat to spoil under the hot prairie sun). The reservations were largely located in the western United States on land not fit for farming. Reservation Indians were forced to live on flour, sugar, and other rations provided by the government instead of their traditional food.

At that time, the policy of the Indian Bureau was to encourage the Natives to abandon the hunting culture and become farmers. In the Second Fort Laramie Treaty, the Sioux were promised livestock ("one good American cow and one pair of oxen") in order to become self-sufficient. The treaty language was largely symbolic; few cows—good or otherwise—and no oxen were delivered. The government failed to live up to its promises once again.

Even though the Lakota had grown dependent on government rations and treaty annuities, those were often late and there was never enough of either. Making matters worse, the Lakota often avoided periodic attempts by the government to take a census of their people, because they feared the consequences if the government found out just how few of them there were left. Consequently, the government gave them fewer rations.

Not all Lakota went to the reservation, however. A large number under the leadership of Sitting Bull, Crazy Horse, and Gall, among others, remained in the unceded territory between the Black Hills of what is now South Dakota and the Big Horn

Mountains in Wyoming. This area was the last of the original land claimed by Indian nations and had not been yet yielded. Here, together with a number of Northern Cheyenne led by Two Moons, the Lakota continued to live as they had for centuries— hunting buffalo and waging war against the Crow.

Sitting Bull was a Hunkpapa (Lakota or Sioux) spiritual leader whose vision during a sun dance predicted a victory over General George Custer's Seventh Cavalry.

(© Courtesy of the Museum of the Rockies)

A Train Ride Through Indian Country

The Second Fort Laramie Treaty promised that the unceded lands would remain the home of the Sioux and Cheyenne as long as they chose to live there. But events were about to change all that. White civilization was continuing to close in on the Natives. The Northern Pacific Railroad, the second transcontinental rail route, was nearing completion. The railroad reached Bozeman, in Montana Territory, from the West, and Bismarck, in what is now North Dakota, from the East. To close the gap between these two routes, a leg was planned along the banks of the Yellowstone River, which served as the northern border for the lands promised to the Indians by the Second Fort Laramie Treaty.

Rather than plan the route along the *north side* of the river on lands not promised to the Indians, the railroad survey line was to follow a course along the *south side* of the river—the northern boundary of the unceded Indian Territory! Thus, the railroad, as planned, would violate the Second Fort Laramie Treaty. The northern side of the river would have been more expensive to build on because the railroad company would have had to build a number of bridges. The southern route was cheaper. The government tried to get the Lakota to allow the railroad to run through their land, but the negotiations failed. Instead of changing the route, the government decided to build the railroad on Lakota territory anyway.

On June 20, 1873, a military expedition was sent out from Fort Rice on the Missouri River to escort the surveying party laying out the line on—treaty or no treaty—the south side of the Yellowstone. Once again, the government was about to violate a treaty it had made with the Indians.

> **Native Voices**
>
> My friends, for many years we have been in this country; we never go to the Great Fathers' country and bother him about anything. It is his people who come to our country and bother us, do many bad things, and teach our people to be band .... Before you people ever crossed the ocean to come to this country, and from that time to this, you have never proposed to buy a country that was equal to this in riches. My friends, this country that you have come to buy is the best country that we have; ... this country is mine, I was raised in it; my forefathers lived and died in it; and I wish to remain in it.
>
> —Crow Feather, Lakota

The Yellowstone Expedition of 1873

Colonel D. S. Stanley was placed in command of the more than 1,500 soldiers sent to guard the surveyors. One young Lieutenant Colonel George Armstrong Custer commanded the Seventh Regiment and its 10 cavalry companies that were part of the expedition.

General Stanley was not overly impressed with the boy general. In a letter to his wife, Stanley described Custer as a "cold-blooded, untruthful, and unprincipled man ...." He continued, "As I said, I will try but am not sure I can avoid trouble with him." Several days later, Custer lived up to Stanley's assessment of him when, perhaps not wishing to play second fiddle, he went off without permission in pursuit of adventure. Stanley wrote his wife:

> I had a little fury with Custer as I told you I probably would. We were separate four miles and I intended him to assist in getting the train over the Muddy River. Without consulting me, he marched off fifteen miles, coolly sending me a note to send him forage and rations. I sent after him, ordering him to halt where he was ... and never presume to make another movement without orders.

I knew from the start it would have to be done …. He was just gradually assuming command and now he knows he has a commanding officer who will not tolerate his arrogance.

Stanley had no more difficulties with Custer after that, and the survey was completed, but not without a few skirmishes with the Indians that resulted in casualties on both sides.

The Lakota Sioux got a brief reprieve when the company building the railroad went bankrupt in the Panic of 1873, stopping the Northern Pacific in its tracks.

There's Gold in Those Hills!

During the Yellowstone Expedition of 1873, the military realized that this part of the Plains was largely void of a military presence. It had Fort Laramie to the South in what is now Wyoming, Fort Ellis in Montana Territory to the West, Fort Abraham Lincoln in the Dakota Territory, but no posts near the Great Sioux Reservation and the unceded Indian Territory. The military decided to locate a site for a fort in the Black Hills, an area between the Lakota on the West and Cheyenne on the East.

For the Lakota and the Cheyenne, the Black Hills (*Paha Sapa* to the Lakota) were—and still are—sacred land. Within the Hills, the Lakota believe creation began. Their most sacred site is Harney Peak, which is believed to be the center of the universe. The Cheyenne, too, regarded the Hills as sacred. Their great prophet, Sweet Medicine, climbed Bear Butte, near Sturgis, South Dakota, and there received the *Arrow Renewal Ceremony* and their system of government from the Supernatural.

On July 2, 1874, an expedition under the leadership of Colonel Custer set out for the Black Hills to determine the best site for a post. The expedition also included several scientists— a sizable contingent of geologists among them.

Tribal Truths

Custer's role in the discovery of gold was clearly known to the Sioux and Cheyenne. Black Elk, in his remembrances, recalls that Custer came to the Black Hills looking for "that gold dust that makes white men crazy. He got rubbed out [killed] for that."

Code Talking

The Cheyenne prophet, Sweet Medicine, received four arrows from the Spirit Beings, or gods. Two were for hunting and two for warfare. When a Cheyenne murdered a fellow Cheyenne, the arrows became putrid and bad luck would dog the tribe. The **Arrow Renewal Ceremony** made the arrows pure again.

Custer made no secret of the fact that he was going to look into the rumors that there was gold in the Hills.

When the expedition returned to Fort Lincoln two months later, Custer reported that there were veins of gold-bearing quartz on the side of almost every hill and under every blade of grass. This was, of course, an exaggeration, but it produced what might have been the desired outcome, for the announcement of this news started a gold rush that brought thousands of miners into the sacred Black Hills.

Treaty? What Treaty?

At first the Army tried to keep gold-seekers out of the Hills, but no sooner was a party turned back than it snuck right back in past the soldiers. A few parties of miners were killed by the Lakota, but that didn't keep more from trying to make their for-

Native Voices

The Black Hills is my land and I love it.
And whoever interferes
Will hear this gun.

—Lakota song

tunes. Because the government couldn't keep whites out of the Hills, Washington decided to find a way to legalize this trespass.

According to the Second Fort Laramie Treaty, any modifications to that treaty required the consent of three fourths of the Lakota. The government sent commissioners to the Lakota to offer to buy the Black Hills, but the Lakota quickly refused, which they had every right to do.

Tribal Truths

During the negotiations for the sale of the Black Hills, Red Cloud, leader of the reservation Sioux, calmly proposed that $600 million might be a fair price for the Black Hills. When the commissioners recovered from that bit of sticker shock, they made a counterproposal of $6 million. Neither side was serious, of course, but Red Cloud didn't want to be accused of not being willing to negotiate.

The Sting of Rejection

The commissioner of Indian Affairs was embarrassed that his representatives were unable to force the Sioux to consent and, in retaliation, he ordered all Indians to report to their respective agencies by January 31, 1876. This ultimatum was both impossible to comply with and was in violation of the Second Fort Laramie Treaty. The government had no right to compel the Lakota to do anything while they were lawfully residing in their own territory. Besides, the order was given in November

1875—the bands of Lakota and Cheyenne were already holed up in their winter camps. To move the villages during the coldest time of the winter would have been suicide.

When only one band showed up by the stated deadline, the commissioner threw up his hands and turned the matter over to the Army. The Army decided that those bands that refused the order were at war with the United States and needed to be compelled to obey by force, if necessary.

The Army Prepares to Make War on the Sioux and Cheyenne

General Phil Sheridan, commander of the western forces, planned his strategy. He would use one of his favorite attack plans—three converging forces:

- ◆ Major General Alfred Terry, commanding the Department of Dakota, was to lead one column of soldiers west from Fort Abraham Lincoln to the Yellowstone Valley.

- ◆ Brigadier General George Crook, commanding the Department of the Platte, was to move up from Fort Laramie to the Yellowstone Valley.

- ◆ Colonel John Gibbon would command the third prong moving eastward from Fort Ellis in Montana Territory. The three prongs would meet in the vicinity of the junction of the Bighorn and Yellowstone rivers and crush the Sioux and Cheyenne, either annihilating them or forcing their surrender.

The Army estimated that there were only 1,000 warriors in the Powder River country and that they would be no match for 2,000 well-trained professional soldiers.

Round One to the Indians

The first blood was drawn in March 1868. General Crook left Fort Laramie on March 1 intending to "get some idea of the country and the difficulties to be overcome in a summer campaign." On the Powder River, the expedition located pony tracks. Colonel J. J. Reynolds took three companies of cavalry with him to follow the tracks, and on March 17, he found an Indian village. Reynolds attacked immediately without bothering to identify the Indians. If he had, he would have found out that they were a Northern Cheyenne village under Chief Two Moons, who was mainly friendly to the whites. In fact, Two Moons, along with some Lakota, grew tired of waiting to begin their annual hunt and was on his way back to the Cheyenne Reservation. Had Reynolds not attacked, Two Moons would not have joined the Lakota at the Little Bighorn.

Reynolds drove into the camp, scattering the Cheyenne and Sioux. The Indians quickly rallied, however, and held Reynolds pinned down from the bluffs overlooking the village. The cavalry retreated, pursued closely by the Cheyenne. The party returned to Fort Fetterman in defeat.

The fight had several unintended results. First, Crook realized that fighting Indians was not going to be a cake walk. Second, a patriotic fervor swept through the Sioux and Cheyenne and, as a result, Natives like Two Moons who had been reluctant to fight were now eager to drive the white soldiers out of their land. And as for Reynolds, he was charged with neglect of duty, for which he was found guilty and relieved of duty for one year.

How Custer Almost Missed His Own Party

The real expedition was scheduled for late spring 1876, when the ground would be dry enough for the troopers to take the field. The campaign was further delayed as the Army waited to hear the fate of one of its officers, George Custer. Custer was to command one of the three columns, but he was in the middle of a battle for his career.

Earlier, Custer was on leave in Washington where he and his wife Elizabeth (Libby) were the toast of the town. Widely popular (with everyone but the men in his command), Custer enjoyed the attention paid him. On one occasion, he let it be known that he was aware of illegal conduct by those responsible for Army procurements out west. Among the people he charged with corruption were President Grant's secretary of war, William Worth Belknap, and Orvil Grant, the president's brother. When called by Congress to testify on the matter, it turned out that Custer's knowledge was based on rumor and hearsay. Even though the gossip Custer spread around Washington was, in fact, true, Grant's enemies weren't pleased by Custer's inability to help their cause. And of course none of this pleased President Grant. Thus, when command positions for the Yellowstone Expedition were being considered, Custer's name was noticeably absent.

The thought of missing what was thought would be the most glorious victory in Plains Indian warfare caused Custer great anguish. He begged General Terry to intervene on his behalf and finally, after the intercession of General Sherman, Custer was allowed to accompany his regiment, the Seventh Cavalry, but under no circumstances was Custer to be given any significant command.

Crook Clashes with the Sioux

In May, as Crook and Terry were converging from the East and the West, General Crook, along with 1,050 officers and men, advanced from Fort Fetterman northward to where the "hostiles" were thought to be gathered. Scouts brought word that the Sioux were probably on the Rosebud Creek, and Crook quickly headed in that direction.

The Lakota knew that trouble was brewing, however, and had scouts follow Crook's men.

On June 17, 1876, Crook clashed with the Sioux under the leadership of their great war leader, Crazy Horse, in the Battle of the Rosebud. General Crook had almost 1,300 men, and the Army estimated that the Indians had approximately 1,500 warriors (Native accounts put their numbers somewhere closer to 1,000). It was, in terms of the sizes of the two groups, an even fight.

Ancient Tales
A week before the Battle of the Little Bighorn, during a sun dance, Sitting Bull sacrificed 100 pieces of flesh and had a vision in which he saw many soldiers "falling into camp," or falling dead from their horses as they rode toward the Indian village. This was an omen that the Sioux would receive a great victory.

This was no well-organized confrontation between two advancing armies but rather a swirling, ever-shifting fight. Crook's troops were split into smaller groups and these into yet smaller pockets in which they engaged in hand-to-hand battle with the Lakota warriors.

Tribal Truths

During the Battle of the Rosebud, Comes-in-Sight, a Cheyenne chief, had his horse shot out from under him. In the din of battle, Comes-in-Sight looked up to see a horse and rider bearing down on him. He swung up on the horse and the two rode to safety. His rescuer? His sister, Buffalo Calf Road Woman, who had come along to help with the horse herds. The Cheyenne always remember this fight as the Battle Where the Girl Saved Her Brother.

No side gained the upper hand. When it appeared that the Natives were going to be routed, Crazy Horse rode among the warriors shouting, "Come on, Lakotas, it's a good day to die." As the day wore on, the fighting became more sporadic and, eventually, the Sioux and Cheyenne withdrew. The Battle of the Rosebud ended in a draw, although Crook would claim victory. Crook withdrew some 40 miles south to lick his wounds in the Big Horn Mountains. Unknown to him at the time, a great battle raged on the banks of the Greasy Grass River.

The Battle of the Little Bighorn

As General Terry and Custer came westward from Fort Lincoln, they located the trail of a large village moving across the plains. This was one of five bands that were camped on the Greasy Grass; four Lakota bands and one Cheyenne village under Two Moon. Scouts followed the trail until it hit the Rosebud Creek. General Terry, Colonel Gibbon, and Custer met on the riverboat, *Far West*, to finalize their strategy. Terry decided he would send Gibbon up the Bighorn and the Little Bighorn, while Custer and the Seventh Cavalry would circle around and come down the Little Bighorn from the South. If the plan worked, the Lakota and Cheyenne would be caught in the middle.

Custer and his cavalry left about noon on June 22. As the regiment rode away, Colonel Gibbon called after Custer, "Now, Custer, don't be greedy. Wait for us." Custer replied cryptically, "No, I won't."

> **Tribal Truths**
>
> Scholars have been debating the meaning of Custer's reply for now well over 100 years. Some believe he was telling Gibbon that he wouldn't be greedy, while others believe he meant, "No, I won't wait for you." The real truth is buried in Grave 1, Section 27, Row A of the West Point Cemetery.

Custer at Crow's Nest

Custer's orders were to travel south, keeping the Wolf Mountains on his right until he reached the Little Bighorn valley; then he was to follow the river northward until he located the Indians. Instead, Custer, led by hired Crow army scouts to find the so-called hostiles, crossed the Wolf Mountains directly into the Little Bighorn two days ahead of Gibbon. Custer was up to his old tricks again, but this time he'd pay a high price for his insubordination.

On June 25, 1776, Custer stopped the march and climbed to a high point on the divide between the Rosebud and the Little Bighorn known as the Crow's Nest. From there, his Crow scouts, with eyes more accustomed to seeing the smallest detail on the vast plain, could see clearly the valley below and the thousands of lodges. Custer, however, couldn't see the village—five villages, actually—nor any smoke from cookfires.

Custer Decides to Attack

During the night, one of the mule packs from Custer's party came loose and had scattered supplies along the trail. When a soldier was sent back to recover the goods, he discovered several Lakota warriors examining the contents of the pack. The Army had lost the element of surprise.

Custer decided to attack at once. Believing the Indians would scatter at the first signs of soldiers, he divided his regiment into four units. He ordered Major Marcus Reno to cross the river with 112 soldiers and attack the village from the South. He took 231 men and rode down the ridge paralleling the river, intending to attack the village at the earliest opportunity. Custer left 130 soldiers to guard the pack train and sent Captain Frederick Benteen and 125 troopers off to the South with instructions to search the ravines for escaping Indians.

Reno and Benteen Fall on Hard Times

Reno crossed the river and attacked the village. The Hunkpapa Sioux chief, Gall, with hundreds of warriors, repelled Reno's charge and forced him to retreat with his men across the river and into the bluffs above. More than a third (nearly 40) of Reno's soldiers were dead or missing by the time the survivors reached the river bluffs.

Tribal Truths

When Gall came out to meet him, Reno ordered his men to dismount and then to mount again. He ordered a retreat to the trees along the Little Bighorn and once more ordered the troops to dismount. Even though he was harshly criticized for cowardice in battle, his confusion is understandable: As Reno charged the village, he was riding next to Bloody Knife, Custer's favorite Arikara scout. Bloody Knife was shot in the head, spattering blood and brains all over Reno's face.

Meanwhile, Benteen received an urgent message from Custer: "Come on. Big village. Be Quick. Bring packs." Benteen rode in the direction that Custer traveled but found Reno surrounded and trapped by the Lakota and Cheyenne instead. Reno and Benteen were pinned down and were unable to support Custer. As nightfall came, there was no word from Custer.

Tribal Truths

No one is sure exactly how many Lakota and Cheyenne there were at the Greasy Grass. The village consisted of a number of smaller camps, including a Cheyenne camp, the Hunkpapa of Gall and Sitting Bull, the Miniconjous, Sans Arc, Oglala (under Crazy Horse), and smaller groups of Blackfeet Sioux, Two Kettles, Yankton, Santee, and even a few lodges of Arapaho. The entire village, consisting of approximately 1,500 lodges, was spread out down the river about 3 miles. It is believed that there were between 12,000 and 15,000 Indians in the encampment, of whom at least 4,000 or 5,000 were men of fighting age.

Where's Custer?

No one knows for sure what happened to George Custer. There are two principle sources for knowledge about Custer's fate: Native accounts and the archaeology of the battle site. Neither is complete or accurate.

After having left Reno, Custer went north, more or less parallel to the Greasy Grass River. It's likely that he saw the warriors sprint out of the village to counter Reno's attack on the southern part of the encampment and assumed that the Lakota and Cheyenne were fleeing. Believing Reno had things well in hand, Custer may have continued along the ridge looking for a ford in order to reach the village and support Reno's offensive. But at that time, as now, the banks of the Little Bighorn were quite steep, forcing Custer to continue farther along the river to find a crossing.

> **Ancient Tales**
>
> The Indians have a joke about Custer waiting for those 20 minutes. Beaver Heart, a Cheyenne warrior who fought Custer, said that when the scouts warned Custer about the village, he laughed and said, "When I get to the village, I'm going to find the most beautiful girl and take her." So that's what Custer was doing for those 20 minutes— looking for an Indian bride.

It is believed that Custer and five companies (approximately 230 men altogether) reached a point on the ridgeline where he could see the village below. Apparently he dispatched two companies to investigate a ford below at the head of Medicine Tail Coulee. They may have reached the river, but, in any case, they were driven back up another draw where Custer and the other three companies later joined them.

According to reports from Crow and Cheyenne witnesses, Custer waited for approximately 20 minutes after regrouping, either looking for another crossing or waiting for Benteen to reinforce him. In either case, no help came and that delay may have cost him his life. Had he retreated, he might have lived to fight another day.

Custer's Last Stand

As Custer waited, the Lakota and Cheyenne rallied their warriors in the village below. Gall, having driven Reno back across the river, led his warriors against Custer's southern flank. Crazy Horse's Oglala (Sioux) fighters, and Two Moon's Cheyenne warriors, circled around and cut off Custer's escape from the North. The remaining soldiers formed a tight ball atop Custer's Hill where they were finally overrun, and Custer was killed.

Although the fight in which Custer died is often called his "last stand," some scholars speculate that Custer made no such heroic last stand, but was killed early in the battle. Others suggest that he took his own life, following the so-called code of "save the last bullet for yourself."

Tribal Truths _____

Not all the Natives that day were fighting the soldiers. Custer had under his command 26 Arikara, 6 Crow, and 4 Dakota (an eastern cousin to the Lakota), all serving as scouts. Four scouts, Curley, Goes Ahead, Hairy Moccasin, and White man Runs Him, rode with Custer as far as Medicine Tail Coulee where Custer released them from further service. One of the scouts, Curley, then 19 years old, remained nearby and witnessed the battle. Other tribes criticized the Crow for aiding the Army, but what is often forgotten is that the battle took place on lands the Crow claimed.

Native sources and memories are silent about when Custer died or about who killed him. Scholars suggest that the Lakota and Cheyenne warriors feared reprisals if they told the truth about Custer's killer. More than likely, it was like Spotted Blackbird, a Lakota warrior, said: "If we could have seen where each bullet landed we might have known. But hundreds of bullets were flying that day." It is certain that Custer died from either a gunshot to the side or from one to the head. Either would have been fatal. As for Custer's body, he avoided being scalped or mutilated. He cut his hair short before leaving Fort Abraham Lincoln and thus had no hair to scalp and, because he was wearing his buckskin coat, the Lakota and Cheyenne may have believed that he was a civilian scout.

No one can be certain how many Lakota or Cheyenne died that day. John Stands In Timber, Cheyenne historian and grandson of Lame White Man, a Cheyenne who fought Custer, heard that the Lakota lost 66, while the Cheyenne just 7 men, but certainly there might have been more. Plains custom was that relatives recovered the dead as quickly as possible and took care of the remains immediately.

A Victory Too Well Won

The Battle of the Little Bighorn was over quickly. When asked how long the clash lasted, Indian participants replied, "As long as it takes the white man to eat his noon meal." Even as the battle was raging on the hillside above, down in the village, women were striking their camps and preparing to flee. Earlier in the spring of 1876, the Lakota and Cheyenne bands had come together for their mutual protection, and now that the threat was eliminated, they separated into their respective bands, following tribal customs.

The news of Custer's defeat shocked the nation. America was celebrating the hundredth anniversary of its independence when it learned that one of its heroes had been "massacred." (This was no massacre as Sand Creek had been. Custer attacked a village of not only men, but women and children as well. It was a battle during which Custer was out-manned and out-maneuvered.) Requiems were composed to Custer's memories and the public demanded retribution.

The Army was embarrassed and, with reinforcements, reentered the field. Crook and Terry together brought nearly 4,000 soldiers to the plains to find and crush the "hostile" Indians. General Nelson Miles, with several hundred soldiers, during the daring winter campaign of 1876 and 1877, was able to do what Crook and Terry could not: defeat the Lakota and Cheyenne. One by one, the Lakota and Cheyenne bands were located and returned to the reservation.

Native Voices

Because I am a red man. If the Great Spirit had desired me to be a white man he would have made me so in the first place. He put in your heart certain wishes and plans; in my heart he put other and different desires. Each man is good in his sight. It is not necessary for eagles to be crows. Now we are poor but we are free. No white man controls our footsteps. If we must die, we die defending our rights.

—Sitting Bull, when asked why he didn't surrender

The End of a People's Sacred Dream

At the end of 1877, there were no longer any tribes living on the land in the traditional way. They were all returned to their reservations or to reservations of other tribes to begin their new lives without the bison, and often separated from the land that gave them birth. The federal government entered a new era of policies directed at the Native American; now defeated, they could assimilate into white culture and take their rightful place among their non-Indian neighbors.

As for the sacred Black Hills, the Sioux first refused to sell the hills in 1876 and still stand by that decision. A court awarded the Sioux $105 million in compensation for the land that was taken illegally—a paltry sum indeed when approximately $250 billion (yes, *billion*) worth of gold has been extracted from that land in the last 100 years. The Sioux have refused to accept the money, which today is worth $500 million with interest. The Sioux have vowed never to accept a penny of the money, demanding instead the return of their sacred lands.

The Least You Need to Know

♦ The Battle of the Little Bighorn was the direct result of a series of treaty violations by the American government.

♦ Gold was discovered in the Black Hills, an area sacred to the Lakota and the Cheyenne.

♦ The government tried to force the Lakota to sell the Black Hills.

♦ The Battle of the Little Bighorn occurred during a military campaign designed to subdue the Indians and force them onto reservations.

♦ General George A. Custer attacked a peaceful village of Cheyenne and Lakota people.

♦ The Indians' victory brought more troops to the Northern Plains.

15

The Last Little Wars

In This Chapter

- ◆ The Nez Perce fall victim to government greed
- ◆ Natives take up the Ghost Dance
- ◆ The Wounded Knee Massacre
- ◆ Geronimo and his fellow Apache warriors

After the Battle of the Little Bighorn and the last bands of Sioux and Cheyenne were relocated to reservations, the era of the free and independent Plains Indian hunter and warrior was over. Now tribes had to make the adjustment to a new lifestyle on the reservation.

Reservation life was dismal. By 1881, all the buffalo were gone from the region. Medical attention and food were in short supply. Rations were not sufficient for needs, and suffering was made worse by particularly severe winters. There was too little food, warmth, and comfort in the new environment; freedom of choice was denied the Indians, and almost no work opportunities existed for the males.

Given the plight of reservation Indians, is it any wonder that the Nez Perce, Northern Cheyenne, Apache, and the Lakota made one last attempt to recapture a way of life now past?

The Nez Perce Flight

In 1863, the Nez Perce signed a treaty with the U.S. government in which they gave up land in the Wallowa Valley in Washington, leaving them with a small reservation in what is now Idaho. This broke the heart of the Nez Perce leader Old Joseph, and he made his son, Young Joseph (*Hin-mah-too-yah-lat-kekt*, or "Thunder Rolling Down the Mountain") promise never to give up any more of their homeland.

Native Voices

My son, my body is returning to my mother earth, and my spirit is going very soon to see the Great Spirit Chief. When I am gone, think of your country. You are the chief of these people. They look to you to guide them. Always remember that your father never sold his country.

You must stop your ears whenever you are asked to sign a treaty selling your home. A few more years and the white men will be all around you. They have their eyes on this land. My son, never forget my dying words. This country holds your father's body. Never sell the bones of your father and your mother.

—Old Joseph, Nez Perce leader, to his son Joseph

Young Joseph became chief not long after his father's death in 1871. He continued to fight the government's efforts to move them to the Lapwai Reservation in Idaho. But their land was coveted by the whites when gold was discovered in the nearby mountains.

Even though the Indians wouldn't budget, in 1875 the government issued a proclamation opening up the remaining portions of the Nez Perce homeland for homesteading by white settlers. The government gave the Nez Perce "a reasonable time" to move to the Lapwai Reservation, but Joseph had no intention of moving so far from the grave of his father. In response, the government sent the military to forcibly remove the Nez Perce.

Should They Stay or Should They Go?

The government sent General Oliver Otis Howard to carry out the orders for the Nez Perce relocation. In May of 1877, Howard met with the Nez Perce leaders, Joseph, White Bird, Looking Glass, and Toohoolhoolzote, but the two parties couldn't reach an agreement. Frustrated by Joseph's refusal to comply with the orders to move, Howard arrested Toohoolhoolzote (he was later released) and gave Joseph and his people 30 days to move from the Wallowa Valley.

Concern for the safety of their women, children, and old people, many of whom were with them, finally moved the chiefs to accept the inevitable. They reluctantly agreed to move peaceably. Then they rode over the reservation for several days, selecting sites on which their bands would settle. Howard gave them only 30 days to move even though the Snake, the Salmon, and other rivers would be in full spring floodtide, making their crossing perilous. The bands, torn with sadness and anger, rode home to pack up, gather their stock, and leave their lands.

As they began their move to Lapwai, the Nez Perce held a council. White Bird and Toohoolhoolzote wanted to go to war, while Joseph maintained that it was "better to live at peace than to begin a war and lie dead." Meanwhile, some warriors slipped away from the council and raided nearby ranches, killing 11 white settlers. Such actions, Joseph knew, would not go unanswered by the military. The Nez Perce could not return to the Wallawa Valley, nor were they going to accept life on the Lapwai Reservation. Instead, they were going to fight.

Native Voices

I would have given my own life if I could have undone the killing of white men by my own people. I blame my young men and I blame the white man .... My friends among the white men have blamed me for the war. I am not to blame. When my young men began the killing, my heart was hurt. Although I did not justify them, I remembered all the insults I had endured, and my blood was on fire. Still, I would have taken my people to buffalo country [Montana] without fighting, if possible.

I could see no other way to avoid war. We moved over to White Bird Creek, sixteen miles away, and there encamped, intending to collect our stock before leaving; but the soldiers attacked us and the first battle was fought.

—Chief Joseph, Nez Perce

On to Grandmother's Land

Joseph decided to lead his people to Montana where the Nez Perce went in more peaceful times to hunt buffalo. The Army, led by General Howard, quickly intercepted them. The Nez Perce defeated Howard at White Bird Canyon in what is now Idaho on June 17, 1877, and slipped away across the mountains. The Nez Perce managed to elude the soldiers and joined with Chief Looking Glass at the Clearwater River some 40 miles.

The Nez Perce now numbered about 700, with approximately 200 warriors. Once more they held council and agreed that their only course was to seek refuge across the border in Canada, or *Grandmother's Land*, as the Natives referred to it.

They were in familiar territory, having crossed the Bitterroot Mountains into Montana on numerous occasions, and so they quickly put General Howard behind them. On July 25, they came out of Lolo Pass where they spotted soldiers ahead.

Code Talking

Grandmother's Land was the term used by Natives to describe Canada, after the Queen of England.

Tribal Truths

Tribes often escaped the U.S. military by going to Canada. Sitting Bull went there following the Battle of the Little Bighorn, as had others. The U.S. Army could not cross the Forty-ninth Parallel in pursuit of Indians, and thus Canada was thought of as a place of sanctuary.

Joseph, Looking Glass, and White Bird told the soldiers' captain, Charles Rawn, that the Nez Perce were going to pass no matter what. Rawn attempted to stall Joseph, knowing that Howard was closing in, but after several days, the Nez Perce fought their way around the soldiers and continued to the Big Hole River south of present day Missoula, Montana.

"Fight! Shoot Them Down!"

Hoping to rest and refresh themselves and their horses, the Nez Perce paused at the Big Hole. On the night of August 9, a column of soldiers and volunteers, under the leadership of Colonel John Gibbon, attacked the Indians as they slept. Gibbon ordered that no prisoners, male or female, should be taken. A terrible fight ensued. Although surrounded and outnumbered, White Bird rallied his warriors while Joseph led the women and children out of harm's way.

The Nez Perce managed to escape and inflicted heavy damage on Gibbon and his men at the so-called Battle of the Big Hole, killing 30 soldiers and wounding 40 more. But the toll was higher on the other side of the ledger. Eighty Nez Perce, mostly women and children, were killed. It is likely that all the Nez Perce would have been killed had not White Bird urged his warriors to fight hard, shouting, "Fight! Shoot them down! We can shoot as well as any of these soldiers."

The Nez Perce continued to flee, turning eastward. They entered Yellowstone National Park on August 22. (Yellowstone had been made a national park only five years earlier, in 1872.) They surprised visiting tourists, killing several and capturing others.

Native Voices

I jumped from my blankets and ran about thirty feet and threw myself on hands and knees, and kept going. An old woman, Patsikonmi, came from the tipi and did the same thing, bent down on knees and hands. She was to my left and was shot in the breast. … The soldiers were shooting everywhere. Through tipis and wherever they saw Indians. I saw little children killed and men fall before bullets coming like rain.

—Kowtoliks, Nez Perce, age 15

Americans were not accustomed to having their vacations disturbed by fleeing Indians, and the U.S. Army was embarrassed that it was out-fought and out-smarted by a ragged band of Indians. General Sherman ordered an all-out effort to stop the Nez Perce. The nearest regiment happened to be the Seventh Cavalry, recently brought back to strength after having taken a beating at the Battle of the Little Bighorn a year earlier. But even the Seventh, hungry as it was for revenge, was unable to stop the Nez Perce.

So Close, but Yet So Far

The Nez Perce eluded the Seventh and turned north toward Grandmother's Land and safety. Upon reaching the Bear Paw Mountains in north-central Montana on September 29, the group stopped only 40 miles from the Canadian border to hunt buffalo and rest. They knew General Howard was two days behind and so could afford to tarry for a short while. What they didn't know was that General Nelson A. Miles was closer, having come from Fort Keogh, at Miles City, Montana.

General Miles attacked the Nez Perce camp on September 30 with 600 soldiers and 30 Sioux and Cheyenne scouts. In the first wave, the Nez Perce killed 24 soldiers and wounded 42 others. But as the day wore on, the Nez Perce found themselves short on ammunition and luck. In the fighting, they lost 18 men and 3 women. Among the dead were Joseph's brother, Ollokot, and Toohoolhoolzote. Some Nez Perce slipped away in the night. General Miles requested a council with the Nez Perce, and Joseph complied. Miles insisted that the Nez Perce surrender, but Joseph refused. He was held captive for several days during which time the soldiers resumed their attack. Meanwhile, Howard arrived to reinforce Miles, and Joseph, knowing his people could hold out no longer, surrendered on October 5, 1877. As part of the terms of surrender, the Army would give his people food, clothing, and medical care. Most important, they were assured that they could go home to Lapwai, in Idaho.

Native Voices

Tell General Howard I know his heart. What he told me before I have in my heart. I am tired of fighting. Our chiefs are killed. Looking Glass is dead. Toohoolhoolzote is dead. The old men are all dead. It is the young men who say yes or no. He who led on the young men [Ollokot] is dead. It is cold and we have no blankets. The little children are freezing to death. My people, some of them, have run away to the hills, and have no blankets, no food; no one knows where they are—perhaps freezing to death. I want to have time to look for my children and see how many of them I can find. Maybe I shall find them among the dead. Hear me, my chiefs! I am tired; my heart is sick and sad. From where the sun now stands, I will fight no more forever.

—Joseph, Nez Perce

Cause of Death: A Broken Heart

The surviving Nez Perce, those who didn't escape to join Sitting Bull's people, were shipped to Fort Leavenworth, Kansas, where they were confined as prisoners of war. After 100 of them died of disease, they were sent to Indian Territory. Joseph repeatedly asked—even begged—to be allowed to return home, as General Miles had promised, but no one listened. Joseph and the Nez Perce remained in Indian Territory until 1885. Only 287 now survived. Some eventually were permitted to go to the Lapwai Reservation, but Joseph and 150 others were believed to be too dangerous to allow among the others. They were shipped to Nespelem on the Colville Reservation in Washington, where Chief Joseph died on September 21, 1904. The agency physician listed the cause of death as "a broken heart."

Cheyenne Autumn: The Northern Cheyenne Flight North

With the Lakota, the Northern Cheyenne fought and defeated Custer at the Battle of the Little Bighorn. After the battle, they were forced to surrender, and more than 1,000 of them, under the leadership of the Cheyenne chiefs Dull Knife, Little Wolf, Standing Elk, and Wild Hog, were taken to Fort Robinson, Nebraska. Chief Two Moon's band, numbering some 350, remained in Montana, living at Fort Keogh.

The Northern Cheyenne being held at Fort Robinson hoped to join their tribespeople in Montana, but the government decided to transfer them to Indian Territory to live on the Southern Cheyenne and Southern Arapaho Reservation. The Northern

Cheyenne agreed, with the understanding that if they didn't like living in the South they would be allowed to return to the Black Hills area, their traditional homeland.

So Much for Promises

Once down south, the Northern Cheyenne were miserable. There wasn't enough food for everyone, and many Northern Cheyenne came down with malaria. Starving and sick, the Cheyenne chiefs appealed to the agent in charge of the reservation to allow them to return home, but he refused to grant their request.

Native Voices

These people were raised far up in the north among the pines and the mountains; in that country we were always healthy. There was no sickness and very few of us died. Now, since we have been in this country, we are dying every day. This is not a good country for us, and we wish to return to our homes in the mountains.

—Little Wolf and Dull Knife, Northern Cheyenne leaders

They survived that first winter by eating their dogs, but spring didn't bring them any relief. Warm weather brought out mosquitoes and a new round of malaria.

Finally, frustrated and nearly starving to death, on September 10, 1878, the Northern Cheyenne, under Little Wolf and Dull Knife, slipped off the reservation and headed north.

The Fighting Cheyenne

The Cheyenne who headed northward numbered 297 men, women, and children. Only a third of these were men of fighting age and they had only a few horses. In order to avoid notice, they left their tipis standing at the reservation, hoping to fool the agent and soldiers into believing they were still there.

Some soldiers soon discovered their absence and were sent to find them and bring them back. The Cheyenne made their way through Kansas and into Nebraska, traveling at night to avoid detection. Ten thousand soldiers, from forts Wallace, Hays, Dodge, Riley, and Kearney, together with 3,000 civilians from nearby towns and settlements, joined in the hunt for the Cheyenne.

Saving the Seed of the Beautiful People

Once in Nebraska, the two Cheyenne leaders couldn't agree on their next course of action. Dull Knife wanted to go to Red Cloud's Lakota reservation, while Little Wolf wished to continue northward to the Tongue River country of southeastern Montana. They finally agreed that each would go his own way. Dull Knife and about 150 people turned to the Northwest, and Red Cloud's reservation and 134 continued due north. They split the children, some going with each group, hoping at least that some would survive.

Fort Robinson Break-Out

On October 23, 1878, Dull Knife's band was traveling through a blizzard when they suddenly found themselves surrounded by soldiers from Fort Robinson in Nebraska. Dull Knife told the soldier chief that they wanted no trouble, only to be allowed to join Red Cloud or Spotted Tail, chiefs on the Great Sioux Reservation. The soldiers escorted the Cheyenne to Fort Robinson to await some decision on their fate by the Indian Bureau.

Dull Knife's people were quartered in a log barracks for several months while the government debated what to do with them. While at Fort Robinson, the Indians were forced to give up their arms, but they managed to hide a few weapons. They were given blankets, food, and medicine, and generally were treated well.

Dull Knife's people soon found out that Red Cloud could offer them no sanctuary. Red Cloud was a prisoner on his own reservation and the little food he and his people received from the government was inadequate for even their own needs. So, the Cheyenne pleaded once more to be allowed to go home.

> **Native Voices** _____
>
> Tell the Great Father that Dull Knife and his people ask only to end their days here in the north where they were born. Tell him we want no more war. We cannot live in the south; there is no game. Here, when rations are short, we can hunt. Tell him if he lets us stay here, Dull Knife's people will hurt no one. Tell him if he tries to send us back, we will butcher each other with our own knifes.
>
> —Dull Knife, Cheyenne leader

On January 3, 1879, they finally received an answer from the War Department. General Sheridan's message was simple, "Unless they are sent back to where they came from, the whole reservation system will receive a shock which will endanger its stability. The Indians should be taken back to their reservation."

The military told Dull Knife of Sheridan's orders, but the Cheyenne refused to consider returning south. In response, the Army surrounded the barracks, and on the night of January 9, the Cheyenne broke out of the barracks, fighting with the few weapons they had hidden from the soldiers.

In the first hour of fighting, more than half of the warriors were killed, and many women and children were slaughtered as they tried to escape. When morning came, 65 Cheyenne were returned to the fort, mostly women and children. Thirty-eight remained at large, 32 in one group moving north, pursued by four companies of soldiers. A few days later, these few were trapped in a buffalo wallow. The soldiers fired on them until no fire was returned from the Cheyenne. Only nine survived. Dull Knife had escaped to Red Cloud's agency where he was captured and held.

After months of delays, the few survivors of the Fort Robinson out-break were transferred to Red Cloud's reservation, where they joined Dull Knife.

Little Wolf Makes It Home

Meanwhile, Little Wolf and his followers spent the winter of 1878–1879 hiding out on the plains. When spring came, they started northward for the Tongue River country. Here they met Two Moon, who was scouting for the Army. Two Moon convinced Little Wolf to lay down his weapons and surrender at Fort Keogh. The Cheyenne gave up their guns and went to Fort Keogh where many of the younger men joined the Army scouts and learned to drink whiskey.

Finally in 1884, after years of being moved around and living life in limbo, the government established a reservation for the Northern Cheyenne on the Tongue River, and they were once more reunited.

The Natives Learn a New Dance

In the 1880s, the federal government, in an attempt to turn Native people into whites, prohibited the practice of many traditional ceremonies and forced their children into boarding schools (more on this in Chapter 16). In additional, the terrible conditions on the reservations led to despair among the people.

In the midst of all this despair, a Paiute medicine man named Wovoka (he had been adopted by a white family and was known to them as Jack Wilson) had a vision in which he "died" and went to the other world. There he was united with his ancestors.

He was told by his vision that a new world was coming, that the white people would go back to where they came from, the buffalo would return, and the dead would rise up to be united with their relatives. The message, which combined native beliefs with Christian concepts, gave hope to the Native peoples when they most needed it. Wovoka became a messiah to his people, and his vision began what came to be known as the Ghost Dance movement.

> ### Native Voices
>
> Grandfather [the messiah] says, when your friends die you must not cry. You must not hurt anybody or do harm to anyone. You must not fight. Do right always. It will give you satisfaction.
>
> Do not tell the white people about this. Jesus is now upon the earth. He appears like a cloud. The dead are all alive again. I do not know when they will be here; maybe this fall or in the spring. When the time comes there will be no more sickness and everyone will be young again.
>
> Do not refuse to work for the whites and do not make any trouble with them until you leave them. When the earth shakes [at the coming] do not be afraid. It will not hurt you.
>
> —Wovoka, Paiute Messiah

Tribes living on reservations throughout the West heard of Wovoka and the Ghost Dance. Many, like the Arapaho, Cheyenne, Bannock, Sioux, and Ute, sent emissaries to learn the tenets of the Ghost Dance. What they learned was not complex. Believers danced until they entered a trance wherein they communicated with their dead relatives.

Ghost Shirts and Broken Hoops

To the Sioux, or Lakota, the Ghost Dance offered a hope for the future in a hopeless time. Following the Battle of the Little Bighorn, the Lakota were returned to the reservation, only to find the whites coveting more land. They were left with a few small and scattered reservations in remote and undesirable areas of what is now South Dakota.

The Lakota had always been a proud warrior culture. While their women continued their traditional roles of caregiver, the role of the men was changing. They were asked to take up the plow at a time when even experienced white farmers were failing because of drought and severe winters.

When the Lakota adopted the Ghost Dance, they added an innovation that reflected their warrior past. In their version of the Ghost Dance, they were instructed to construct "Ghost Shirts" that made the wearer invincible to the bullets of the white man. The Ghost Dance inspired the Lakota to believe that they would be able to force the white man to leave Indian land, at gunpoint if necessary. They would soon put their "invincible" shirts to the test.

> **Native Voices**
>
> The whole world is coming,
> A nation is coming, a nation is coming,
> The Eagle has brought the message to the tribe.
> The father says so, the father says so.
> Over the whole earth they are coming.
> The buffalo are coming, the buffalo are coming,
> The Crow has brought the message to the tribe,
> The father says so, the father says so.
>
> —Lakota Ghost Dance song

The Indian agents greatly feared the Ghost Dance movement. They did not want another uprising like the one that nearly wiped out the white population of Minnesota in 1862 (see Chapter 13). So when the Sioux embraced the Ghost Dance, their agents sought help from the U.S. military. In the winter of 1890, some of the Sioux began to gather in the Bad Lands to practice the Ghost Dance. The agent at the Standing Rock Reservation, James McLaughlin, feared that Sitting Bull, the great spiritual leader, would use his influence to rally the people behind the Ghost Dance movement. He ordered the arrest of Sitting Bull.

The Death of Sitting Bull

On December 15, 1890, Indian police, representing the more progressive element of Lakota society, surrounded Sitting Bull's house. He surrendered peacefully but his followers began to gather outside, calling on him to resist.

As Sitting Bull was being led away, his son, Crow Foot, called him a coward, and Sitting Bull pulled away from his guards. One of the Indian police officers was shot and he, in turn, shot Sitting Bull. In the fracas that followed, six policemen were killed or wounded and Sitting Bull and his son, with six other supporters, also died that day.

Tribal Truths _____

After the western reservations were established in the 1880s, the federal government began to enact policies to assimilate Native peoples into mainstream society. As agents on the various reservations tried to break up traditional power structures among the Sioux bands, they created Indian police groups to work for them.

The Indian police were under the authority of the Indians agents and were meant to replace the military on reservations. According to the commissioner of Indian Affairs at the time, Ezra A. Hayt, the Indian police would "materially aid in placing the entire Indian population of the country on the road to civilization." On May 27, 1878, Congress voted to pay $30,000 for 430 privates at $5 a month and 50 officers at $8 a month. By the end of 1878, 30 reservations had an Indian police force, 40 of them had one in 1880, and 59 in 1890.

The Indian policemen were not chosen by the camp council but by reservation authorities, and they represented non-Indian interests. This led to tragedies like the one that happened on December 15, 1890, when 43 Indian police of the Standing Rock Reservation followed Agent McLaughlin's orders to surround Sitting Bull's cabin. In the confusion that followed his arrest, Sitting Bull was killed by two of the policemen, Bull Head and Red Tomahawk.

The Seventh Cavalry Gets Its Revenge

Some Lakota, under the leadership of Big Foot, remained in the Bad Lands, under the watchful eye of the Army. Supporters of Sitting Bull joined Big Foot, raising the concern of the agent in charge and the military. The Army was sent to bring Big Foot and his people back to the reservation.

Big Foot led his people south to seek protection at the Pine Ridge Reservation. The Army intercepted the band on December 28 and brought them to the edge of Wounded Knee Creek to camp. Colonel George A. Forsyth, commander of the Seventh Cavalry, with four companies, surrounded the makeshift camp. Four hundred seventy soldiers, armed with four Hotchkiss guns, guarded 340 Lakota, of whom only 106 were warriors.

On December 29, Forsyth and the Seventh made ready to disarm the Lakota. The soldiers stormed through the village, overturning beds, pushing people away, searching for weapons. The Lakota men became increasingly agitated as they saw their women being bullied about. The search revealed about 40 weapons, most in poor condition.

In the midst of this tense situation, a medicine man, Yellow Bird, walked about calling on the men to resist and reminding them that they were invincible because of their

Ghost Shirts. One Lakota youth managed to keep a gun from the soldiers and, in the frenzy of the moment, he pulled his weapon and fired at the soldiers, killing one.

The troopers reacted instantly, firing into the gathered Lakota with their rifles and Hotchkiss guns. The Lakota pulled their knives and war clubs to defend themselves, but they were outmanned and outgunned. Within minutes, some 200 Sioux lay dead on the ground, together with approximately 60 soldiers, many of whom were killed by friendly fire.

Had the story ended there, it would have been tragic enough. But the Seventh Cavalry charged upon the civilians, the fleeing women and children, and butchered them as they huddled against the banks of Wounded Knee Creek.

No one knows how many Lakota were massacred, but the number approached 300, nearly two thirds of whom were women and children. As the fighting continued, a storm swept over the plains, covering the bodies of the dead with snow.

The dead were buried on New Year's Day, 1891, in a long pit. The bodies were tossed into the mass burial, many naked, stripped of their Ghost Shirts, which were taken as souvenirs by the soldiers of the victorious Seventh. There was no ceremony, no one to mourn the dead, no honor in victory or defeat. A nation's *hoop* was broken, and a nation's dreams ended, as did the Ghost Dance movement.

Code Talking

The great holy man of the Oglala Sioux, Black Elk, referred to the unity of the Lakota people as a **hoop,** the nation's hoop. The circle is a powerful metaphor of oneness and timelessness. That strength was broken at Wounded Knee.

Native Voices

I did not know then how much was ended. When I look back now from this high hill of my old age, I can still see the butchered women and children lying heaped and scattered all along the crooked gulch as plain as when I saw them with eyes still young. And I can see that something else died there in the bloody mud, and was buried in the blizzard. A people's dream died there. It was a beautiful dream ... the nation's hoop is broken and scattered. There is no center any longer, and the sacred tree is dead.

—Black Elk, Lakota

The Apache's Last Stand

The Apache people arrived in the Southwest United States between the fifteenth and late sixteenth century, emigrating from the Mackensie River Valley of western Canada. The Apache are generally divided into seven major groupings, with the Jicarilla, Lipan, and Kiowa-Apache tribes forming the eastern tribes, and the Navajo, Mescalero, Chiricahua, and Western Apache (inclusive of the Tonto, Coyotero or White Mountain, Gileños, and Pinaleños bands) forming the western tribes. In the late 1800s, the Apache made their living raiding against the Mexicans and other southwestern tribes.

In 1871, Congress appropriated funds to settle the Apache of Arizona and New Mexico upon reservations. The government dispatched General Howard, of Nez Perce fame, to move the Apache to reservations and relocate others to more "suitable" areas, away from settlements and trouble. In October 1872, Cochise, one of the most powerful Apache chiefs, signed a peace treaty with Howard, giving the Chiricahua a reservation some 55 miles square in southeastern Arizona. One emerging war leader who lived in this settlement was Goyathlay ("One Who Yawns"), better known to the white men as Geronimo.

> **Native Voices**
>
> I was born on the prairies where the wind blew free and there was nothing to break the light of the sun. I was born where there were no enclosures.
>
> —Geronimo, Apache

The Apache settled down to life under the protection of the Army. Here, many learned the life of farmer and found peace. But for other Apache, the reservations were safe places where they could return after raiding white and Mexican settlements. Enough of the Apache continued to live off the reservations, in the mountains, to worry the federal government. General Crook sent out word that all bands of Apache away from their reservations would be considered hostile. He instructed his commanders to accept the surrender of the Apache or hunt them down until they were killed or captured.

Throughout the 1870s and early 1880s, Geronimo and Victorio, an Apache chief, continued to raid on both sides of the U.S.-Mexico border. Even Geronimo's arrest in 1877 didn't stop the marauding. Victorio established a stronghold in Mexico and recruited an army to make war against the United States. Before the end of 1879, he had a band of 200 Mescaleros and Chiricahuas. He raided Mexican ranches, and into Texas and New Mexico, killing settlers and striking against cavalry, and then dashing back into Mexico. Victorio was finally killed by Mexican soldiers on October 14, 1880, and it appeared that the Apache resistance against white encroachment was over.

However, in the spring of 1885, a small group—42 warriors and 92 women and children—of Chiricahua Apache fled their reservation under the leadership of Geronimo and disappeared into the mountains of Arizona and Mexico. General Crook, who knew the Apache as no other white man did, persuaded most of the "hostile" Apache to surrender after a strenuous 10-month campaign. Geronimo, fearing severe punishment, slipped away with 32 Apache. Geronimo's fears were justified when Crook was replaced by General Nelson Miles, who imprisoned the Indians who had surrendered.

Miles chased Geronimo and the others unmercifully for five months, finally convincing Geronimo and his small band of followers to surrender. In the end, not only were Geronimo's little band exiled, but so were the entire Chiricahua Apache, numbering nearly 500. They were rounded up and sent into imprisonment in Florida, where many died, suffering the ill effects of life in the tropical lowlands. In 1894, they were sent to Fort Sill, Oklahoma, and it was not until 1913 that the Apache were allowed to join the Mescalero Apache on their reservation in New Mexico.

Yet another nation's hoop was broken and scattered.

The Cheyenne, Nez Perce, Apache, and Lakota fought to resist what may have been inevitable. Each tribe fought to keep a way of life alive, but in the end, each reluctantly accepted or was forced to accept a life confined to a reservation. Perhaps the Lakota song is correct: "The old men say the earth only endures. You spoke truly. You are right."

Native Voices

The soldiers never explained to the government when an Indian was wronged, but reported the misdeeds of the Indians.

—Geronimo, Apache

Native Voices

There was a time we could escape the white soldiers. But now the very rocks have become soft. We cannot put our feet anywhere. We cannot sleep, for if a coyote or fox barks, or a stone moves, we are up—the soldiers have come.

—Delche, Apache chief of the Chiricahuas

The Least You Need to Know

◆ The Nez Perce chose to flee to Canada rather than to accept life on the Lapwai Reservation.

◆ The Northern Cheyenne fled Oklahoma to return to their homeland in Montana.

♦ Wovoka, a Paiute mystic, founded the Ghost Dance movement.

♦ The Lakota developed a more militaristic version of the Ghost Dance in the hopes of using it to keep whites from taking what remained of their land.

♦ Hundreds of Sioux were massacred at Wounded Knee when the Army attempted to disarm men returning from a Ghost Dance in the Bad Lands.

♦ The Apache also suffered at the hands of the government.

Chapter 16

Getting "Civilized"

In This Chapter

- ◆ Christianizing the Indians
- ◆ Erasing Indian culture
- ◆ The Dawes Act divides Indian land
- ◆ Finally, Indians become American citizens

From 1850 through the 1880s, the federal government followed a policy of acquiring Native land and isolating Indian people upon reservations. Native peoples tried to defend their homelands, but ultimately they couldn't resist the military might of the American Army. Scattered tribes held out for many years, but finally even they were forced to accept the reservation system.

But the U.S. government wasn't satisfied with simply keeping Indians on reservations. Once the last band was herded onto reservation land, the government began to force the American Indians to assimilate into non-Indian society, relying on a triple-pronged approach: Christianity, education, and land policies.

Come to Jesus, My Savage Brother!

Even though most Native peoples had their own spiritual and religious practices, the government believed that their beliefs were both savage and backward, therefore being a hindrance to the so-called "civilization" of the Native peoples. Between 1880 and 1934, the federal government spent a lot of time trying to convert Native peoples to Christianity. They had varied levels of success.

Putting a Stop to Those Old Heathenish Dances

Because non-Indians didn't understand the beliefs of Indian people nor the religious rituals they performed, Native spiritual ways were thought to be incompatible with civilized living. Some Christians thought that the rituals held by Native peoples amounted to the worship of false and pagan gods. These rites seemed so foreign that non-Indians simply refused to acknowledge that these practices had any value at all. The federal government tried to stamp out many of the traditional religious ceremonies.

One of the first efforts by the Office of Indian Affairs was to outlaw certain traditional ceremonies and to limit the influence of "medicine men." Secretary of the Interior, Henry M. Teller (1882–1885), made the following comment about Native ceremonies:

> … the continuance of the old, heathenish dances, such as the sun-dance, scalp-dance, & c. These dances, or feasts, as they are sometimes called, ought, in my judgement, to be discontinued.

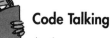

Code Talking

A **give-away ceremony** is not so much a religious ritual as it is a social custom. When a person is honored for deeds well done, instead of receiving gifts, he or she gives gifts to those who helped that person succeed. The same government that had been butchering Indians for years believed that such acts of generosity were not civilized. Go figure.

In order to discourage the practices the secretary found so objectionable, the Office of Indian Affairs created a list of "Indian Offenses." These offenses included taking part in such rituals as the sun dance, or even being present at such ceremonies, holding a *give-away ceremony*, visiting a medicine man, and having more than one wife.

Punishments were spelled out for each of these offenses. A man who had more than one wife, for example, would receive "a fine of not less than twenty dollars, or work at hard labor for a period of twenty days, or both, at the discretion of the court." Someone who took part in a sun dance could be punished "by withholding his or their rations for a period not less than fifteen days, nor more than thirty days, or by incarceration in the agency prison for a period not exceeding thirty days."

> ## Tribal Truths
>
> Because of the government's policy to suppress traditional religious exercise, some tribes lost their ceremonies; others continued to hold their rituals out of view of the Indian agents. Sadly, the Crow Indians of Montana forgot how to perform their original sun dance during this era of suppression. When they were once again allowed to hold their ceremonies in the early 1940s, the Crow had to adopt the Shoshoni version of the sun dance.

Pick a Religion, Any Religion ... as Long as It's Christian

The Office of Indian Affairs put a great deal of effort into providing religious instruction for Native peoples—whether they wanted it or not. In the 1890s, Congress appropriated funds to religious groups to administer schools among Indian people. Ironically, the source of these funds was the proceeds from the sale of Indian land.

Additionally, the Office of Indian Affairs allowed religious denominations to establish missions on western reservations for the spiritual conversion of the Natives. The only difficulty was that there was no agreement as to which denomination should have the monopoly on Indian souls. To solve this, the commissioner of Indian Affairs simply divided the reservations among those churches willing to set up shop. So through the luck of the draw, Natives became Lutherans, Unitarians, Episcopalians, Methodists, or Reform Dutch!

Constitution? We Don't Need No Stinking Constitution!

At this point, readers at all familiar with the First Amendment to the U.S. Constitution might be questioning the federal government's actions. The First Amendment to the Constitution reads as follows: "Congress shall make no law respecting an establishment of religion, or prohibit the free exercise thereof." Yet, the government had an established policy of denying Native peoples the right to practice their own religion and of systematically forcing the practice of Christianity upon them.

How did the United States get away with this? Native peoples, not being citizens of the United States, had no political power. The United States was free to violate its own basic rights for the "good" of Indian people. Was it right? Certainly not! The consequence is that many Indian people were deprived of their cultural heritage simply because their ways were different.

Killing the Indian to Save the Man

The Office of Indian Affairs believed that education would ultimately be the key to assimilating Native peoples into mainstream American society. The problem was, however, that public education is financed by the taxpayer, and Indian people at that time paid no taxes. Local school districts refused to accept Indian children because their parents didn't contribute to school funding. The federal government was forced to open and pay for schools for Indian children.

The first off-reservation *boarding school* was Carlisle Indian Industrial School. It opened on October 6, 1879, in Carlisle, Pennsylvania—a non-Indian community far away from Native villages. The school's founder, and indeed the founder of the Indian boarding school system, was Captain Richard Henry Pratt, a retired military officer who saw service during the Civil War and the Indian wars.

Code Talking

Indian **boarding schools** were schools established in the 1880s away from reservations. Indian children lived at the schools until they reached age 18. While at the schools, children received an education and learned a trade.

Native Voices

The superintendent [of the school] lined up all the boys and went down the line, saying to each boy, "You're a farmer, you're a blacksmith, you're a carpenter." That's how they decided what trade you would learn.

—Potawatomie Elder

The principle mission of the school was simple: "Kill the Indian and save the man." Pratt believed that students at Carlisle should be removed from what he believed were the degenerating effects of reservation life and be forced into a regimented existence modeled after Army life. Like Carlisle, the other Indian boarding schools were often far away from Native villages to keep the Indian children from their parents' influence. Children were rounded up and sent to Carlisle, Chemawa (Salem, Oregon), Haskell (Lawrence, Kansas), or the dozen or so other boarding schools.

Attendance was compulsory. Indian agents scoured the reservations, sweeping up all school-aged children. Many escaped, hidden under beds or out in the hills by their parents. Children went in at six years of age, and many stayed until they were eighteen. The government provided transportation to the school. However, if a child wished to come home during holidays or summers, their parents had to pay. Most parents were too poor to bring their children home, so they stayed away until they graduated. While there, the children lived in dormitories, dressed in military uniforms, marched to class, and generally lived a strict and controlled life. Girls learned home economics and secretarial skills while boys learned the building trades or farming.

In the majority of the boarding schools, the children attended school only four hours a day, or even less. The rest of their time was devoted to "vocational training." All the hard menial labor required to raise food, produce milk and butter, repair shoes, launder clothing, and otherwise operate the institution was performed by the students. Most of the work tasks were in no way related to the students' "education." The situation was worse than reform schools during that same time period.

Tribal Truths

One of the first acts that an Indian boy experienced when he was taken to boarding school was to have his hair cut off—all of it. This was ostensibly because of head lice, but more to eliminate tribal identity. Among the Plains, a person only cuts his or her hair when in mourning; the more hair you cut, the closer you were to the deceased. Imagine being six years old, speaking no English, and having someone shave all your hair off!

Making matters worse, because they were fed so little food, the students were malnourished. Researchers at the time found their living conditions appalling. Beds were placed in every spot that there was room, with little light or ventilation.

The Outing System

Pratt worried that if children were allowed to return home, even during the summer months, they would have to be retrained when they returned to school in the fall. He developed what became known as the *outing system*. During summer vacation, Indian children were placed with white families, as free sources of labor.

Code Talking

The **outing system** was developed to prevent children from "backsliding," that is, from going back to their traditional ways. Indian children were placed in white homes during summer vacation where they continued to become "civilized."

Lost Children, Lost Generations

The Native children in boarding schools were prevented from practicing their native ways, prohibited from speaking their native languages, and generally expected to become white. Some ran away. Some died of disease and heartache. Some survived.

To understand the impact that this system had on Native peoples, one has to realize that between 1880 and 1950, fully two thirds of all Indian people educated were educated in the boarding school system and at the 132 on-reservation day schools that were added in the 1930s. Sociologists today generally agree that many social challenges Native peoples face today can be traced, at least in part, to the boarding school system. There were at least two generations of Native peoples who were subjected to this experience, removed from their families and culture, forbidden to practice their native ways, and severely punished for doing so. It is no wonder that some Indian people didn't make the adjustment.

I should note that not every Indian who was educated at the Indian boarding schools had negative experiences. My parents attended Haskell Indian Industrial Training School, now Haskell Indian University, in Lawrence, Kansas—my father in the 1920s and my mother in the late 1930s. My mother was trained as a secretary and my father became a cobbler. Both spoke fondly of their boarding school experiences, and had friendships with classmates that lasted a lifetime.

Forcing Mr. Indian Between the Plow Handles

During the early reservation period, the Office of Indian Affairs was resolved to force Natives to enter mainstream American society. The government wanted to promote self-sufficiency and an independent spirit among its Indian charges. What better example of these qualities than the American farmer!

The difficulty with promoting farming among Indian people was that reservation lands were held communally. So the government had to establish a mechanism to provide for individual land ownership so that Natives could follow the example of their farming neighbors.

On February 8, 1887, Congress passed the *General Allotment Act*, or Dawes Act. The act provided that a reservation was to be surveyed and divided into 160-acre parcels to be allotted to individual Indians. The allotted land was to be held in trust by the federal government for a period of 25 years, after which the allottee received clear and negotiable title. The Dawes Act was not a homestead act; that is, the person who received an allotment was not required to live on it or even farm it. Many did not, or could not. The provisions of the Dawes Act regarding the size of the allotment were as follows:

To each head of a family, one-quarter of a section [160 acres];

To each single person over 18 years of age, one-eighth of a section;

To each orphan child under 18 years of age, one-eighth of a section; and,

To each other single person under 18 years now living, or who may be born prior to the date of the order of the President directing an allotment of the lands embraced in any reservation, one-sixteenth of a section.

The Dawes Act was thought to be the solution to the "Indian problem," but in practice it proved more beneficial to non-Indians than to Natives. The act actually provided a mechanism for non-Indians to acquire Indian land. Because some Native peoples did not farm the reservation land, white neighbors pressured Congress to allow access to this idle land for white benefit. Colorado congressman James Belford spoke for most non-Indians living in the western United States when he stated that "an idle and thriftless race of savages cannot be permitted to guard the treasure vaults of the nation."

Code Talking

The **General Allotment Act,** or Dawes Act, was an act passed by Congress in 1887 that provided for the survey and assignment of individual allotments to Indians.

The author of the General Allotment Act, Senator Henry Dawes of Massachusetts, believed he was proposing a solution that was for the Indian's own good. He observed the following:

> Inasmuch as the Indian refused to fade out, but multiplied under the sheltering care of reservation life, and the reservation itself was slipping away from him, there was but one alternative: either he must be endured as a lawless savage, a constant menace to civilized life, or he must be fitted to become part of that life and be absorbed into it.

The purpose of the Dawes Act was to bypass tribal organizations and deal directly with individual Indians. President Theodore Roosevelt called the General Allotment Act "a mighty pulverizing engine to break up the tribal mass."

Be Like Whitey ... or at Least Give Him Your Land

Under the provisions of the Dawes Act, after each person who was eligible to receive an allotment got one, the reservation was typically thrown open for homesteading by non-Indians. Proponents of the Dawes Act believed that this would have a positive effect on Indian people. Natives would see their white neighbors laboring on their homesteads and want to emulate their success. In application, the homesteading of reservation land created a checkerboard of ownership, causing confused jurisdictions and hard feelings between Indian and non-Indian neighbors. On several reservations, like the Flathead Reservation in Montana, tribal members are a minority on their own reservation!

Tribal Truths _____

In the case of the Turtle Mountain Chippewa of North Dakota, there was not enough reservation land to allot to all eligible Indians. Some Turtle Mountain people received allotments on the Fort Peck Indian Reservation in Montana (Assiniboine and Sioux) and others received allotments on public lands elsewhere in Montana. The result was that some Turtle Mountain allottees had to leave their homes and move to Montana.

In Uncle Sam We Trust

Making matters even worse, once 25 years had passed and the owner had free and clear access to the land, it was taxable property, and was therefore subject to seizure in the event of nonpayment. In all, individual Native peoples lost as much as 23 million acres of land, either from seizure or sale. The government was asking Indian people who had been hunters and warriors to be transformed into yeoman farmers in only 25 years. Even for those tribes that were agriculturally based, often it was the women who farmed, not the men.

Indian Land Sold and Alienated, 1887–1934

Type	Acres
Surplus Reservation Land Sold	22,694,658
Allotted Land Sold or Alienated	23,225,472
Ceded Reservation Land	38,229,109
Miscellaneous Losses	3,474,456
Total	87,623,456

Bully for You!

As if things weren't already bad enough, the late 1880s and 1890s couldn't have been worse for agriculture in the western United States. White farmers and ranchers failed and were forced into bankruptcy when harsh winters and dry summers killed off their livestock. Fully two thirds of the ranchers in Montana and the Dakotas failed. One rancher in the Dakotas gave up farming and went back home to New York and entered politics. His name was Teddy Roosevelt! Yet the government expected Indians to become farmers during this time.

Splitting Heirs

Last, the allotment of reservation land was a one-time deal—the act didn't provide for future generations. When an allottee died, the allotment was divided among surviving heirs. Each heir then possessed an interest in the original allotment. This process is referred to as *fractionation*. As each generation passed on, the interests became smaller and smaller and the number of heirs greater and greater; today, some heirs may possess the equivalent of one square foot of reservation land. Try farming that!

Code Talking

As the land allotted to individual Indians passed from generation to generation, ownership was often divided among an increasing number of heirs. It is now common for as many as 100 to 300 individuals to hold undivided interests in a single allotment. This division of ownership interest is referred to as **fractionation.**

A Policy Doomed to Fail

Historians agree that the Dawes Act was a disaster. If its purpose was to free the Indian, the cost of that freedom was indeed great. The act actually provided a mechanism by which Indian people lost nearly 90 million acres of land. Before the passage of the General Allotment Act, the total area of all reservations (1887) was nearly 130 million acres. By 1934, the amount of land owned by tribes and individual Indians shrunk down to only 43 million, a net loss of 67 percent.

The irony of the General Allotment Act is that it was a policy promoted by so-called friends of the American Indian. This act was supposed to free Indians and encourage them to take their place in mainstream America. What it did, in practice, was "free" the American Indian from 87 million acres of land and reduce that which remained into small, unusable plots. Although hindsight is said to be 20/20, it's hard to imagine how promoters of this policy didn't see its many faults from the beginning.

Tribal Truths

As Native peoples, my parents were not citizens of the United States at their birth. My mother was born the year the General Citizenship Act was passed. I have in our family's archives her citizenship papers. I guess that makes me a first-generation American!

The First Americans Finally Become Citizens

As a part of the policy of civilizing Natives, Congress extended American citizenship on American Indians on June 2, 1924. The first Americans would be the last people to be officially recognized as Americans.

Citizenship was offered largely because of American Indian participation in World War I. Thousands of Native peoples fought in both the Canadian and U.S. armed forces. Some people in Congress, led by Charles Curtis, a senator from Kansas, believed that Indians should be "rewarded" for their service with American citizenship.

> **Tribal Truths**
>
> It is estimated that more than 12,000 American Indians served in the U.S. military in World War I. Approximately 600 Oklahoma Indians, mostly Choctaw and Cherokee, were assigned to the 142nd Infantry of the 36th Texas-Oklahoma National Guard Division. The 142nd saw action in France and its soldiers were widely recognized for their contributions in battle. Four men from this unit were awarded the Croix de Guerre, while others received the Church War Cross for gallantry.

However, being a citizen and being allowed to exercise the rights of citizenship are two different things! Many states didn't allow American Indians to vote after they received citizenship. The state of New Mexico did not allow Natives in that state to vote until 1948, and then only under threat from the federal courts.

In order to impress the importance of American citizenship, the Office of Indian Affairs created a scripted ceremony. An Indian man wearing buckskin clothing was brought forth to read a condemnation of his traditional lifestyle after which the man shot an arrow out onto the prairie, symbolizing the casting off of the old ways. The fellow then ducked into a tipi, emerging minutes later wearing shirt, pants, vest, spats, and shoes to begin life as a new man and a new citizen. Talk about high theater!

Some American Indians believe that American citizenship is not such a great honor. They believe that accepting American citizenship is to accept the sovereignty of the United States over tribal affairs. Some tribes, like the Onondaga, issue their own passports. According to the courts, however, the General Citizenship Act of 1824 grants citizenship whether a tribe or individual wants it or not.

Freed from Savagery? Shackled Anew!

Efforts and policies of the U.S. government that forced the American Indians to assimilate into the dominant society characterized the period between 1880 and 1934. The United States tried to eradicate Native culture through its education and land policies. The goal was to force the American Indian into the mold of the dominant society and for Indians to take their place as American citizens.

Instead, the American Indian had less to work with than before, less land, and little left of his and her traditional culture. Instead of solving the "Indian problem," the General Allotment Act created problems that may never be completely resolved.

The Least You Need to Know

♦ After 1880, Natives were confined to reservations, and the federal government attempted to assimilate them into mainstream white society.

♦ In order to "civilize" the American Indian, the federal government forced Native peoples to become Christians.

♦ The government created the boarding school system as a method of teaching Indian children American ideals and culture.

♦ The General Allotment Act, also known as the Dawes Act, provided for the survey of the reservations and the distribution of allotments to tribal members.

♦ The policy of the American government between 1880 and 1934 was to make American Indians into farmers.

♦ American Indians have been citizens of the United States since 1924.

♦ Policies of the Dawes period designed to assimilate the American Indian worsened the condition of Natives by separating them further from their land and cultures.

Chapter 17

The Indian New Deal

In This Chapter

- ◆ Making sense of the Meriam Report
- ◆ John Collier to the rescue
- ◆ A change in Indian policy
- ◆ The "Vested Rights" of tribal governments

Beginning in 1934, the federal government radically changed its policy toward American Indians. Gone were the destructive land deals of the Dawes era. The federal government finally admitted that its reservation land policies were a failure and that a change in direction was needed for Native lives to improve. The government decided that for American Indians to be self-sufficient, tribes needed to be equipped for the current environment. Tribes, the government decided, needed a system of governance.

The Problem of Indian Administration

Changes in Indian policy began with the publication in 1928 of a report, officially titled "The Problem of Indian Administration" but popularly called the Meriam Report. This study was commissioned by the secretary of the interior and conducted by the Institute for Government Research Studies in Administration (or the Brookings Institute). The technical director of the survey was Lewis Meriam, hence its title.

The purpose of the study was to assess the economic and social condition of the American Indians and to make recommendations for the improvement of those conditions. The study was comprehensive. The team visited reservations, communities, schools, and hospitals.

The Meriam Report recommended what amounted to a reversal of policies that were adopted during the Dawes period. It recommended that care be taken when dividing up land among individuals. In addition, the Meriam Report was highly critical of the boarding school system and the health system. Despite the critical nature of the report, there was no immediate response from policy makers.

Code Talking

The Institute for Government Research Studies in Administration released the **Meriam Report,** or "The Problem of Indian Administration," in 1928. The report was highly critical of the federal government's Indian policies and made sweeping recommendations for change.

Native Voices

We have got a real friend in John Collier. He really likes Indians. In past time, we had Commissioners against us who tried to stop our ceremony dances and our dances-religious. They nearly destroy us, call our ways bad or immoral or something, and put in the paper they are going to stop us. But John Collier fight for us ... and saves us. Now, he look far ahead and it is like he is putting a wall all around us to protect us—and this Wheeler-Howard Bill is this wall.

—Antonio Luhan, Taos Pueblo

John Collier and a New Deal for Indians

Perhaps the Meriam Report would have continued to gather dust on the shelf of the secretary of the interior had John Collier not entered the picture. He was a social worker by training and had established a training school for social workers in 1915.

After a trip to New Mexico, Collier became an advocate for the revival and support of Native American cultural life on communal lands held by self-governing tribes. He founded the American Indian Defense Association and campaigned for policy reform throughout the 1920s. He soon won respect among reformers for his advocacy for Native peoples.

When Franklin D. Roosevelt was elected president in 1932, he appointed Collier commissioner of Indian Affairs. Collier wasted no time in putting his stamp on Indian Affairs. His crowning achievement was the passage by Congress of the Indian Reorganization Act of 1934, also known as the Wheeler-Howard Act.

Getting Reorganized

The Indian Reorganization Act changed federal Indian policy in several ways, including the following:

- Helping Indians who wanted land obtain it and preventing Indian land loss

- Stabilizing Indian tribes by vesting them with real, though limited, authority

- Permitting Indian tribes to equip themselves with the devices of modern business organization, through forming themselves into business corporations

- Establishing a system of financial credit for Indians

- Supply Indians with means for collegiate and technical training in the best schools

- Open the way for qualified Indians to hold positions in the Federal Indian Service (Bureau of Indian Affairs)

The Indian Reorganization Act (IRA) stopped the allotment of land to individual Indians and provided a mechanism for some tribes to acquire land they had lost by the General Allotment Act. The IRA also provided funding for American Indians to attend college, something not available in the Dawes period.

> **Code Talking**
>
> The **Indian Reorganization Act,** or Wheeler-Howard Act, permitted tribes to form tribal governments and incorporate as business corporations.

Boilerplate Bureaucracies

During the Dawes period, the federal government bypassed traditional tribal governments in favor of dealing directly with individual Indians. Those traditional governments went the way of the buffalo. The Indian Reorganization Act, however, encouraged strengthening tribal governmental organizations as a way to promote self-sufficiency. The trouble was that many tribes no longer had a governmental structure, traditional or otherwise. So, the government helped them create new ones.

Most tribes first adopted written constitutions soon after the Indian Reorganization Act was passed in 1934. The early IRA constitutions were "boilerplate" documents fashioned after drafts by lawyers from the Department of the Interior. One of the main features of the IRA government was that all actions of the tribal governments were subject to the supervision of the Bureau of Indian Affairs. One hundred eighty-one tribes reorganized under the Indian Reorganization Act while 77, including the Navajo, the largest tribe in the United States, rejected the IRA.

Some tribes rejected the IRA because they wished to reestablish their traditional forms of government while some tribes, like the Navajo and Crow, didn't want their governments to be subject to the authority of the Bureau of Indian Affairs. In theory, those tribes that didn't accept the IRA were not subject to the approval of the Bureau of Indian Affairs, but all tribes operated under the authority of the secretary of the interior.

> **Native Voices**
>
> It's not self-government because self-government by permission is no self-government at all. Everything that the Indian Reorganization Act brought in under the guise of self-government was subject to the approval or the concurrence of the Secretary of the Interior or his authorized representative—the superintendent. These Indians have never made policy decisions; they have never been able to use creative thinking.
>
> —Ramon Roubideaux, Sioux, who ultimately accepted the IRA

Vested Rights

One of the most important parts of the Indian Reorganization Act was section 16, which describes the *vested rights* that tribal governments possessed. They include the following rights:

- The right to employ legal council, the choice and fixing of fees to be subject to the approval of the secretary of the interior.

- The right to prevent the sale, disposition, lease, or encumbrance of tribal lands, interests in lands, or other tribal assets without the consent of the tribe.

- The right to negotiate with the federal, state, and local governments.

- The right to determine tribal membership.

- The right to tax.

- The right to exclude nonmembers from tribal territories.

- The right to regulate domestic relations.

- The right to regulate commerce and trade.

> **Code Talking**
>
> **Vested rights** are those rights and powers that the Indian Reorganization Act grants to a tribal government.

These rights allow a tribal government to do business as a business corporation. Tribal members are like investors in a corporation who receive benefits from commonly held assets of the "company." Thus, if a tribe sells coal reserves on tribal land, all members of the tribe can benefit. The tribe can use these resources to provide services to its members, such as education, health, and police protection.

> **Tribal Truths** _____
>
> Under the IRA, tribes set their own membership criteria. Most require a member to have at least one-quarter degree tribal blood (not total Native blood) in order to be enrolled. Some tribes are more liberal. The Cherokee Nation of Oklahoma require applicants for registration to be able to connect to an ancestor who is listed with a roll number and a blood degree on the 1899–1906 Dawes Commission of Final Rolls.

Making Way for Qualified Indians

Yet another important provision of the IRA permitted what is known as "Indian Preference." Indian Preference means that if there are qualified Indian applicants for a job vacancy in either the Bureau of Indian Affairs (in the Department of the Interior) or in the Indian Health Service (within the Public Health Service), a selection must be made from those qualified applicants, and non-Indian applicants are not considered for the position.

The U.S. Supreme Court has held that the Indian Preference Law does not constitute harmful racial discrimination or violate the due process clause of the Fifth Amendment, but is reasonably and rationally designed to further Indian self-government. The Indian Preference Law is a distinct statute that does not violate Title VII of the Civil Rights Act of 1964, as amended. The logic of the application of Indian preference is simple. The Bureau of Indian Affairs (BIA) and the Indian Health Service (IHS) are two government agencies that not only provide services to Native peoples but also enact policies that affect Indians.

> **Tribal Truths** _____
>
> In 1934, when the Indian Reorganization Act was passed, 34 percent of the Bureau of Indian Affairs employees were Native Americans. Today, 90 percent of BIA employees are American Indians. Shouldn't the agencies that serve Indian people employ Indian people?

A Fair Deal: The New Bureau of Indian Affairs

The Indian Reorganization Act in 1934 provided a vehicle for tribes to create their own government vested with real, though limited, authority. Tribes were encouraged to become self-sufficient and self-governing business corporations. The role of the Bureau of Indian Affairs changed from paternal "Great White Father" to an advisor. The tribal governments were empowered to act for the benefit of enrolled members, and the bureau's philosophy was to support those efforts by providing advice and assistance.

The Least You Need to Know

♦ The Meriam Report, published in 1924, was highly critical of federal Indian policy, as represented by the General Allotment Act.

♦ John Collier became commissioner of Indian Affairs in 1932 and led dramatic changes in Indian policy.

♦ The Indian Reorganization Act (IRA) ended the allotment of land to individual Indians and permitted tribes to establish tribal governments and incorporate as business corporations.

♦ Tribes acquired certain "vested" rights via the IRA, such as the right to establish tribal membership and the right to tax.

Chapter 18

Back to the Bad Old Days

In This Chapter

- ◆ The "termination" policies of the 1950s
- ◆ Role of House Concurrent Resolution 108
- ◆ Public Law 280
- ◆ The failure of the termination policy
- ◆ Relocating Indians to the cities

Federal Indian policies in the 1950s and the 1960s nearly destroyed the earlier good works of Commissioner of Indian Affairs John Collier. In an attempt to "free" the American Indian, the federal government terminated its relationship with a number of Indian tribes and, in the process, nearly eliminated their existence as a tribal people.

We're Finished with You

Pro-Indian reformer John Collier resigned as commissioner of Indian Affairs in 1945, and for the next five years, the BIA continued to pursue the policies he advocated. However, that all came to an abrupt end in 1950, when Dillon S. Myer was appointed as the new commissioner for

Indian Affairs. Myer, it seemed, was determined to undo all of Collier's hard work for the good of the Indians. One of his earliest acts was to end programs aimed at Indian development and to begin what he termed "withdrawal programming." Also called *termination*, it refers to the withdrawal of federal support of Indian tribes.

Myer was no friend of the Indians. While commissioner, he interfered with the election of tribal officers on the Blackfeet Reservation, sold some land belonging to the San Ildefonso Pueblo without tribal consent, and challenged the right of tribes to select their own attorneys. He even supported a bill introduced in Congress that would have authorized Indian service employees to carry arms and arrest Indians without warrants. It is unclear why he pursued such policies, but publicly he characterized his philosophy as "freeing the Indians." Who needs such "liberties"?

Code Talking

Termination refers to the withdrawal of federal support from an Indian tribe and an end of the trust status accorded to Native land.

Tribal Truths

During World War II, Dillon S. Myer was in charge of the internment camps in which persons of Japanese ancestry were placed, following the hysteria that came after the bombing of Pearl Harbor. He brought the same policy of forced removal and coercive methods to Indian affairs.

Myer's termination policy included the following acts:

♦ The unilateral abrogation of all federal responsibilities owed to the tribes and their citizens and all treaty and other agreements between the governments of the various tribes and the United States.

♦ The abolition of tribal governments.

♦ The eradication of reservations and all tribal holdings of lands and assets.

♦ The elimination of the federal bureaucracy dedicated to the support of Indian programs and the fulfillment of treaty guarantees.

♦ The consequent reduction of the federal budget.

Myer advocated an end to health, economic, and educational benefits provided for by the Indian Reorganization Act. He saw the return of the boarding school system where Indian children could be removed from the ties of family and reservation, and he ordered the end to classes that stressed Native culture.

The Zimmerman Report

Even though Myer didn't "liberate" the Indians until 1950, the roots of the termination movement began in 1947 when Acting Commissioner of Indian Affairs William

Zimmerman was asked to appear before the Senate Post Office and Civil Service Committee to provide a list of tribes that, in his opinion, could be separated from federal jurisdiction. Zimmerman provided the committee with three categories of tribes—those that could be immediately released from federal jurisdiction, those that might be released in the near future, and those tribes that might never be released.

Zimmerman's criteria were (1) the degree of acculturation of a particular tribe, (2) the economic well-being of the tribe, (3) the willingness of the tribe to be released from federal supervision, and (4) the willingness of the state to assume jurisdiction of services formally provided by the government. The list of tribes that might be immediately terminated included the Klamath, Osage, Menominee, and Flathead tribes.

Myer stated in 1951 that the two long-range objectives of the Bureau of Indian Affairs were "(1) a standard of living for Indians comparable with that enjoyed by other segments of the population, and (2) the step-by-step transfer of Bureau functions to the Indians themselves or the appropriate agencies of local, state or federal government."

In theory, termination should be the natural outcome of a successful program begun by the Indian Reorganization Act. Tribes should, after some time, have become completely self-governing and self-sufficient, no longer needing the supervision of the Bureau of Indian Affairs. In theory, tribes would be freed from the limitations imposed by bureau policies. But Myer was determined to make termination happen well before most tribes were capable of surviving the transition.

House Concurrent Resolution 108

The high point of the termination effort came with the passage of House Concurrent Resolution 108 (HCR 108), adopted by both the House and the Senate on August 1, 1953. The resolution stated that it was the opinion of Congress that it was the policy of the government, as rapidly as possible, "to make the Indians … subject to the same laws and entitled to the same privileges and responsibilities as are applicable to other citizens."

A congressional resolution has no standing in law. It does not even require presidential signature. It only expresses the opinion of the current Congress. But HCR 108 caused panic in Indian country and for good reason.

Twelve termination acts were passed from 1954 to 1962 dealing with the Alabama and Coushatta tribes of Texas, California reservations, the Catawba tribe of South Carolina, the Klamath tribe of Oregon, the Menominee tribe of Wisconsin, the Ottawa tribe of Oklahoma, the Ponca tribe of Nebraska, the Uintah and Ouray Ute mixed bloods of Utah, western Oregon bands (600 of them), and the Wyandotte tribe of Oklahoma. Later, some of these actions were reversed and some terminated tribes received federal recognition.

Public Law 280

One of the prerequisites for termination was that the state would have to be willing to assume jurisdiction over some aspects of Indian affairs. However, no mechanism was in place for this to occur. Indian affairs had always been the responsibility of the federal government, and states weren't prepared to take it on.

To remedy this, in 1953 Congress passed Public Law 280, giving states power to extend their civil and criminal law over Indian reservations. Public Law 280 extended state law over reservations in Wisconsin, Minnesota (except Red Lake), Nebraska, California, and Oregon (except several tribes on the Warm Springs Reservation). Public Law 280 required no Indian consent until it was amended in 1968.

Trying to Burn the Tipi Down

Tribes greatly feared termination. The loss of federal supervision, they believed, would lead to the loss of the reservation and their culture. In retrospect, the Natives were correct.

> **Native Voices**
>
> It is important to note that in our Indian language, the only translation for termination is to "wipe out" or "kill off." You have caused us to jump every time we hear this word … how can we plan our future when the Indian Bureau threatens to wipe us out as a race? It is like trying to cook a meal in your tipi when someone is standing outside trying to burn the tipi down.
> —Earl Old Person, Blackfeet tribal chairman and chief

Making matters worse, the federal government ignored the criteria developed by Zimmerman. Tribes were often terminated from federal supervision without their consent, and states were often not interested in assuming jurisdiction. On one reservation in Nebraska, when the tribe was terminated, the state refused to assume criminal jurisdiction, meaning that the former reservation had no system of law and order. No study, as recommended by Zimmerman, was ever made of the several bands in western Oregon, except to note that some had timber resources. The Alabama-Coushatta Reservation was turned over to the state of Texas with no real plan. Several bands of Paiute were terminated even though they were dirt poor (the reason for terminating them was that they never received services from the government anyway). It was a frightening time for Native Americans.

The Best of Times, the Worst of Times: A Tale of Two Tribes

Two wealthy tribes, owners of valuable timber, were terminated at the same time: the Menominee of Wisconsin and the Klamath of Oregon. These two tribes represent two different termination scenarios—both of them negative.

The Menominee were a prosperous tribe. They had several tribal enterprises, a healthy income from timber sales, and paid all the expenses for Bureau of Indian Affairs services. Their success was their undoing.

Tribes were supposed to agree to terminate their relationship with the government, but according to the records, the Menominee didn't vote for termination. No one knew what it meant. When tribes were terminated, the tribal assets were liquidated and distributed to tribal members. The people assumed they were receiving a portion of their monies held in the U.S. Treasury—they didn't understand that by accepting the payments, they were consenting to ending their relationship with the government.

When the Menominee were terminated, a new county was created, comprising the former reservation, and tribal board of executives selected to manage their resources. Their first years after termination were difficult because of low timber prices and inadequate revenues.

Native Voices

Termination represented a gigantic and revolutionary *forced* change in the traditional Menominee way of life. Congress expected us to replace our Indian way of life with a complicated corporate style of living. Congress expected immediate Menominee assimilation of non-Indian culture, values, and life styles. The immediate effect of termination on our tribe was the loss of most of our hundred-year-old treaty rights, protections, and services. No amount of explanation or imagination prior to termination could have prepared us for the shock of what these losses meant.

—DRUMS Committee, Menominee

In the spring of 1970, a grass-roots organization entitled DRUMS (Determination of Rights & Unity of Menominee Shareholders) was established to restore the reservation to federal status. Fortunately, DRUMS' hard work paid off. In 1973, President Nixon signed the Menominee Restoration Act into law. Public Law 93–197, the

Menominee Restoration Act, made provision for the return of the Menominee Indians to full tribal status and the return of tribal assets to trust status.

The Klamath, too, had plenty of timber and were paying the bureau for services. After tribal assets were liquidated, the Klamath were given the option of taking their share of the assets or allowing it to remain in a block to be managed as a trusteeship. When they learned that individual shares were worth $44,000, most of the Klamath withdrew the money. The result was a disaster.

Much of the wealth derived from the sale of the Klamath's heritage was lost to sharp dealings by merchants and unscrupulous attorneys who mishandled, embezzled, or engaged in self-dealing from trust accounts of those determined to be incompetent, or by hundreds of other schemes meant to separate the Klamath from their funds. In 1980, the Klamath tribes began to work in earnest for restoration of federal recognition, and in 1986, the tribe was restored as a federally recognized tribe. Now their efforts are focused on restoring their land base.

Moving to the Concrete Prairies

So what happens when Native peoples no longer have a reservation or land upon which to live? The federal government's answer was to ship them off to the cities. There was a general shift in America toward urban living after the Second World War. But the federal government under Commissioner Myer made *relocation* a part of federal Indian policy.

The idea was simple. Reservation families were relocated to cities such as Minneapolis, Chicago, Denver, Los Angeles, and Oakland. The bureau paid for the cost of moving, placed them in jobs, and helped them find housing. The idea was that Native peoples would assimilate into white society and not burden the Bureau of Indian Affairs again. In 1955, 3,400 Indians were already living in low-rent apartments or housing developments in the cities. By 1957, close to 10,000 more were working in construction and light industries in the concrete prairies.

Some prospered in the cities and never returned. Others worked and lived in the cities for a time but

Code Talking

Relocation was a federal program begun in the 1950s in which Indian families were moved (relocated) to cities where jobs and housing for them was found.

Tribal Truths

Everyone swears it's true. There was a family from Browning, Montana, who was driven to Oakland on relocation by the agency superintendent. He arranged their housing and a job and began the long drive back to Montana. When he arrived back on the reservation, the relocated family had already moved back.

eventually returned to the reservations. Others were simply swallowed up by the cities, becoming skid-row casualties.

> ## Native Voices
>
> They said the government wanted to put a man on the moon and it could be done all right, but nobody knew how to get the guy home again after he landed on the moon. These guys said all the government had to do was put an Indian in that rocketship and tell him he was being relocated and then, after he got to the moon, that Indian would find his own way home again and the government wouldn't have to figure that part out at all.
>
> —Watt Spade, Cherokee

Urban Indians

In the 1970s, urban Indian centers were established in many large communities with significant Native populations. Funded by grants from federal government programs like the Comprehensive Employment and Training Act, these centers offered social services such as job and education counseling as well as offering a place where Natives could learn about Native heritage. Native peoples who had been long-removed from their reservation communities and those who had never known the reservation found places where they might feel comfortable being Indian. Not surprising, the urban centers also spawned activism, like the American Indian Movement, started in Minneapolis, Minnesota, to combat police brutality against Native peoples in the Twin Cities.

Joining the Big Wide River of Mainstream America

The policies of the 1950s—on the surface, anyway—seemed reasonable. The Bureau of Indian Affairs was perceived as a barrier to Native development and, by releasing tribes from bureau support, those tribes could prosper. And perhaps most important, the government, having eliminated the bureau, could save money.

The consequences, however, were predictable. Native peoples are strongly connected to the land, and when disconnected from the land, they don't fare well. Relocation, on one level, represented an opportunity to begin a new life, but Native peoples generally found that life away from their land isn't necessarily a life worth living.

Native Voices

Why is it so important that Indians be brought into the "mainstream of American life"? What is "the mainstream of American life"? I would not know how to interpret the phrase to my people in our language. The closest I would be able to come to "mainstream" would be to say, in Indian, "a big, wide river." Am I then to tell my people that they will be "thrown into the Big Wide River in the United States"?

—Earl Old Person, Blackfeet tribal chairman

For tribes that were terminated, the results were disastrous. Terminated tribes were separated from their lands and, ultimately, from their heritage. As Earl Old Person, Blackfeet chief, observed, "It is important to note that in our Indian language, the only translation for termination is to 'wipe out' or 'kill off.'"

The Least You Need to Know

♦ Termination refers to the ending of the government's responsibilities and services to selected tribes.

♦ Termination offered a way for the government to get out of the Indian business.

♦ For the most part, tribes that were terminated didn't fare well.

♦ The federal government tried a policy of relocating some Indian people to the cities, hoping that they would assimilate into mainstream American society.

♦ Relocation led to an increase in the urban Native population as well as a loss of cultural ties for those who relocated.

Part 4

Modern Indians, Modern Challenges

Although most American Indians don't live on reservations, to many they remain a home, a place where the culture is still actively practiced, a place where (if they're lucky) the native language is spoken, a place that they just may return to someday.

That doesn't mean that life is all rosy on reservations. They are places of historic poverty, social distress, and economic depression. As you will learn in the following chapters, reservations have their own governments with the same kinds of challenges that all governments face.

Other chapters in Part 4 make clear the importance of spirituality to Native peoples, and continued protection of their rights to follow traditional practices and beliefs.

Indians Take the Reins: Tribal Self-Determination

In This Chapter

- ◆ Handing power back to the Indians
- ◆ The BIA gets a new role
- ◆ Making sense of sovereignty
- ◆ How tribes get federal recognition
- ◆ Fine-tuning the government-to-government relationship

As the federal government's policy toward American Indians ranged from elimination to assimilation to separation over the years, Indians could count on one thing: What they wanted was rarely taken into consideration. For nearly 200 years the federal government, through the military or the Bureau of Indian Affairs, simply told the tribes what would be done and how it would be done. Voices from the various tribal governments were ignored.

But as you know by now, the tribes could be as stubborn as the federal government when it came to determining how they should live. In the face of changing federal Indian policy, the tribes always asserted that they were sovereign nations—regardless of what the federal government claimed.

Finally, in the late 1960s and early 1970s, changing social attitudes, Indian activism, and an administration favorable to Indians helped bring about dramatic changes in the U.S. government's attitude and policy toward the first Americans. It may have taken close to 500 years, but the Natives were finally beginning to get the treatment they deserved.

Tricky Dick Deals the Natives an Honest Hand

While most history books focus on President Richard Nixon's involvement in the Watergate scandal, forever associating "Tricky Dick" Nixon with dirty politics, Native historians have long recognized Nixon as having left a far more important and lasting legacy to Indians: self-determination.

> **Tribal Truths**
>
> It is perhaps ironic, and certainly arguable, that Richard Nixon, so much the poster child for the corruption of American politics, probably did more for Native peoples than any other American president. Because of his efforts, Congress passed legislation to strengthen tribal governments, repeal termination, and set aside funds to aid the preparation of native leaders to administer programs run be BIA.

On July 8, 1970, President Richard M. Nixon's administration handed much of the decision-making regarding how they should be governed to the tribes themselves, establishing a policy of self-determination. In his "Special Message on Indian Affairs," President Nixon stated that the goal of all new federal Indian policy should be "to strengthen the Indian sense of autonomy without threatening his sense of community." Unlike previous attempts to establish Indian autonomy, Nixon promised to continue to offer federal support—both financial and administrative—until the tribes no longer needed it.

This Is Not Your Father's Bureau of Indian Affairs

The Bureau of Indian Affairs backed Nixon's policy of self-determination. In 1970, Commissioner of Indian Affairs Louis R. Bruce distributed to his staff "a statement of the policies, which will hence-forth guide the Bureau in its administration of Indian affairs." It was intended to change the bureau's focus from one of managing Indian affairs to helping Indians manage their own affairs. Further, it reaffirmed the trust status of Indian land and gave tribes the option to take over any or all BIA program functions; more important, however, it gave tribes the right to reestablish BIA programs if the need arose.

In theory, the BIA was to become advisor, rather than the paternalistic "Great White Father" it had been.

The Indian Self-Determination Act

The formal acknowledgement of this new direction in federal Indian affairs came in 1975, when Congress passed the Indian Self-determination Act. It gave tribes the authority to contract with the federal government to operate programs that serve tribal members. Under the new policy, tribes could contract to run their own law and order, education, or forestry programs, to name a few examples. Rather than run the program for the tribe, the BIA would give the tribes the funds to run the program themselves. Tribes could contract to administer all former bureau programs or only one or two. The ultimate goal was for tribes to administer all of their own programs, but only when they became ready to do so.

The law has since been amended to give tribes increased participation in the management of federal Indian programs. Also, under the self-determination law and amendments to it, tribes exercise broader discretion over funds and designs of tribal programs so that they can tailor them to local needs.

Enactment of the self-determination law in the mid-1970s marked the beginning of the federal government's acknowledgment of tribal *sovereign* rights.

> **Code Talking**
>
> **Sovereignty** is the supreme, absolute, and uncontrollable power by which any independent state is governed. It is the international independence of a state, combined with the right and power of regulating its internal affairs without foreign dictation.

Termination by Any Other Name?

At first, tribes were suspicious of this new approach. They had, after all, been burned by changes in federal policy in the past. Some thought the federal government was once again preparing to terminate Indian programs under the guise of self-determination. However, the tribes cautiously accepted self-determination, and it has become the foundation of tribal governments. Based on the policy of self-determination, tribes now make decisions for Indian people that used to be made by the federal government.

Who Rules Whom

The relationship can get complicated between the federal government and tribes, as the sovereign tribal nations exist within the borders of the United States, and Indian sovereignty is a product of several overriding principles. The essential three principles are as follows:

◆ The Constitution vests Congress with plenary *power* over Indian affairs, meaning that Congress's power of Indians is full or great. The power is not absolute, however, and is limited by the U.S. Constitution.

◆ Indian tribes retain important sovereign powers over "their members and their territory," subject to the plenary power of Congress.

◆ The United States has a trust responsibility to Indian tribes, which guides and limits the federal government in dealings with them.

Thus, federal and tribal law generally has primacy over Indian affairs in Indian country, except where Congress has provided otherwise. For example, Congress authorized the Environmental Protection Agency to delegate responsibilities to states for implementing and enforcing national standards within their jurisdiction, including Indian reservations. The relationship between Indian tribes and the federal government is further determined by prior agreements. When tribes signed treaties with the government, those tribes established a legal association that remains today. Some tribes, however, for a variety of reasons, either severed that relationship or never established one in the first place. For these tribes, the federal government has established a method for seeking federal recognition and thereby "legal" status.

Hey, Uncle Sam, Recognize Me!

For tribes seeking federal recognition, the stakes are high. A tribe must petition the federal government for this status, which carries economic, political, and social benefits, from health care and educational benefits, to money for housing. More important, federal recognition validates a people's culture and history as unique and special. For a tribe like the Duwamish of Washington State, Chief Seattle's people, or the Little Shell Tribe of Chippewa, it means that they really didn't disappear into history.

The federal government has established two methods by which Indian tribes can seek federal recognition. A tribe can seek recognition through an act of Congress or it can petition the BIA for acknowledgement. The standards that must be met to achieve recognition are very high and the process can be time-consuming, requiring many years of research and review. However, if a tribe can make it through the BIA process, there can be no question about its legitimacy. A tribe must demonstrate that it meets seven criteria to obtain BIA recognition:

1. Show that it has been identified from historical times to the present on a continuing basis as an American Indian tribe.

2. Show that it has comprised a distinct community continuously, from first sustained contact with the Europeans to the present.

3. Show that it has maintained political influence or authority over its members as an autonomous entity since historical times.

4. Present a tribal constitution or other governing document.

5. Provide a membership list of persons descended from the historical tribe.

6. Demonstrate that the membership does not consist of persons who are members of other American Indian tribes.

7. Show that it is not the subject of congressional legislation that expressly forbids or terminates recognition.

Once a tribe files its petition for federal recognition, the BIA will review it for any obvious deficiencies. After correcting its petition to comply with BIA's recommendations, the tribe must formally declare that it is ready for the BIA to make its decision regarding tribal status.

> **Native Voices**
>
> We are a scattered tribe. We weren't claimed by the whites. We weren't claimed by the full bloods. They used to call us persons with no souls. Now at least we have an identity.
>
> —Ed Lavenger, Little Shell Tribal Elder

> **Tribal Truths**
>
> Only 15 tribes have received federal recognition through the "Federal Acknowledgement Process" since 1978. Sixteen petitions for recognition have been denied in that same space of time.

As It Should Be: Gov to Gov

For more than 560 tribes, federal recognition carries the additional importance of a unique and historical relationship with the American government. The federal government interacts with Native tribes now as it had 200 years ago: nation to nation. This association is embodied in the "government-to-government relationship" recently acknowledged by the Clinton administration.

On April 29, 1994, President William Clinton issued an historic executive memorandum titled "Executive Memorandum: Government-to-Government Relations with Native American Tribal Governments." In this memo, which was distributed to all heads of the executive departments and federal agencies, Clinton affirmed the importance of Native sovereignty, stating that "the United States government has a unique legal relationship with Native American tribal govern as set forth in the Constitution of the United States, treaties, statutes, and court decisions." The document further states that, "As executive departments and agencies undertake activities affecting Native American tribal rights or trust resources, such activities should be implemented in a knowledgeable, sensitive manner respectful of tribal sovereignty."

Finally, American Indians got the R-E-S-P-E-C-T they deserved!

Guiding Principles of the Government-to-Government Relationship

President Clinton's directive requires that in all activities relating to or affecting the government or treaty rights of Indian tribes, the executive branch shall …

- ◆ Operate within a government-to-government relationship with federally recognized Indian tribes.

- ◆ Consult, to the greatest extent practicable and permitted by law, with Indian tribal governments before taking actions that affect federally recognized Indian tribes.

- ◆ Assess the impact of agency activities on tribal trust resources and ensure that tribal interests are considered before the activities are undertaken.

- ◆ Remove procedural impediments to working directly with tribal governments on activities that affect trust property or governmental rights of the tribes.

- ◆ Work cooperatively with other agencies to accomplish these goals established by the president.

Each department in the federal government reviewed its programs and procedures to ensure that it adheres to principles of respect for Indian tribal governments, that it honor the United States's trust responsibility to Indian tribes, and to assist Indian tribes as domestic dependent nations within the federal system.

A Parade of Presidential Policies

President Clinton's executive memorandum builds on the firmly established federal policy of self-determination for Indian tribes. Working together with Congress, previous presidents affirmed the fundamental policy of federal respect for tribal self-government. President Johnson recognized "the right of the first Americans … to freedom of choice and self-determination." President Nixon strongly encouraged "self-determination" among the Indian people. President Reagan pledged "to pursue the policy of self-government" for Indian tribes and reaffirmed "the government-to-government basis" for dealing with Indian tribes. President George H. Bush recognized that the federal government's "efforts to increase tribal self-governance have brought a renewed sense of pride and empowerment to this country's native peoples."

Tribal Truths

The mandate to protect religious liberty is deeply rooted in this nation's constitutional heritage. The government seeks to ensure that American Indians are protected in the observance of their faiths, and also recognizes the significant federal interest in aiding tribes in the preservation of their tribal customs and traditions. In performing its duties in Indian country, the federal government will respect and seek to preserve tribal cultures.

Tribalism in the Twenty-First Century

Indians, haunted by history, wonder if the government-to-government relationship will be sustained in the future. Native peoples have seen policy changes in the past that radically contradicted those they replaced. They know from experience that the current policy of cooperation and consultation can easily be replaced by one of government interference and control.

The test of greatness for the United States in the future will not be its military might or how this country is perceived internationally. The real test will be how the United States treats its own citizens, and, in particular, how it treats Native peoples.

Words like *sovereignty*, *self-determination*, and *self-government* are meaningless until the federal government allows tribes to achieve true autonomy. Tribes need adequate funding to maintain and strengthen their economies and governments, just as other world nations require assistance to maintain their cultural and political identities. The United States must recognize its responsibility to the First Americans. The foundation we build today will impact Native peoples for the next seven generations and beyond.

The Least You Need to Know

◆ President Richard M. Nixon was, arguably, the most supportive president of tribal self-government.

◆ In theory, the Bureau of Indian Affairs is a service organization and not a management agency.

◆ The federal government maintains full control over American Indian tribes.

◆ Tribes that are not now acknowledged as "federally recognized" must undergo a lengthy application process.

◆ Federally recognized tribes enjoy a political relationship with the American government that acknowledges the United States's trust responsibility with Native peoples.

◆ In 1994, President Bill Clinton signed an executive memorandum making it the policy of the federal government to support and respect tribal sovereignty.

Chapter 20

When Rights Collide: Hunting, Fishing, and Gathering

In This Chapter

- ◆ Defending the right to hunt, fish, and gather
- ◆ Regulating reservation hunting and fishing policies
- ◆ Subsistence as an essential Native tradition
- ◆ Why whaling is important

Before Euro-Americans came to this continent, most tribes depended extensively on three methods of obtaining their food: hunting, fishing, and gathering. Many tribes were mobile, following the game herds while other tribes, like those in the Pacific Northwest, relied on fish runs to survive. Many treaties established between the Indians and the federal government guaranteed the Indians the right to continue hunting, fishing, and gathering on their traditional lands, but more and more, these rights are being challenged, particularly by non-Indian sports groups and environmentalists.

We Reserve the Right to Hunt and Fish

Nearly every tribe in the United States has a treaty with the federal government, and nearly every tribe has relinquished land. In exchange for the land, the treaties and agreements often stipulated that tribes retained the right to continue to hunt, fish, and gather food. In the language of the treaties, tribes retained the right to "hunt and fish in their usual and accustomed places" or "usual and accustomed grounds and stations" in the case of the fishing tribes of the Northwest.

Code Talking

In signing the treaties, the tribes reserved many of their aboriginal rights, including land, hunting, and fishing rights, and the right to self-government. This concept is embraced in the **Reserved Rights Doctrine.** This doctrine was first established by the Supreme Court in *United States* v. *Winans*, 198 US 371 (1905) when the Supreme Court held: "The treaty was not a grant of rights to the Indians, but a grant of rights from them—a reservation of those not granted."

Even if treaties and agreements are silent on the issue of the rights of tribes to hunt and fish as they had in the past, those rights may still be protected. The Supreme Court has ruled that a treaty is "not a grant of rights to the Indians, but a grant of rights from them." Any right not explicitly extinguished by a treaty or a federal statute is considered to be "reserved" to the tribe. This principle, called the *Reserved Rights Doctrine*, has consistently been upheld by the courts.

Treaty rights regarding fishing and hunting were easy to keep as long as few non-Indians lived in or around those "usual and accustomed places." In recent years, however, these treaty provisions have caused a great deal of conflict between Indians and non-Indians.

On the Rez

Conflicts between Indians and non-Indians over hunting and fishing rights do not exist on the reservation because tribes regulate all matters within their respective territories. Furthermore, on many reservations, there are still plentiful game and fish that not only provide sustenance to tribal members but also serve as a commercial resource for the tribal economy.

Because the regulation of hunting and fishing is a local matter, tribal laws vary widely. Some tribes establish rules governing the season, place, and manner of hunting and fishing and enforce these regulations in tribal courts. Other tribes put no restrictions on when, where, or how members may hunt or fish.

Because tribal courts do not, as a general rule, have jurisdiction over non-Indians, federal regulation makes it a federal crime for non-Indians to hunt or fish on an Indian reservation without permission of the tribe.

In short, an Indian tribe has the right to regulate hunting and fishing on the reservation, although it is up to the federal government to prosecute nonmember's caught poaching on reservation land.

Tribal Truths

The Mescalero Apache, through careful management, have managed to grow their elk population from 13 head in 1966 to more than 1,200 head today. The tribe issues 50 elk hunting licenses a year to nonmembers.

Off the Rez

Conflicts arise between Natives and non-Indians when tribes act on their rights to hunt and fish on nonreservation land—places where Indians have fished and hunted for hundreds of years.

Among the earliest conflicts with respect to fishing rights were those in the Northwest where tribes were guaranteed the right to fish "at all usual and accustomed grounds and stations." These "usual and accustomed grounds and stations" were not identified in the treaty but there's little question that they included places both on and off reservations.

Fish-ins, Marlon Brando, and the Boldt Decision

In 1963, the state of Washington ruled against the rights of the Quillayute, Nisqually, Muckleshoot, and other indigenous nations of the Pacific Northwest to fish with nets, as they traditionally had, regardless of prior treaties. The state mandated that all Indian fishing had to be done with hook and line according to Washington fish and game laws. The tribes appealed to the courts for relief.

Tribal Truths

Non-Indian commercial fishers caught salmon by the millions of tons in the Pacific and Puget Sound, but the state blamed declining fish runs on Indian netting and lawlessness. The state didn't like that Indians didn't follow state-mandated seasons, didn't get licenses, and didn't heed catch limits. Tribes claimed the real culprits in the salmon's decline were commercial fishing, dam-building, and logging. Decades of research would eventually corroborate this.

In an attempt to increase public awareness of the importance of fishing to tribal people, individuals attempted to exercise their still-in-question fishing rights in what were called "Fish-Ins." The most dramatic incident in what would come to be known as the Puyallup-Nisqually fishing rights movement occurred in 1964 when actor Marlon Brando and Episcopalian canon John Yaryan joined tribal member Robert Satiacum to fish in the Puyallup River. All three were arrested amidst a media frenzy. None of the three were ever formally charged, but for the first time the public was drawn into the controversy.

Hook, Line, and Billy Club

One of the most frightening series of events occurred in 1964 at Frank's Landing on the Puyallup River, south of Tacoma, Washington. The police and tribal members clashed when the officers attempted to arrest Natives who were fishing. This set off an emotionally charged battle during which game wardens beat Indians with flashlights and leather-covered clubs.

> **Tribal Truths**
>
> In 1972, Richard Oakes, an organizer of the Puyallup-Nisqually fishing rights movement was found dead. Tacoma, Washington authorities claimed Oakes shot himself in the stomach. Others, such as the American Indian Movement, contend he was murdered for his support of Indian fishing rights.

Indians and non-Native allies protested the police brutality, attracting even more national interest in the controversy, and more fish-ins were planned. Actor/advocate Dick Gregory came to the Northwest to take part in the fish-ins. Unlike Brando, Gregory was arrested and sentenced for illegal fishing. He fasted during his time in jail, bringing continued media attention to the movement.

The Feds Step into the Fray

On August 27, 1973, the United States, representing 14 Indian tribes, sued the State of Washington. George H. Boldt, senior judge of the Federal District Court in Tacoma, Washington, presided over what would become a landmark case in Native American rights, *United States* v. *Washington.*

The case boiled down to two questions: First, did Indians have treaty rights to fish off their reservations? And if the answer to question one is yes, then did these treaties reserve the tribes a specific portion of the salmon and steelhead swimming through their "usual and accustomed" fishing places?

On February 12, 1974, Judge Boldt issued his ruling. He held that the tribes did indeed have definable rights to salmon, steelhead, and other fish. In the second part of his ruling, Boldt interpreted the tribes' right to take fish "in common with" non-Indian citizens, meaning to share equally. The treaty tribes, he opined, were entitled to catch 50 percent of the harvestable fish passing through their fishing areas. The Supreme Court upheld Boldt's ruling in 1979.

As a result of the Boldt decision, the federal government was held to have a legal obligation to regulate the ocean fishery to ensure that a reasonable number of salmon reached tribal fishing places on the Columbia River. In 1980, Congress passed the Northwest Power Act, which, for the first time, mandated that Columbia River power production and fisheries be managed as co-equals. It called for a fish and wildlife program to make up for losses caused by federal water development in the Columbia River basin. Tribes and the federal government began to work together to manage fisheries in the basin.

The Rise of American Indian Activism

The fish-ins at Frank's Landing in the 1960s demonstrated to many Native peoples the importance of social activism. When Indians demonstrated on the Washington State Capitol steps in support of their fishing rights, they were joined by other activist groups, including the Peace and Freedom Party, Socialist Workers Party, Black Panthers, and Students for a Democratic Society, all organizations already seasoned in the serious game of social protest.

This spirit of activism had an impact on Native peoples. In 1968, the American Indian Movement (AIM) was founded in Minneapolis, Minnesota. Dennis Banks (Anishinabe), Clyde Belcourte (Ojibwa), and other community activists originally started the organization to curb police harassment of Indians living in Minneapolis. As the organization grew, AIM broadened its mission to represent other urban Indian issues (such as education and employment), protect the traditional ways of Native peoples, and intervene in cases relating to treaty and aboriginal hunting and fishing rights.

Escape to Alcatraz?

In a move to draw attention to Native American causes, in 1969, a number of Natives, calling themselves Indians of All Tribes, occupied Alcatraz Island in San Francisco Bay. They laid claim to the island, citing a nineteenth-century agreement that granted Indians first rights to government surplus lands (Alcatraz prison had been closed and the island declared surplus property). The occupation grew until in involved hundreds of Indians and their supporters. The occupation lasted for 20 months and served as a rallying point for Indian activism.

The Trail of Broken Treaties

In 1972, Indian activists took their causes directly to the federal government. AIM organized a caravan, called the Trail of Broken Treaties, from San Francisco to Washington, D.C., to highlight the mistreatment of Native peoples. When they reached Washington, AIM presented a 20-point position paper on Indian rights to the Nixon administration. Unsatisfied by the response by the government, AIM took over the BIA building for six days. The government negotiated an end to the occupation of the BIA building with promises that it would investigate Indian concerns. Later, in 1973, the Nixon administration formally rejected the 20 points that had been presented during the Trail of Broken Treaties demonstration, but the occupation brought Indian rights to the national agenda.

Wounded Knee II

The climax of the American Indian Movement came in 1973 during the siege of Pine Ridge and the occupation of the tiny South Dakota reservation town of Wounded Knee. AIM leaders Russell Means and Dennis Banks went to the Pine Ridge Reservation to protest the administration of Richard (Dicky) Wilson, then chairman of the tribal council. Many, though not all, tribal members believed that Wilson had a tyrannical hold on reservation resources such as jobs and social services.

Tribal Truths

Wilson formed a paramilitary police force called the Guardians of the Oglala Nations (which became known as the "GOON" squad) to squash attempts by tribal members to give support to AIM.

Wilson called for federal marshals to help counter AIMs presence on the reservation, calling AIM members trouble-makers and militants. More than 200 AIM sympathizers gathered at the site of the 1890 Wounded Knee Massacre to demonstrate. They were surrounded by more than 300 U.S. Marshalls, FBI agents, and BIA police officers armed with guns, armored personnel carriers, and other military hardware.

Two Indians were killed in the 71 day stand off which finally ended on May 3 in a negotiated settlement. Of the 563 people arrested, 185 were indicted, but only 15 were convicted of charges ranging from interfering with a postal inspector to trespassing. AIM leader Russell Means was charged with 37 felonies, but after three years of trials and hearings, he was cleared of all charges.

After the siege, repression on the reservation increased. AIM supporters were harassed and a number of them were murdered by unknown assailants. Despite the efforts of AIM and their supporters, conditions on the reservation remained unchanged.

Spear a Pregnant Squaw, Save a Walleye: Things Get Really Ugly

Treaty rights conflicts between states and Indian tribes reached a new low in 1985 when Ojibwa Indians in Wisconsin sought to exercise their right to spear walleye on lakes off their reservations.

The conflict was bitter, pitting pro-treaty Natives and their supporters with the non-Indian sport-fishing men and women, some of whom threatened to use armed force against Indians who tried to exercise their rights. At first, Native fishermen were reluctant, fearing for their safety. When they did try to exercise their rights, Ojibwa fishermen were shot at and harassed by shouting, sign-carrying "sports enthusiasts." One particularly vicious sign expressed their resentment and hatred: "Spear a pregnant squaw, save a walleye."

Local law enforcement agencies and Wisconsin Department of Natural Resources wardens refused to protect spear fisherman and their families from violent protesters even after the courts upheld their rights. Finally, U.S. Chief District Judge Barbara B. Crabb issued an injunction against the most violent group—Stop Treaty Abuse—and Wisconsin and federal marshals were called in.

What's the Big Deal?

People unfamiliar with the controversy might be surprised by the vehemence with which some non-Natives reacted to Indians invoking their treaty rights. What could possibly be wrong with Native people continuing to do what they had been doing for hundreds—even thousands—of years? It all boiled down to two things: 1) Non-Native sport fisherman feared that Indian fishermen would take fish in such numbers that there would be few left for them, and 2) they believed the federal courts had granted the Ojibwa special privileges by allowing them to harvest fish using methods that were illegal for other fishermen.

Whereas individuals were concerned about potential scarcity and special privileges, many states feared a loss of revenue (fearing a decline in fishing and hunting license sales) and the loss of their authority over natural resources in their states.

> **Tribal Truths** _____
>
> States have shown themselves to be unwilling to concede what they believe to be their rights in favor of a negotiated compromise. For example, Washington State and Wisconsin spent several years in litigation and millions of dollars before accepting treaty rights. State officials have even ignored federal court decisions.

During the first season, Natives took 2,061 walleye by spear. Harvests grew steadily for the next three years, with 6,940, 21,321, and 25,974 walleye, respectively, speared by Natives. During 1989, a sudden recurrence of cold weather at the end of the spawning season curtailed fishing activity and only 16,053 walleye were taken.

In contrast to the number of walleye harvested by sports fishermen, the number taken by spear fishermen was astonishingly low. To take just one example, angling accounted for 672,303 walleye in 1988. This constituted 96 percent of the total catch!

Everyone Wins

Ironically, this conflict has resulted in better fish management for the state of Wisconsin. The Department of Natural Resources realized that the Indian spear fishing doesn't constitute a greater threat to the resource than sport fishing using hooks and lines. In response to these findings, the Wisconsin Department of Natural Resources set minimum-size restrictions on waters where Native fishermen are expected to take a significant proportion of the harvestable walleye population. The result is a healthier fish population for all who fish. Clearly, Wisconsin walleye managers are in a far better position today to ensure sound management than they were a decade ago.

Alaska's Subsistence Hunting

For some people, hunting and fishing is not so much a "right" as it is a necessity. For Native peoples in Alaska, *subsistence hunting* is more than a cultural display or historic element of their heritage; it is a way of life.

During territorial days in Alaska, subsistence hunting and fishing was recognized as necessary. A special game law allowed "any Indian or Eskimo, prospector, or traveler" to hunt and fish out of season "when he is in need of food." In the rough-and-tumble gold-rush days on the Klondike, game was plentiful and people hunted to put food on the table.

 **Code Talking**

Subsistence hunting (and fishing) means to take game for survival as opposed to for sport or commercial purposes.

The government slowly chipped away at aboriginal hunting and fishing rights, however. After Alaska became a state in 1960, it sought to manage its resources and better regulate hunting and fishing. Subsistence was still recognized by both the state and the federal governments, but it wasn't viewed as having priority over regulations in place to keep game fish and animal populations stable.

Then in 1971, Congress passed the *Alaska Native Claims Settlement Act* (ANCSA). In the course of settling Native land claims, aboriginal hunting and fishing rights were extinguished. However, the settlement did provide for Natives subsistence hunting and fishing and handed regulatory power to the state and Department of the Interior.

Native Alaskans brought several cases before the state of Alaska, arguing that the state subsistence laws were inadequate to address the needs of Native Alaskans who depended upon subsistence hunting and fishing for their livelihood.

Code Talking

The **Alaska Native Claims Settlement Act** was passed in 1971 to resolve land claims brought by Alaska Natives.

An arrangement between the State of Alaska and the federal government ensued in 1990, granting dual-management of Alaska lands, whereby the State of Alaska retains management on state and private lands, and the federal government, through the secretary of the interior, controls management of fish and game on federal lands. Prior to 1994, federal management regulations excluded marine and navigable waters from the secretary of the interior's jurisdiction, leaving fish stocks (59 percent of the rural subsistence diet) without protection. An Athabaskan grandmother named Katie John was instrumental in making those fish available to Native Alaskans.

The Katie John Case

In 1984, Katie John and fellow villagers petitioned the Wrangell-St. Elias National Park and Preserve to allow them to resume fishing at Batzulnetas, the traditional site of Katie John's family's fish camp. Because the camp was at the headwaters of the Copper River (considered a navigable waterway), it fell under the state of Alaska's jurisdiction. The state declined the request. Represented by the Native American Rights Fund, they next sued the United States in federal court, claiming that the federal government had unlawfully excluded navigable waters from subsistence fishing. Finally, in 1994, the U.S. District Court for the District of Alaska, Judge Russell Holland, ruled that the federal government could protect rural Alaskans' subsistence needs by taking over fisheries management in all navigable waters running through and adjacent to federal lands. The State of Alaska, with the help of the state legislature, appealed, claiming state sovereignty to manage fish in navigable rivers located on federal lands.

In May 2001, the 9th Circuit Court of Appeals in San Francisco handed down a ruling that Katie John had the right to continue to subsistence fish at the headwaters of the Copper River. Katie John, now in her 80s, had won the first round in a long, drawn-out legal battle to keep her annual fish camp, one that she and her grandparents had routinely visited every year since she was born.

> ## Native Voices
>
> As we sat near a stream where [Katie John's] father and mother fished for salmon to feed their family, she relayed to me a simple yet compelling message: Katie John only wants to protect her right to subsistence so she can raise and provide for her family the best way she knows how, in the way taught by her parents and earlier generations. She had fought the federal government and then the state for 10 years. She was tired but said she would never walk away from them by giving up on subsistence.
>
> —Alaska governor Tony Knowles

Following Katie John's victory, the State of Alaska had to decide whether or not to appeal the decision to the U.S. Supreme Court. Alaska governor Tony Knowles decided not to appeal, leaving the lower-court decision stand. "I cannot oppose in court what I know in my heart to be right," Knowles said. "I know—we all know—what Katie John does is not wrong. It is right—right for her, right for her family, right for her village. Yet today, the State of Alaska is not protecting that most basic of rights—for every Alaskan to provide for themselves and their families."

A Whale of a Controversy

Sometimes tribes exercise their right to hunt and fish not because of politics or subsistence, but rather for reasons of cultural renewal—as a means of expressing their traditional identity. Recently, the Makah of Washington State decided to hunt whales in the Pacific Ocean for this reason.

Culture of Whale Hunters

The Makah were once renowned whale hunters. For thousands of years, leaders of extended family lineages organized the hunts, which brought the hunters great prestige and demanded much of them both physically and spiritually. The Makah were traders as well. One of the valuable trade goods they produced was whale meat and oil. The importance of whaling was recognized in their settlements with the U.S. government. The 1855 Treaty of Neah Bay provided that "The right of taking fish and of whaling or sealing at usual and accustomed grounds and stations is further secured to said Indians in common with all citizens of the United States ....”

Like many Pacific Northwest tribes, the Makah had been prevented from continuing their cultural practices by assimilation policies of the federal government and diminishing whale populations due to commercial whaling. The Makah accepted the limitations that assimilation placed on them and discontinued the practice of many of the traditional elements of their culture, including whale hunting. The last documented Makah whale hunt occurred in 1926.

Native Voices

No one can say we don't have the right to whale, or that we are not a whaling people ... It's who we are.

—Keith Johnson, Makah Whaling Commission

Commercial whaling at the turn of the century had decimated whale populations. In 1946, the United States signed the International Convention for the Regulation of Whaling (ICRW). The ICRW established an International Whaling Commission (IWC) to regulate the whaling industry. The IWC's purpose wasn't to end whaling, but rather to manage it in order to “provide for the conservation, development, and optimum utilization of the whale resources,” taking into consideration “the interests of the consumers of whale products and the whaling industry.” Still, whale populations continued to decline.

The gray whale population dropped from 30,000 to several thousand early in the twentieth century, prompting the United States to place grays on the endangered species list in 1969. Since then whale populations have made a slow recovery as the IWC increased its protection measures, most recently with a ban on commercial whaling in 1986. These conservation efforts have allowed whale populations to increase to about 25,000. The sustainable yield for this species has been estimated to be about 400 to 600 whales.

Return to the Hunt

In the late 1970s, the Makah took a renewed interest in their language and culture. Their treaty rights and their traditional songs and stories all made it clear that Makah's identity is intimately tied to whale hunting. After struggling to regain their right to fish in traditional ways as well as to hunt other sea mammals such as seals and sea lions, whaling was a next logical step.

The Makah, like many of their neighbors in western Washington State, were carvers of totem poles.

(© Corbis)

When the United States removed the gray whale from the endangered species list in 1994, the Makah notified the federal government that they planned to resume whaling, in accordance with their treaty. The Makah received federal support but they were also asked to obtain permission from the IWC. Although the Makah believed the treaty gave them the sufficient right to whale, they agreed. The United States brokered a deal and the Makah received permission to hunt gray whales under international law.

Back at Neah Bay, Makah preparations for the hunt were underway. Gray whales migrate every year from the Bering Sea to winter in the Baja peninsula. Their trip south in winter and north in spring creates two hunting seasons for the Makah at Neah Bay. The Makah established the Makah Whaling Commission, composed of representatives from 23 traditional whaling families. The commission hired a veterinarian to select a humane killing method for the hunt.

The hunt was not a reenactment of an ancient hunt, although the Makah tried to retain traditional elements. When the whale was spotted, the crew set out in a canoe, but was followed by a high-speed chase boat to ensure the whale didn't escape if it was wounded. The crew trained for the hunt, both physically and spiritually (individuals undertook spiritual preparations known within family tradition).

The hunt was to follow a specific plan. The crew would approach the whale from the left and strike it with a harpoon, and would then immediately shoot it with a retrofitted, Word War I anti-tank rifle. This high-powered weapon (twice the power of an elephant gun) was designed by the Makah tribe to kill the whale humanely. Once the whale has been killed, a man must dive into the water and sew the whale's mouth shut so that it will not sink; then the vessels tow the whale to a place where it can be ritually butchered and distributed to individual families, who will either freeze it or preserve it with smokehouse equipment around the reservation.

United Against the Hunt

The opposition against the Makah whale hunt brought together some strange bed-fellows. Approximately 250 animal rights groups and 27 conservation organizations opposed the hunt. Some organizations opposed any kind of hunting and fishing while others feared that the Makah were interested in commercial whaling. Yet other organizations were against the hunt because of the negative image hunting brought Washington's eco-tourism industry. Representative Jack Metcalf of Washington opposed the hunt because he opposed Natives receiving "special rights" like hunting and fishing rights.

Tribal Truths

The Makah largely supported the hunt. In a 1995 referendum, 73 percent of the tribal members were in favor of resuming whaling. One opinion poll has reportedly shown 85 percent of tribal members in support of whaling. When the Makah were offered potentially substantial financial assistance in exchange for abandoning their whaling rights, tribal members overwhelmingly rejected the offer. However, some Makah people are (or were) opposed to the hunt for different reasons. A few have opposed the killing of any gray whales. Other Makah were concerned that proper ceremonies cannot be followed because that knowledge has been lost. Another group opposed the hunt, at least initially, because they didn't believe they were properly consulted.

The Hunt

The Makah had set their first hunt for the fall of 1998. A convoy of protest vessels occupied of Neah Bay in an attempt to prevent them from taking a whale. The protest plus the Makah's agreement to hunt only migrating whales (which delayed the hunt and forced them to travel farther from shore than they traditionally had), prevented them from taking a whale that first season.

The Makah gave it another go the following spring, and on May 17, 1999, a Makah canoe harpooned a 30-foot gray whale and, after a short fight, brought the three-year-old whale to the beach where more than 2,000 tribal members and their families waited. After over 70 years, the Makah ate whale. Only the eldest remembered its taste.

> ### Native Voices
>
> They said, "We lost our focus; they said we need to back up, to see where this whole thing is headed, to see what's going on." I don't blame them. There's a lot of pressure on us. It's hard to contend with sometimes. We are looking at how we can straighten out our canoe. Get back to things.
>
> —Keith Johnson, Makah Whaling Commission Chairman

Future hunts will not be such media spectacles. Future hunts will not be political exercises. Future hunts will be family affairs, clans who take to the sea to feed themselves and their relatives for another year.

All or Nothing

Restoration of an ancient tradition? Needless killing of an innocent creature? Reclamation of a sovereign right? Special rights?

For Native peoples, protecting what few sovereign rights that remain is the most important fight left to them. Without such rights, as archaic as some may think they are, Natives have no claim on their history or culture. Without such rights, Native peoples are not unique, not sovereign nations.

The Least You Need to Know

- Native tribes have the right to hunt and fish in their "usual and accustomed places" as defined by treaties.

- Tribes manage the regulation of hunting and fishing on their own reservations.

- Some tribes have the right to hunt and fish in areas off their reservations.

- In *United States* v. *Washington*, the tribes of the Pacific Northwest had their right to share fish equally with non-Indian citizens upheld.

- Tribes in Wisconsin have the right to spear fish in lakes off the reservation.

- Natives in Alaska won an important case that upheld their right to subsistence fish on navigable rivers.

- Despite public sentiment to the contrary, the Makah tribe of Washington continues to carry out their right to hunt whales.

Chapter 21

Indian Education: Unto the Seventh Generation

In This Chapter

- ◆ Getting by without formal education
- ◆ Early Indian-controlled schools
- ◆ Federal support for Indian education
- ◆ Native higher education achievement
- ◆ The tribally controlled community college movement

Every society needs a system of transmitting knowledge from one generation to the next. This process provides a smooth transition from youth to adulthood. For Native peoples even before the arrival of Columbus, a well-educated community was necessary for survival.

Traditional Native education was informal—there were no classrooms, grades, or teachers per se. The whole community was charged with ensuring that a child grew up knowing his or her role in the society in which he or she lived. Approaches to learning were developed based upon the values Native societies revered. Each person was expected to perpetuate what he or she learned from childhood to adulthood, learning practical skills and wisdom. Like all other aspects of Native life, this, too, slowly started to change once Euro-Americans arrived on the scene.

The newcomers to the Americas wasted no time in setting up formal education for Indian children. Over time, three different groups—religious institutions, the colonial and federal governments, and tribes themselves—established education systems. Each had a different philosophy about what kind of education was in the best interest of Indian children.

Preacher Teachers

The Jesuit priests established the first schools for Native peoples in Havana, Cuba, in 1568. These schools were used by the Spanish explorers and colonists as a means of "civilizing" Native peoples and acculturating them into European life ways. As the Spanish continued their explorations and conquests onto the American continent,

Tribal Truths

The Jesuit and Franciscan presence is still felt, particularly in the Southwest, where a great number of Indian people are Catholic.

they further extended their assimilation of the Native peoples. Schools continued to be an important vehicle for that goal. Some schools, particularly those in the American Southwest founded after 1590, provided labor, in the form of Native students, to Spanish colonists. The French Jesuits and Spanish Franciscans both used education as a method of converting Indian people to Catholicism.

The English Protestant religious groups were most active in the early colonies on the Eastern seaboard. There, the colonial governments supported religious education for Native peoples; the colonial government employed the missionaries who taught at such schools. Two individuals, John Eliot and Dr. Eleazer Wheelock, used education to spread their Puritanical views, taking two different routes.

The Apostle to the Indians

John Eliot, later known as the "Apostle to the Indians," first began learning the Algonquin language, spoken by most New England Indians, from Indians captured during the Pequot War.

He came to Massachusetts in 1631 and become pastor of the church in Roxbury the next year. For the next 58 years, he not only pastored the congregation at Roxbury but ministered to the surrounding Indians as well. By all accounts, Eliot was beloved among his Indian disciples. Eliot organized towns for Indian converts where they could preserve their own language and culture and live by their own laws. Approximately 14 of those towns were established with the total converts numbering about 4,000.

The Natives Go to Dartmouth

Dr. Eleazer Wheelock was the headmaster of the Moors Charity School, which later became Dartmouth College. His philosophy was to remove Indian children from their family and tribe and board them in schools far from the influence of Native culture. Wheelock, as the first president of Dartmouth College, supported the enrollment of Indian students during the earliest years of its existence. In 1775, the Continental Congress approved the expenditure of $500 to educate Indians at Dartmouth. Many of his Indian students sickened, died, or were spoiled by the amenities of white civilization. By 1768, he had aroused the enmity of Sir William Johnson, the superintendent of the affairs of the Six Iroquois Nations, who withdrew all Indians from the Six Nations from his school.

> ### Native Voices
>
> We know you highly esteem the kind of Learning taught in these Colleges, and the maintenance of our young Men, while with you, would be expensive to you …. Several of our young People were formally brought up in the Colleges of the Northern Provinces; they were instructed in all your Sciences; but, when they came back to us, they were bad Runners, ignorant of every means of living in the Woods, unable to bear either Cold or Hunger, know neither how to build a Cabin, take a deer, or kill an enemy … they were totally good for nothing.
>
> —Canassatego, Iroquois, in his reply to an offer by the Virginia Legislature inviting them to send six youths to be educated at Williamsburg College of William and Mary

The work of these early educators exemplified the attempts of the church-sponsored, government-supported educational institutions. The aim of these efforts was to Christianize the American Indian and, by doing so, to civilize Indians as well. Of the two pioneer educators, Wheelock's boarding school idea would become central to the U.S. federal educational philosophy.

The Federal Boarding Schools Revisited

In each of the periods of federal Indian policy, from treaty-making, removal, termination, and self-determination, education of Indian youth has always been considered part of the solution to the "Indian Problem." Central to that view was the philosophy that only by immersing Indian children in the mainstream educational system will Indian children be acculturated and thus civilized. The federal government's role in education was, therefore, to provide a mechanism to accomplish that goal.

As noted in Chapter 16, the federal government implemented a policy of off-reservation education in boarding schools for Indian children, beginning in 1879. Children were prohibited from practicing their own cultures or from speaking their aboriginal languages. In return, children received agricultural and industrial training.

The consensus is that the boarding school system was a dismal failure. The goal of the federal school system was to promote the integration of Indian people into mainstream American society. Removal of children from their homes proved not to be an effective method of accomplishing that goal. The system created several generations of Native peoples who were accepted in neither the white nor the Indian worlds.

Indian Schools: Education on Their Own Terms

While some Native peoples avoided adopting a more systematic and formal educational program, others used the American model of education to establish tribal schools. In the late eighteenth century, the Cherokee, Chickasaw, Creek, Choctaw, and Seminole nations responded to federal pressure to assimilate by establishing their own schools, banks, courts, and other institutions.

> **Native Voices**
>
> Children must be taught or they will not know anything; if they do not know anything, they will have no sense; and if they have no sense they will not know how to act.
>
> —Native proverb

After they were forced to move to Indian Territory, the tribes became known as the "Five Civilized Tribes" and reestablished the political, economic, and educational system they had begun while living in their traditional homelands in the East.

Cultivating the Rosebuds

The federal government wasn't the first to establish boarding schools for Native Americans. One of the first Indian boarding schools, the Cherokee Female Seminary, was founded in 1851 by the Cherokee Nation in Oklahoma. Students at the Cherokee Female Seminary, who called themselves Rosebuds, took courses in Latin, French, trigonometry, political economy, and literary criticism, a curriculum that precluded any discussion of Cherokee culture or language.

For 50 years, more than 3,000 Cherokee women attended the Cherokee Female Seminary. The school offered a rigorous curriculum from elementary grades through high school that was patterned after that of Mount Holyoke Female Seminary. It offered no instruction in the Cherokee language or culture, but it was open only to full- and mixed-blood Cherokee girls. Many of the seminarians were acculturated Cherokees.

Tribal Truths

The most Cherokee seminary graduates from one family were the six children of William and Jananna Ballard. Ruth Ballard Fleming, my grandmother, was one.

The Public Schools

In 120 of the nearly 400 treaties that it negotiated with Indian people, the government promises to furnish a teacher and school building for the education of Native children in exchange for millions of acres of Native land. This arrangement conferred upon the federal government the unique responsibility to administer a federal educational system for Native peoples. As with all things relating to Native peoples' rights, the government was slow to recognize its obligation.

Because most Indian families in the late nineteenth and early twentieth centuries lived on reservations, public school education was unavailable to them. By 1920, more Indian children were attending public schools, their tuition paid for by the government. As more and more non-Indian people came to the reservations, some homesteading on land made available by the Dawes Act, the federal government responded by assisting public school development and funding.

The most important progress was made in 1934 when Congress passed the Johnson-O'Malley Act, which allowed the federal government to sign contracts with states for Indian students' education in the public schools (typically, public education is funded by the state government). Later, in the 1950s and 1960s, Congress passed several "Impact Aid" bills that provided payments to school districts in lieu of taxes to compensate school districts impacted by federal activity. Impact Aid was initially meant to assist schools impacted by the military build-up in 1959 and the 1960s, but was broadened to include Indians living on reservations. The major criticism of such funding was that the costs were applied to the general support of the schools themselves, either to operating

Native Voices

With education you are the white man's equal; without it you are his victim.

—Chief Plenty Coups, Crow

costs or to school construction. Little money was directed specifically to Indian children, who suffered from high dropout rates and underachievement.

Tribal Truths

Only about 7 percent of Indian students in the United States attend schools funded by the Bureau of Indian Affairs. Approximately 5 percent attend private or parochial schools. Thus, the majority of Indian children are being educated in public schools. According to data available in 1990, this represents nearly 400,000 students enrolled in kindergarten through high school.

Unfortunately, Native children rank at the bottom, or nearly so, on most measures of educational success. There are a number of studies of dropout patterns of Native children that yield different numbers (some scholars believe that the dropout rate is close to 40 percent), but all agree that Native students drop out of school at a significantly higher rate than non-Natives. Factors contributing to dropout include boredom with school; lack of relevance of schooling with Native life; and the quality of the interaction between students, their peers, and school personnel. Because the largest number of students tend to drop out during their adolescent and pre-adolescent years, reasons for leaving school may have more to do with a lack of social integration than with scholastic shortcomings.

Fixing the System

Native children's lack of success in the school systems made it clear that reforms were necessary. The most recent reforms in Indian education are a product of the self-determination movement in the 1970s. Congress, acting upon the advice of Native educators and parents, enacted several pieces of legislation directed at the improvement of Indian education.

Tribal Truths

Tired of the urban public schools' failure to address the growing urban Native population's needs, Native peoples opened alternative schools. Red School House in St. Paul, Minnesota, and Heart of the Earth Survival School in Minneapolis, Minnesota, stressed Native culture, history, and language.

Two of the more effective bills were the Indian Education Act of 1972 and the Indian Self-Determination and Education Assistance Act of 1975, which allowed tribes to contract for the administration of services (including schools) previously provided by the Bureau of Indian Affairs (see Chapter 19). Other legislation allowed for local control of school boards in BIA schools. This legislation provided Native peoples with the means to create school environments and curricula that respond to local needs.

The heart of the reform movement of the 1970s was greater control over educational programs at the local level. Among the earliest tribal schools was Rough Rock Demonstration School (Arizona) and Ramah High School (New Mexico), both on the Navajo reservation. The Ramah School was the first tribally controlled high school since the Cherokee and Choctaw schools had closed in the early 1900s.

Speaking Two Tongues: Bilingual Education

Part of the reforms in Indian education included the integration of Native languages and culture into the curriculum. Prior to the 1970s, the philosophy of educating Native children focused on providing a vehicle for Native peoples to assimilate into mainstream society. Native language use and cultural study was not viewed as consistent with that goal. But since the 1970s, the importance of Native language retention has been recognized as an integral part of education. Across the United States, nearly 100 bilingual programs are operating in schools that have a considerable number of Native children. Some programs are language retention programs designed to teach the Native language to nonspeakers.

Tribal Truths

The number of fluent speakers of some languages is in steady decline, and bilingual programs are viewed as one way to halt the decline.

In other communities, where people still speak Native languages, bilingual programs in the schools help Native speaking children learn English. Proponents believe that, when properly done, bilingual education is superior to English-only programs of instruction. Admittedly, some people—both Indian and non-Indian—don't believe that public school is an appropriate venue for native language instruction. They argue that children's parents should teach them their Native language and culture.

Supporters of bilingual education in public schools won a victory when President George H. W. Bush signed the Native American Language Act in 1990. It declares that it is the policy of the United States to "preserve, protect, and promote the rights and freedom of Native Americans to use, practice, and develop Native American languages." The act encourages the use of Native languages in schools where there are large enrollments of Native children.

American Indian Higher Education

In 1935, Bureau of Indian Affairs commissioner John Collier reported that only 515 Indian students were attending colleges and universities. There were few programs for Native students, except the several education programs for Indians and non-Indians who might teach on or near an Indian reservation. There were, at the time, three BIA-run technical institutes: Haskell Institute in Kansas, Chilocco Indian School in Oklahoma, and the Institute of American Indian Arts in New Mexico. In 1963, Haskell Institute developed a college preparatory program, and two years later, Haskell became a federally sponsored junior college.

Code Talking

BIA scholarships provide supplemental financial assistance to eligible American Indian/ Alaska Native scholars entering college seeking a baccalaureate degree. It is awarded to applicants recognized by the secretary of the interior as a member of a tribe who has at least one fourth degree Indian blood. Recipients must be admitted for enrollment to an accredited institution and demonstrate financial need.

Although the Indian Reorganization Act of 1934 recognized the need for qualified Indians to receive technical and university education, no programmatic responses followed. In 1961, only 626 Indian students received BIA support to further their education in colleges and universities. By 1964, the number of students receiving *BIA scholarships* increased to 1,327 students. Even though more students were attending college, the impact was not very dramatic. In 1968, only 181 American Indians earned college degrees.

Opening the Pipeline

The social unrest of the late 1960s and early 1970s brought attention to the dismal conditions in ghettos, barrios, and Indian reservations. For Native peoples, this was an era during which great strides were made in self-government. The Indian Self-Determination and Educational Assistance Act of 1975 gave tribes a greater voice in administering their own services, including educational programs. Tribal leaders recognized that they needed business managers, doctors, nurses, lawyers, engineers, teachers, and other professions if their tribes were going to achieve true self-government. As a result of more BIA and tribal funding for education, a huge increase in the number of Natives of college age, and changes in bureau policies, college enrollments of Native students increased by nearly 500 percent in the 1970s.

As Native students landed on American college campuses, they were influenced by other ethnic minorities who demanded more relevant curriculum and more people of color among the student body and faculty. Responding to those demands, colleges and universities established ethnic studies programs and strove to create a more diverse university community.

Native American Studies Programs

Native students demanded that colleges recognize their value by creating Native American Studies (NAS) programs. Like the Black Studies programs, Native American Studies (also called Indian Studies or American Indian Studies) wanted academia to recognize their histories and cultures as worthy of study.

Indian leaders hoped that Native American Studies programs would provide Native scholars with access to the university community, where they would train young Indian students who might ultimately return to the reservation. Indian activists believed that NAS programs would also counter the Euro-American or mainstream teachings of manifest destiny and white stereotypes of Native culture and history.

Tribal Truths

Many Native students want an education that they can bring back to the reservations to help their people. Many do so at great sacrifice, with the knowledge that they could make more money and get more prestige working elsewhere.

Many Native American Studies programs offer courses in history and culture. Other programs focus on providing support services for students, such as counseling, academic advising, and financial aid. No matter what their focus, all Native American Studies programs strive to promote strong relationships between the academic community and Native peoples. NAS is committed to the preservation and survival of Native American peoples and cultures.

The emergence of Native American Studies programs corresponds with the increase in Native enrollment in colleges and universities. By 1976, Indian student enrollment increased to 76,000. By 1982, that enrollment increased to 87,700 students.

Today, more Indians than ever are attending colleges or universities. In 1988 and 1989, 3,954 Indians received Bachelor's degrees, 1,086 earned Master's degrees, and 85 were awarded Doctoral degrees. This is a remarkable change from the 181 Indian college graduates in 1966. However, even if these numbers were doubled, it would not represent parity with other groups.

Tribal Colleges

Currently, 36 percent of all students enrolled in institutions of higher education are attending two-year junior or community colleges. For Native students, 60 percent of all students in higher education attend two-year programs. This is a significant trend, suggesting that the two-year college is addressing a substantial need in the Native

Tribal Truths

Although tribal colleges are, in the main, located on reservations and controlled by the tribe, non-Indian students are welcomed and make up a sizeable enrollment at some schools.

Code Talking

The **American Indian Higher Education Consortium (AIHEC)** was founded in 1992 to provide support and leadership to the tribal college movement.

community. The most important feature of this movement is the development of tribally controlled community colleges.

In 1968, the Navajo tribe created the first tribally controlled community college in the United States. Those first tribal colleges provided vocational training in carpentry, plumbing, and other trades. As they developed, they added college preparation, and now nearly all tribal colleges are accredited by the same agencies that govern public and private colleges. Others followed the Navajo's lead, until now there are 33 tribal colleges and universities in the *American Indian Higher Education Consortium (AIHEC)*.

Tribal colleges and universities are located in 12 states, mainly in the West and one Canadian province. While most are found on American Indian reservations, a few, like D-Q University and Haskell Indian Nations University attract students from around the country.

Tribally Controlled Community Colleges in North America

Tribal College	State or Province
Bay Mills Community College	MI
Blackfeet Community College	MT
Cankdiska Ciolana Community College	ND
College of Menominee Nation	WI
Crownpoint Institute of Technology	NM
D-Q University	CA
Diné College	AZ
Chief Dull Knife College	MT
Fond du Lac Tribal and Community College	MN
Fort Belknap Community College	MT
Fort Berthold Community College	ND
Fort Peck Community College	MT
Haskell Indian Nations University	KS
Institute of American Indian Arts	NM

Tribal College	State or Province
Keweenaw Bay Ojibwa Community College	MI
Lac Courte Oreilles Ojibwa Community College	WI
Leech Lake Tribal College	MI
Little Big Horn College	MT
Little Priest Tribal College	NE
Nebraska Indian Community College	NE
Northwest Indian College	WA
Oglala Lakota Community College	SD
Red Crow Community College	Alberta
Salish Kootenai College	MT
Sinte Gleska University	SD
Sisseton Wahpeton Community College	SD
Si Takna College	SD
Sitting Bull University	ND
Southwestern Indian Polytechnic Institute	NM
Stone Child Community College	MT
Turtle Mountain Community College	ND
United Tribes Technical College	ND
White Earth Tribal and Community College	MN

Native Voices

It was the busiest time of my life. We helped each other write reports, grants, curriculum, and a new catalog. I remember being there before 8 A.M. and staying until 6 P.M. I drove home, made a sandwich, and was back by 7:30 P.M. I would work until 10 or 11 P.M. and I was never alone. The hard work was okay; we felt that we were accomplishing something.

—Tribal College Administrator, on the struggle to establish a new tribal college

Supporting the Tribal College Movement

Tribal colleges are seriously underfunded, and their existence is often in jeopardy. They were greatly helped when, in 1978, Congress passed the Tribally Controlled

Community College Act, providing limited federal support for tribes wishing to start tribal colleges. Then, in 1994, tribal colleges gained land-grant status under the *Morrill Act*, giving them more access to federal funding.

A New Paradigm for Higher Education

The tribal colleges vary with each community they serve. Some are well established and financially secure. Some have well-manicured campuses with buildings built by the students in the trades programs, while at some tribal colleges classes are held in church basements and community centers. The one thing that the tribal colleges share is the mission of providing higher education in the reservation community to address local needs and desires. They are accountable to their community, the formally educated leadership, as well as to the elders who are the caretakers of the traditional knowledge.

Code Talking

The **Morrill Act** was signed by President Abraham Lincoln, which provided public land to several states to establish and support colleges whose curricula would include agriculture.

Toward the Future

Today, more Native peoples are attending elementary, secondary, and institutions of higher education than ever before. Their success depends on the ability of those educational institutions to respond to their needs. If traditional educational efforts fail to succeed, tribes and Native organizations will need to seek alternative programs and schools. Above all, Native peoples need to take control of their own education.

The Least You Need to Know

- ◆ Education is not an invention of the white person: Native peoples had informal educational systems that enabled them to survive and prosper before the arrival of Europeans.

- ◆ The first formal educational institutions for Native peoples were supported by religious organizations.

- ◆ The Cherokee, among others, founded schools that consisted of mainstream curriculum.

- ◆ The government is obligated to provide education to Native Americans in 120 treaties.

◆ Indian children have higher dropout rates and lower achievement scores than non-Indian students.

◆ The establishment of Native American Studies programs at colleges and universities contributed to the increase in the number of Native students in higher education.

◆ The tribally controlled community college movement is the most significant development in Native higher education in the last 30 years.

Chapter 22

Bitter Medicine: Indian Health and Well-Being

In This Chapter

- ◆ Native beliefs about illness and health
- ◆ Traditional cures for sickness
- ◆ Native contributions to modern medicine
- ◆ Major health challenges for Native peoples

Our ancestors realized that in order to survive, one has to be healthy. A culture must likewise be in good health to survive and thrive. If the people themselves are not in good health, then how can they expect their culture to be healthy?

Before tackling the health issues facing Indians and their community today, we'll take a look at how Native Americans have traditionally treated illnesses.

Traditional Perspectives on Health

Various cultures have different explanations for illness. And while some illnesses are just accepted, like toothaches and colds, some were attributed to spiritual or religious causes (and therefore spiritual or religious cures).

> **Native Voices** _____
>
> Why must people be ill and suffer pain? We are all afraid of illness. Here is this old sister of mine; as far as anyone can see, she has done no evil; she has lived through a long life and given birth to healthy children, and now must suffer before her days end. Why? Why?
>
> —Aua, Inuit

Navajo Wellness and Being

Some cultures see illness as a state of being rather than as something with an organic source. For example, as noted in Chapter 4, the Diné (Navajo) believe that one should live in accordance with all things in one's environment. This state of being is referred to as *hozho*. This Navajo term is complex and lacks an easy translation. Essentially, hozho is a state of being marked by living in balance and harmony with all things around you. Navajo refer to "walking in beauty" to describe thinking, acting, and living in hozho.

Dualism and Antagonism

In mainstream Western society, duality tends to dominate ideas—good vs. evil, emotion vs. reason, body vs. spirit. One tries to resolve these apparent conflicts by choosing one over the other. The Navajo view these as complementary. When one exists without the other, it is incomplete. Good and evil do not exclude one another. Each needs the other. The Navajo idea of balance is to embrace both rather than choosing one and banishing the other.

> **Native Voices** _____
>
> Rather than trying to control nature, one should try to achieve balance with it. White people deal with flooding on a river by building a dam, while a Navajo would simply move to higher ground.
>
> —Navajo adage

Navajos don't view dualism as antagonistic. That is, good doesn't battle evil; each just "is." They are found in each person's character and in their view of the everyday world. People are a mixture of good and evil, and one seeks to find a balance between the two. Certainly, a Navajo will seek to avoid evil, but would not conceive of a world absent of it.

Navajos see the central focus of living as balance and harmony among the natural, the human, and the supernatural. Rather than seek to control these elements, the Navajo seek to establish harmony and balance in their lives.

In keeping with this perspective, Navajo medicine is directed at the whole person—what some might call mind, body, and spirit. Whereas Western concepts of medicine typically separate mind and body, treating one but not the other (and, in fact, Western medicine tends to compartmentalize the body through medical specialization), Navajo medicine treats the whole package.

Illness and Ceremonials

Because wellness is living in harmony and balance, when someone is ill, he or she is out of balance. The Navajo acknowledge that living in harmony is difficult, as there is chaos all around us. Consequently, it's not unusual for people to get out of harmony and become ill, usually as a result of their own actions, whether intentional or not.

According to the Navajo tradition, to determine the cause of sickness, one must go to a diagnostician. These are men and women who have a gift for "seeing" the cause of illness. Two such types of Navajo diagnosticians are hand tremblers and crystal gazers who, through prayer, concentration, and the use of pollen, pinpoint the cause of illness. Once a diagnostician identifies the cause of the illness, he or she directs the patient to a medicine person to perform the proper ceremony of healing.

Ancient Tales

Navajo ceremonial life centers on curing. The origin myths of curing ceremonies follow a general pattern. They are accounts of an individual (Navajo, of course) who has become separated from his people and cured of some specific ailment by the gods. The individual returns to his people and teaches them the proper ceremony of healing. The myths are filled with ceremonial details and serve as guidelines for the conduct of the ceremony.

Songs of Prayer and Power

Among the Navajo, there are more than 50 different healing ceremonies. They are called *sings*, *chants*, or *ways*. The ceremony is presided over by a "singer" who might also be called a medicine man. This person will conduct a ceremony—usually lasting between two and nine days—that restores the patient back to hozho and wellness.

Code Talking

The terms **sings**, **chants**, and **ways** are synonymous with "ceremony," healing rites among the Navajo. Each ceremony is associated with an element or elements of the creation story.

The sings have specific curative properties. For example, the Bead Chant cures skin disease caused by thunder, lightning, or snakes, the Night Chant cures nervous disorders, and the Evil Way cure *ghost sickness*. The Blessing Way chant is precautionary, rather than curative. It ensures health, prosperity, and general well-being.

> ### Code Talking
>
> **Ghost sickness** is caused when a person has come into contact with the spirit of the dead. When a person dies, his or her spirit, if not allowed to go freely, can cause illness and harm to people nearby. So, when someone is near death, the person is moved outside in order not to trap the spirit within the home. If a person enters a home where someone died, he or she can be inflicted with ghost sickness.

The Place Where Gods Come and Go

The healer or "singer" conducts the sing on behalf of the patient. During the course of the ceremony, he may use songs, prayers, dances, lectures, herbs, and sweat baths to treat his patient. He will also paint a design on the floor using colored sand. These designs are called sandpaintings in English, although the Navajo term for them translates to mean "the place where gods come and go."

Sandpaintings illustrate aspects of the Navajo creation story. More than 500 different paintings correspond to specific ceremonies and phases within a ceremony. No matter what painting is used, it represents perfection and is thought to be the portal for the gods when they journey to heal. The patient is placed on the sandpainting to absorb the healing power from the gods and restore the patient's hozho. When the ceremony is over, the sand is gathered up, taken outside, and scattered in the wind.

Healing in Other Traditions

Beliefs about the causes of illness differ from one Native culture to the next. In some cultures, illness is thought to be the result of some action taken by the patient or contact with something or someone that is harmful, while in others, illness is thought to be caused by supernatural beings as a punishment for wrongdoings. In some societies, witches or sorcerers are believed to be responsible for illness.

No matter the cause, Native cultures all believe that proper diagnosis of an ailment is critical to establishing a course of treatment. After a diagnosis is made, the healer can perform the proper ceremonies to eliminate the underlying cause of sickness.

Although traditional cultures often had effective cures, sometimes patients didn't survive or improve. In such instances, Natives believed that the healer was too weak to counter the supernatural agents of the illness.

Native peoples have used traditional medicines to cure all sorts of ailments for centuries. These medicines consist of herbs and plants that are available where they live. The following table gives a short list of plants used as medicine by tribes in the Pacific Northwest.

> **Tribal Truths**
>
> When my father was diagnosed with throat cancer, a Flathead healer, an herbalist, mixed up a centuries-old infusion for my father that included winterberries. His cancer went away. My father, a practical person, also had radiation therapy. Which cured him, traditional medicine or modern science? To my father, it really doesn't matter.

Selected Indian Medicines

Plant	Symptom
Black spruce	Cough
Wild rhubarb	Arthritis
Tamarack bark	Stomach trouble
Spruce needles	Eye infection
Lichen	Ulcers
Sage	Colds
Bear root	Diarrhea
Willow Leaves	Bee stings

Bad Karma?

The Inuit (Eskimo) thought that illness was sometimes the result of actions that offended the supernatural beings. If a man failed to follow proscribed hunting rituals and, therefore, offended the spirits of the game, he might get sick as a result. Particularly ill-tempered or offensive people also might become ill because of their attitudes. When a person became sick, the Inuit healer questioned the patient, asking him or her to try to recall any offensive behaviors. If the patient remembered what he or she might have done to cause the illness, the healer could treat it.

Lost and Found

Several Native theories of disease are based on a belief that illness is the result of soul loss. According to the Inuit, the soul normally leaves the body in sleep and returns before the person awakes. If the soul doesn't return, has been lost or stolen, a person can become ill and eventually die. The cure for soul loss is to retrieve the soul. During a ceremony, the task of the healer is to enter the dream realm to recover the soul and return it to its rightful owner.

Get Out!

Illness also can be caused by the intrusion of a foreign object, particle, or substance into the human body that must be found and removed. The Navajo, for example, believe that witches cause illness by blowing a foreign object into the body. In those cases, the alien article can be removed by psychic surgery (magically reaching into the body and extracting it) or by sucking the object out with a tube, usually made from a bone.

Native beliefs in supernatural causes and treatments of illness have a common theme. Faced with the unfortunate universal truth that all people get sick and die, people appealed to the supernatural as a way of dealing with what they could not control. Curing ceremonies provide a vehicle for humans to try to understand and influence the supernatural.

> **Native Voices**
>
> I have made your sacrifice.
> I have prepared a smoke for you.
> My feet restore for me.
> My legs restore for me.
> My body restore for me.
> My mind restore for me ....
> —Navajo healing prayer

> **Tribal Truths**
>
> Many uninformed people resent what they believe is free medicinal care given to Native peoples. They may not realize that many treaties provided medical care as a part of negotiated land cessions. Thus, the doctors and clinics were "bought and paid for" when tribes gave up millions of acres of tribal land.

Modern and Traditional Ways

The initial introduction to European styles of medicine to most Indian tribes came from traders, missionaries, and (later) army physicians. The missionaries hoped to convert the Natives to Christianity, saving the soul and the body. When the Army was in charge of the Indian agencies, they brought Army doctors to dispense drugs and care for the sick. By providing health care to reservation Indians, the agents hoped to reduce faith that Indians had in traditional healers and traditional medicine. Discrediting traditional medicine people was one method of promoting assimilation. Physicians and hospitals soon became a familiar sight in Indian communities and modern health care became increasingly available.

Small pox, measles, and cholera killed hundreds of thousands of Native peoples before they built up immunity to them or before contemporary medicines were introduced to cure or prevent many diseases. During the nineteenth century, a number of physicians were employed to treat Native children at boarding schools. A part of the treatments were inoculations against communicable diseases such as smallpox. As a result of these innoculations, diseases that once ravaged Indian communities were, in the main, brought under control.

Cure Worse Than the Disease?

Many Native peoples were initially suspicious of Western medicine. It was difficult for the Natives to accept the concept that microorganisms and germs, which cannot be seen by the naked eye, could cause death. Traditional societies that regarded illness as curable only through the combined energies of the family, clan, or tribe could not understand why patients suffering from tuberculosis, for example, had to be isolated and taken far away to sanitariums, sometimes never to return. For Navajo people, hospitals were places where people went to die and therefore were thought to be inhabited by malevolent spirits.

The differences in how medicine is perceived was a major barrier to Indian acceptance of modern medical treatments. For some cultures, the modern treatments are the opposite of those in traditional societies. For example, among the Navajo, there are supernatural and natural causes for illness and treatment must address both (see the following table for other difference). If a patient feels that a health-care provider doesn't acknowledge the spiritual nature of illness, the patient may not seek help from white medicine. Because of these differences in perceptions, the Indian Health Service on the Navajo reservation employs Navajo "medicine men" who consult with Western trained physicians.

Traditional Medicine vs. Modern Medicine

Indian Medicine	Modern Medicine
Wellness-oriented	Illness-oriented
Patient treated in family or community setting	Patient treated alone and isolated from family
Focuses on "why" illness occurred	Focuses on "how" illness occurred

continues

Traditional Medicine vs. Modern Medicine   (continued)

Indian Medicine	Modern Medicine
Includes natural and supernatural causes	Emphasizes natural causes
Expects multiple causalities	Usually links illness to single cause
Treatment primarily holistic	Treatment primarily physiological
Treatment personal and reciprocally oriented	Treatment impersonal and complaint-oriented

Put This in Your Black Bag

Just as Natives slowly accepted the "white men's" medicine, white people have adopted many of the Indians traditional remedies. These medicines, of course, are not new. Because of the value of traditional remedies among tribal people of the Americas, many herbal medicines have been integrated into modern medicine. Historian Virgil Vogel identified at least 170 botanical drugs in contemporary pharmacology that had been originally discovered and used by Native peoples. Some of the better known drugs include digitalis, quinine, belladonna, cocaine from coca leaves, curare, and ipecac.

The cure for cancer, AIDS, and other modern disorders may be found in traditional treatments in the jungles of South America or in the Canadian woods. Western researchers are now seriously exploring ethno-pharmacology, and questioning indigenous healers about plants and herbs used to cure disease.

Stick Out Your Tongue: Taking the Community's Temperature

The history of the relationship between Native tribes and the federal government is unique. Initially, the government provided health care to Native peoples to halt the spread of epidemics, which were caused by contact between Euro-Americans and Natives. Later, the government agreed to provide health care in exchange for tribal land. Today, the government continues to fulfil its treaty obligation to provide health care for Native peoples. Now, more than half of all Native Americans receive health care from the federal Indian Health Service, a division of the Public Health Service.

Before the non-Indians came to this continent, Native peoples were relatively healthy. While tribes had to contend with shortages of food when droughts came or when game could not be found, people didn't have the option of choosing a bad diet. They ate foods that were naturally healthy. Furthermore, tribes in the Americas didn't have European disease to deal with and, while not disease free, they could usually treat the diseases that they confronted using their traditional remedies.

After tribes were placed on reservations, their health rapidly deteriorated. Confinement on reservations contributed to the continued spread of small pox and other deadly diseases. With little or no game, the federal government supplemented their diet with rations that usually included flour, sugar, and lard. These foods, often high in fat and sugar, were unlike the traditional diets that included lean meat, fruits, and vegetables. Researchers contend that Indians' change in diet has had a significant negative impact on Native Americans' health today.

Some Very Sick Indians

Health concerns today among the Native peoples of the United States have reached a critical stage. The Indian Health Service reports the following frightening facts about Indian health:

- Indian deaths due to alcoholism are more than four times greater than that reported for the general population, and deaths from accidents are more than double.

- Natives suffer from tuberculosis four times greater than for all races.

- The homicide rate is 57 percent higher than for all races.

- The rate of suicide among Natives is 27 percent greater than the general population.

- Death from diabetes is one and a half times greater than in the general population.

- The five-year survival rate for all cancers for American Indians is the worst for all ethnic groups.

The factors for these horrific statistics are many and complex. Today, American Indians are among the poorest, least educated, and most neglected populations in the United States. Poverty, social problems, and disease are unparalleled among major minority groups.

Diagnosing the Problem

A variety of factors contribute to the sorry state of Native American health, including behavior (like reckless driving, drinking, or poor eating habits), environment (poor housing, sanitation, and poverty), and availability and quality of health services. Making matters worse, Indian people tend not to seek treatment for treatable illnesses like influenza, upper respiratory infections, and otitis media (ear infection) until those ailments become serious. Obesity, diabetes, high blood pressure, and pneumonia— all afflictions that affect Native Americans in great numbers—are highly treatable or controllable through education, yet Indian people are slow to seek treatment or education.

And while other serious problems like accidents, violence, suicide, and behavior problems are more difficult to treat because their causes are complex and often unknown, research indicates alcoholism is an important contributing factor. Heavy drinking is the cause for fetal alcohol syndrome (FAS) and is a major factor in suicide, homicide, and behavior-related disorders.

Diabetes and the American Indian

Native Americans are at a higher risk of developing diabetes than non-Native people. Prevalence of type-II (adult-onset) diabetes among Native Americans in the United States is 12.2 percent of those over the age of 19. Diabetes is a disease of the body's metabolism—how it processes food. When someone has diabetes, his or her body does not control blood glucose (sugar) levels and doesn't use glucose properly. People get diabetes when they have insufficient amounts of insulin in the blood or respond poorly to it.

Medical researchers have proposed a number of theories relating to weight, genetics, and diet to explain why Native Americans are more susceptible than the general population to diabetes:

Tribal Truths

One tribe in Arizona, the Pima, has the highest rate of diabetes in the world! About 50 percent of the adults between ages 30 and 64 have diabetes.

◆ **Weight:** One of the causes of diabetes is being overweight. Thirty-seven percent of all Native Americans are overweight and 15 percent are obese.

◆ **Genetics:** Some researchers believe that Native Americans carry a gene they call the *thrifty gene*, so-called because they believe a gene was in place to help the ancestors of Native peoples live through famine and the long hard winters by storing fat in certain cells. Some research indicates that the thrifty gene, in recent generations, has increased the possibilities for Native Americans becoming diabetic. The thrifty gene is no longer a helpful gene to Native Americans.

◆ **Diet:** Native Americans have been introduced to new foods that were not part of their diet from long ago. Fast food and other preservatives have been added to their diet.

Code Talking

The **thrifty gene** is thought to enable Native peoples to store fat in their bodies to be used during times of famine. Famine no longer threatens Native peoples but the gene may now contribute to a greater risk of diabetes.

Other lifestyle factors may also contribute to the prevalence of diabetes among Native Americans. They no longer hunt or grow crops for food, for example, and they probably exercise less, thereby contributing to excessive fat being stored in the cells.

So what is the answer? Studies with Native Hawaiians and other Native groups have demonstrated that if Native peoples return to former food habits, their problems with obesity, diabetes, high blood pressure, and heart disease decrease. Native people, like all people, have to increase exercise, limit sugar intake, and eat healthier. As with many health-related ailments, education is the key to controlling diabetes.

Nobody Loves a Drunken Indian

There is no doubt that alcoholism is a major health concern among Native Americans. As noted previously, Native peoples suffer alcoholism at a rate four times that of the general population.

Research explaining the prevalence of alcoholism among Native peoples is inconclusive but suggests a number of possible origins. Some suggest that it is a behavioral problem, a learned (or rather mislearned) behavior. Scholars point out that Native peoples learned to drink alcohol from those who were abusers—fur traders, trappers, and soldiers. Indians learned to binge drink, encouraged by fur traders who gave the Natives alcohol to facilitate the trade relationship.

Tribal Truths

While alcoholism rates are high among Native Americans, an Indian Health Service study also found that more Natives *do not drink at all* compared to the general population.

Other scholars hypothesize that there may be a genetic link to Native alcoholism. Because of the relatively recent introduction of alcohol to Native populations, they have not been able to make genetic adjustments to this poison. The body may lack the ability to accommodate the presence of alcohol in the system and so it causes greater negative reactions. At least one study has suggested that pregnant Native women may lack the ability to synthesize alcohol so that it affects the fetus, causing birth defects, specifically fetal alcohol syndrome.

Regardless of cause, alcohol is a destructive presence in Native lives. Studies have concluded that alcohol use and abuse are major contributing factors in the commission of crimes, auto accidents and deaths, spousal and child abuse, and suicide. No one knows, truly, why Native Americans are more susceptible than others. The only sure way of avoiding the ravages of alcohol is to abstain from drinking and live healthy lives.

What the Future Holds

The medical system serving Native Americans can help reverse the destructive trends by becoming more culturally aware of the people it serves and addressing preventive measures that reflect the community as well as the individual. Although Native communities have access to some of the best medical facilities and personnel in the United States, improvements can certainly be made. For example, health-care workers can become more culturally aware of the people they serve and employ preventive measures that reflect the community as well as the individual.

Yet, the major challenge to Native health is not the medical system or even Native access to health care. The biggest challenge is within the community. How does a community change its lifestyle to address the medical conditions of its people? Alcoholism, stress, unemployment, and poor eating habits are difficult circumstances to address.

The answer has to come from the community itself. A combination of culturally sensitive, community-wide efforts is needed to give the control over the health of both individuals and the community back to the community.

The Least You Need to Know

- Native peoples generally believed that illness had supernatural origins.
- Traditional Native healing ceremonies give power to individuals for healing disease.
- The federal government began to provide health-care services to Native peoples as a part of treaty obligations.

- The Indian Health Service, a division of the Public Health Service, provides health care for many Native Americans.

- Native peoples have higher alcoholism and diabetes rates than any other population in the United States.

- Living a healthy life, eating right, and abstaining from alcohol are the keys to the survival of Native peoples.

Chapter 23

Gambling on the Future: Tribal Economies

In This Chapter

- ◆ Battling poverty on and off reservations
- ◆ Challenges for mineral-rich tribes
- ◆ Gaming as an economic savior
- ◆ Reservations move "offshore"

The key to the survival of American Indian reservations in the future is going to depend on whether they can establish viable economic substructures to provide services and employment for their residents. Because not all reservations are alike, owing to differences in locale, resources, and tribal values, there is no single template for economic success.

The Bottom Rung of the Economic Ladder

According to the 2000 U.S. Bureau of Census data, there are 2.4 million American Indians and Alaska Natives. And they are at the bottom, or nearly so, on every measure of economic prosperity. American Indians and

Alaska Natives had a median household income of $30,784, based on a three-year average (1997–1999). This is lower than for non-Hispanic Whites ($43,287) and Asians and Pacific Islanders ($48,614), and about the same as Hispanics. Based on a three-year average (1997–1999), the poverty rate for American Indians and Alaska Natives was 25.9 percent. This is higher than the poverty rates for non-Hispanic Whites (8.2 percent) and Asians and Pacific Islanders and approximately equal to the poverty level of Hispanics.

This profile represents all American Indians and Alaska Natives. However, because the greatest pockets of poverty and economic depression exist on reservations, the profile of this subgroup is even more shocking. The 1990 census counted approximately 440,000 American Indians living on reservations and trust land. This represented about 22 percent of all American Indians. Even though over 70 percent of all American Indians do not live on a reservation, approximately 33 percent maintain some contact, living on or near the reservation.

Reservation Blues

In 1989, 31 percent of American Indians were living below the poverty level (the 2000 census data is not yet available, but these statistics should not have radically changed). Compare this to the national poverty level, which was about 13 percent. Twenty percent of the reservation population lacked complete plumbing facilities!

Tribal Truths

On the Rosebud Sioux Indian Reservation in South Dakota, the unemployment rate is more than 80 percent and the annual per capita income is about $4,000.

Nationally, 38 percent of American Indians were unemployed. On some reservations, half the Native population was not employed.

These are bleak statistics, ones that any government would be, and should be, ashamed of. Yet for tribal governments, poverty, unemployment, and inadequate living conditions are the norm, not the exception. The challenge for every tribal government is finding ways to end this cycle of poverty and develop programs that will stimulate the reservation economy.

Third World Countries in America

Many reservations have tried to address the economic and social problems that have plagued their communities. Federal assistance seemingly hasn't accomplished as much as was hoped, and tribal efforts are long on promises and short on accomplishment. Why is it that, decade after decade, reservation economies fail to improve conditions for Indians? After all, with such high unemployment rates, there is an available labor force on most reservations. One of the barriers, however, is that low educational attainment and high dropout rates mean that the available labor pool lacks the necessary qualifications for many better-paying jobs, even if they were available.

Past attempts to find solutions to the chronic unemployment on reservations have had limited success. Reservations are historically isolated communities, far from modern conveniences and transportation hubs. In the 1970s and 1980s, tribes actively pursued industrial development by establishing their own manufacturing companies or attempting to attract companies to relocate to reservations.

The major barrier faced by tribes seemed to be cultural in nature. Outsiders viewed absenteeism and chronic tardiness as measures of a poor work ethic when perhaps tribal members were ill-prepared to conform to time schedules not recognized by their particular worldview. Managers who were tribal members found it difficult to reprimand or fire relatives and friends. As a result, many attempts to establish programs to address the social and economic ills of the reservation communities largely failed.

Tribal Truths

A & S Industries on the Fort Peck Indian Reservation in southeastern Montana solved the problems related to tribal members managing their own people by contracting with an outside management company for the administration of their tribal enterprise.

Paper Millionaires

Today, American Indian land constitutes less than 3 percent of the total area of the United States. Most of the reservations in the West are on lands that are ill-suited for agriculture, and most reservations are rural and isolated. Yet, that land may hide as much as 25 percent of the United States' mineral wealth.

It is estimated that as much as 10 percent of the United States's oil and gas reserves lies under Indian land. Reservation land may contain as much as 33 percent of all the low-sulfur, strippable coal. One half of this nation's privately owned uranium resources are to be found in Indian country (this amounts to approximately 11 percent of the world's known uranium reserves!). In addition to these resources, tungsten, bentonite, copper, and phosphate exist in unknown, but probably significant, quantities.

The abundance of mineral wealth on Indian lands is incalculable, and there is no doubt that tribes are literally sitting on a fortune. So the big question is, why aren't tribes actively exploiting this potential?

Historically, industry and government have conspired to exploit Native peoples' natural resources. In some cases, the Bureau of Indian Affairs, who served as trustee of those resources, negotiated horribly unfair deals with oil and coal companies. In the 1960s, the BIA negotiated fixed-rate contracts for the extraction of coal on the Navajo reservation, but by the end of the 1970s, the price of coal increased by more than 400 percent without the tribe benefiting by one cent. Leases were historically negotiated at less than market rates without regard to quality or quantity.

In the 1970s, tribes began to assert more control over their resources by overturning the bad deals made by the bureau and by making better deals on their own. In 1974, the Northern Cheyenne of Montana succeeded in having their unfair coal leases cancelled. Secretary of the Interior Rogers Morton agreed to cancel the leases because the BIA had not negotiated favorable or responsible terms for the tribe. New guidelines requiring all leases to be approved by both the tribe and the energy companies were developed. Timing played an important role in tribes gaining control of their own economic futures. The embargo of foreign oil in 1973 (with the associated domestic shortages and long lines at the gas stations) left oil-rich tribes holding the upper hand in price negotiations.

OPEC by Any Other Name?

To the distress of American oil firms, 23 tribes formed the Council of Energy Resource Tribes (CERT) in 1975. Their interest was to better prepare tribes for the renewed onslaught on Indian lands. CERT hired geologists and engineers to help tribes manage their energy resources. The public became concerned because it feared that tribes would become an Indian version of OPEC, the Middle Eastern cartel that sets oil prices and production outputs. It didn't settle non-Indian concerns when CERT hired a former oil minister from Saudi Arabia as a consultant! Nevertheless, with the help of CERT and their specialists, member tribes were able to negotiate better contracts, improving their position as resource managers.

So Why Ain't I Rich?

The impression that some might get, given how many resources they own, is that all Native Americans should be millionaires! Not all reservations have coal, oil, gas, or uranium under their lands. Just 13 reservations were involved in oil and gas development in 1983. Ten coal mines on the Crow Reservation of Montana and the Navajo and Hopi reservations in the American Southwest accounted for approximately 3.5 percent of the total U.S. coal production in 1983. So not all reservations are equally blessed.

Of course, some reservations do have vast mineral deposits under their lands. The Northern Cheyenne reservation in southeastern Montana is sitting on an estimated 5 billion tons of coal. The tribe has, to date, resisted any attempt by coal companies to mine the coal, even though the royalties they might receive would mean the tribe could be rich.

For the Cheyenne, the decision not to mine their coal is based not on economic factors but on cultural beliefs. The Cheyenne believe that the earth is their Mother and, therefore, sacred. One does not rip off the skin of Mother to dig up what is below. For them, there is no choice to be made. There will be no open pit strip mines on their reservation.

The Crow, with whom the Cheyenne share a contiguous boundary, have no such qualms. They have several very successful coal mines on their reservation that generate income for the tribe and create employment opportunities for its members.

> **Tribal Truths**
>
> Income from mining can help tribes develop the infrastructure of their reservations, raise the educational levels of their members through training programs, and reduce the high rates of unemployment so endemic on Indian reservations. Wages in the mining industries tend to be higher than average, and tribes can negotiate employment quotas as a part of the cost of doing business on the reservation.

The Downside of Mining

Besides potential conflicts with cultural beliefs, there are other disadvantages to opening up one's land to mining. Full-scale mining means an influx of non-Indians on the reservation, with associated demands on social services, housing, medical care, and schools. As evident from the oil patches of North Dakota and Wyoming, criminal activity, alcoholism, and suicide seem to follow the mining industry. Tribal law and order and social services departments may not be able to address such issues without appropriate planning and resources.

As trustee of reservation land, the BIA has the responsibility to protect Native lands and resources. The bureau has historically been ill-equipped to deal with such issues as environmental impacts and mining contracts, leaving Native peoples open to further exploitation.

Still, the risks for some tribes may be worth the troubles. In 1976, Navajo royalties and mineral leases yielded nearly $13 million of revenue. This is, surely, not the expectation for every tribe, but the potential is there for some. Whatever the case, tribes seem content to sit on their respective minerals until such time when (or if) they are ready to take advantage of them.

Gaming: The New Buffalo

Gaming has always been a part of American Indian culture and economics. People played games of chance and skill, made bets on the outcome of horse and foot races, and generally enjoyed any opportunity to wager as a part of both secular and religious ceremony. Today, gaming has become a part of the economic development for many tribes. It is often the only viable source of employment and governmental revenues available to tribes. It has replaced the buffalo as the staff of life for survival. The proceeds of gaming operations are used for subsistence, cultural preservation, and to improve local economics.

Bingo!

Large-scale Native gaming began in the early 1980s when several tribes began to offer bingo games with prizes larger than were allowed under state law. When the states threatened to shut down the bingo halls on the reservations, the tribes sued in federal court for the right to conduct gaming on their own lands. The courts ruled on two cases, *Seminole Tribe* v. *Butterwork* (1979) and *California* v. *Cabazon Band* (1987), that if state law criminally prohibited a form of gambling, then Indian tribes could not engage in that activity. However, if the state civilly regulated a form of gambling, then tribes within that state could operate such activities free from state control. In essence, the courts formally recognized the tribes' rights to conduct gaming operations on their own lands so long as such games were not criminal by state law.

> **Code Talking**
>
> The **Indian Gaming Regulatory Act** of 1988 established standards and regulations for the conduct of gaming on Indian lands and for the promotion of tribal economic development, tribal self-sufficiency, and strong tribal government.

This was an important win for Indian tribes; however, it wasn't a total victory. Congress, pressured by the states and fearful that unregulated gaming on Indian reservations might attract organized crime, passed the *Indian Gaming Regulatory Act* (IGRA) in 1988, which in effect authorized casino gambling on Indian reservations and provided a regulatory framework and oversight body for the industry in the form of the National Indian Gaming Commission (NIGC).

The Games People Play

Federal law regulates two distinct types of gambling on Indian land. Class II gambling consists of bingo, keno, pull-tabs, punchboards, and nonbanking card games (games in which players play against each other rather than against the house). Class

II gambling is governed by a tribal ordinance that must meet federal guidelines and be approved by the National Indian Gaming Commission.

Class III gambling consists of common casino games such as roulette, craps, and banking card games such as blackjack. It also includes all mechanical or electronic gambling machines such as slot machines and video poker devices. Class III gambling is conducted under a compact that each tribe negotiates with the government of the state in which it is located. Compacts can specify which party has civil and criminal jurisdiction over gambling enforcement. The compacts can apply those state laws to Class III gambling that each party believes necessary for regulation.

An Indian tribe doesn't have complete authority to conduct any type of gambling it wishes. The state must already permit a type of gambling for any non-Indian before it can be conducted on Indian land. The non-Indian gambling need not be commercial or profit-making; gambling by nonprofit organizations for charitable purposes, or even private social betting, can provide a basis for Indians to claim the right to conduct comparable forms of gambling.

> **Tribal Truths**
>
> Class I gaming generally includes social and traditional games and is within the exclusive jurisdiction of Indian tribes. It consists of "charitable gambling" such as church bingo with nominal prizes and traditional tribal games like hand games or stick games. These kinds of games are not subject to federal regulation.

Just the Facts

Many people object to tribes running gaming operations. For some, they are against any kind of gaming, whether Indian or not. Others object to what they believe is a special privilege extended to Indian tribes. Still others believe that Indian gaming is a front for organized crime or is otherwise ripe for corruption.

Here are the facts about Indian gaming:

- Less than one third of all federally recognized tribes have gaming operations. Some tribes have rejected gaming because of potential conflicts with traditional values. For others, gaming is impractical because of their remote location.

- Tribal revenue from gaming amounted to nearly $13 billion in 2001—a lot of money, but less than 10 percent of the total gaming industry. Furthermore, the Indian Gaming Regulatory Act requires that all revenues from tribal gaming be used *solely* for governmental or charitable purposes. Much like a state that runs a lottery, tribal governments determine how gaming revenues are to be spent

Tribal Truths

The Spirit Mountain Community Fund, the charitable arm of the Confederated Tribes of the Grand Ronde Community, awards 6 percent of profits from the Tribes' Spirit Mountain Casino to worthy and deserving charities and organizations in Oregon. Many non-Indians benefit from this charity.

within the parameters set by the law. In contrast to the opulent spending by commercial casino operators (like Donald Trump, an outspoken critic of Indian gaming), tribes use gaming revenue to build houses, schools, roads, and fund health care and educational programs.

♦ Indian gaming has created more than 300,000 jobs in the communities on and around gaming operations. Nationally, 75 percent of those employed by Indian gaming are non-Indians! For Native communities where unemployment has been historically high, gaming has provided jobs where none previously existed.

♦ Indian gaming is regulated on three levels. The tribes are the primarily regulators. State regulation is also present, given that gaming requires a compact or agreement between the tribes and the state. Finally, a number of federal agencies enforce gaming laws, including the National Indian Gaming Commission, the Interior Department, the Justice Department, the Federal Bureau of Investigation, the Internal Revenue Service, and the Treasury Department.

Ancient Tales

The old axiom about the three factors needed for success in any business—location, location, location—applies to Indian gaming. In most cases, reservations are in isolated and rural locations. For the Northern Cheyenne reservation in Montana, a large-scale gaming operation simply isn't feasible, given its distance from any major community. The Golden Eagle Casino, however, which is owned by the Kickapoo tribe in Kansas, is only 45 miles from Topeka, a major metropolitan area.

Betting on the Future

The real question Native Americans need to ask about any economic program they adopt is whether it is sustainable. Some people believe gaming isn't sustainable, because there will be a point at which the local community will reduce its patronage, thereby decreasing revenue for the gaming industry. Furthermore, because gaming, in the main, requires state support, the future of gaming rests at least in part on the whims of each state administration.

Offshore Banking: Reservations Are Islands, Right?

There was a time when if you thought of offshore banking and tax-sheltered investment accounts, the Cayman Islands and Switzerland came to mind. Now, Indian reservations may make a run at international banking commerce, without the sandy beaches or views of the Alps.

At least two tribes are already offering services ordinarily not available in the United States. The First Lenape Nation Bank and the Apaches' First Americans Trust Company, both in Andadarko, Oklahoma, are in the offshore banking business. Most of their advertisement is via the Internet and their deposits arrive in the mail or by wire.

Because of the reservation's semi-sovereign status, the two banks use numbered accounts and offer privacy and safety from most legal demands for money, notably judgments of U.S. courts. The two banks also don't report deposits of over $10,000, as federal law requires. Recent concerns over the funding of terrorist activities will no doubt result in the regulation of these accounts by the federal government. Like with the gaming industry, the federal government has the right to regulate any tribal industry if it wishes.

Because offshore banking is a rather recent development in Indian country, there is no sense of how it might impact tribal economies. One can imagine that, if the recent history of the evolution of the gaming industry on Indian reservations is any indication, Congress will use its plenary powers to pass legislation regulating offshore banking practices on Indian reservations.

Tribal Truths

In April 1999, the Blackfeet Tribal Business Council passed its own foreign capital depository act, allowing the creation of tribally chartered companies to serve as sheltered investment vehicles. Glacier International Depository Ltd. on the Blackfeet reservation in Montana was the nation's first foreign capital depository.

Tribal Truths

Indian tribes aren't the only governments looking at international banking as an economic solution to their financial woes. In 1997, the state of Montana passed legislation clearing the way for its bid to become an "offshore" banking haven.

Feeding the Goose That Lays the Golden Eggs

While tribes may be hitching their futures on gaming and their natural resources, clearly they must consider diversification. Those that can generate capital through highly productive enterprises such as gaming and mining might do well to look to other industries that would be self-sustaining, should their main source of revenue disappear. For example, some tribes are attempting to develop tourism—typically a clean and renewable industry—where the locale is scenic or historic.

One economic model that likewise seems logical is for a tribal government to promote retail development, which encourages tribal members to purchase goods on site, rather than funneling money to reservation "border towns." Success at the retail level may spawn a light manufacturing trade for export off the reservation.

Whatever the case, tribal members are the only people who can determine the economic future of a reservation.

The Least You Need to Know

- There are 2.4 million American Indians and Alaska Natives in the United States; 440,000 of them live on reservations.

- Reservations are pockets of poverty with high unemployment and few economic advantages.

- Reservations have an estimated 25 percent of the United States's mineral wealth, consisting of coal, oil, gas, and uranium.

- Less than one third of all federally recognized tribes have some kind of gaming operations.

- Gaming revenues for American Indian tribes amounted to nearly $13 billion in 2001.

- Some tribes have established offshore banking operations as a form of economic development.

Chapter 24

Protecting Traditional Beliefs and Practices

In This Chapter

- ◆ The meaning of the Peyote Way
- ◆ Defending Indian religious rights
- ◆ Why bones matter
- ◆ The New Age movement and Native traditions

Native people have always had a spiritual side. But because their beliefs were different from Christian philosophy, Euro-Americans thought that Natives' religious beliefs were backward, savage, and unintelligent. During the period of assimilation, political and religious forces combined to separate Natives from their traditional practices. Some Native peoples lost their traditions entirely while others preserved only remnants of their religious ceremonies.

Today, many Native peoples have returned to their traditions, overcoming 500 years of pressure to leave them behind. Tribal people are reclaiming values that once enabled them to overcome whatever obstacles they faced.

And although the courts have upheld Native peoples' rights to practice their religions, they must remain vigilant. It is only by ensuring the right to practice their beliefs that they will remain a distinct culture. Native people are like the proverbial miner's canary—if Native cultures are not protected, then all cultures are vulnerable to elimination.

A Revival of Traditional Beliefs

Tribal Truths

As a boy on the Northern Cheyenne Indian reservation in Montana some 35 years ago, I recall attending a sun dance ceremony in which only four or five men were taking part in the ritual. Now there are a hundred or more who endure the rigors of the sun dance rites.

The renewed interest in ancient traditions is particularly strong among those Natives who have assimilated into mainstream American society and found that there is something missing in their lives. For those people, returning to tribal traditions adds meaning to their lives.

Native perspectives of the universe and its workings obviously differ greatly between and even among tribes. Therefore, it is difficult to be very specific about any revitalization movements among Native peoples. I've selected a few examples that indicate the direction these movements have taken and the problems they have encountered along the way.

The colorful outfit of the American Indian dancer reflects Native people's renewed energy and appreciation for their traditional cultural practices.

(© Corbis)

Native Voices _____

But why should I mourn at the untimely fate of my people? Tribe follows tribe and nation follows nation, like the waves of the sea. It is the order of nature, and regret is useless. Your time of decay may be distant, but it will surely come, for even the White Man whose God walked and talked with him as friend to friend, cannot be exempt from the common destiny.

—Seattle, Dwamish leader

The Peyote Way

One of the most controversial Native American religious movements of the last 100 years is the Peyote Way or peyotism, so called because its followers use the hallucinogen peyote, or _Lophophora williamsii_. An essential element of the Peyote Way is the peyote ceremony, a formalized, all-night prayer meeting, usually held in a tipi, hogan, or "peyote house" especially set aside for that purpose. Although it varies significantly, followers of the Peyote Way often incorporate Christian elements, such as testimony and the recognition of Jesus Christ as a divine being, into their ceremonies.

As in the traditional vision quests of the Plains tribes, participants in the peyote ceremonies experience visions—auditory and visual hallucinations that are induced by the peyote—that they believe are revelations from the supernatural. Besides the use of peyote, adherents of the Peyote Way may fast and seek solitude for quiet contemplation—all traditional modes of worship among traditional tribes.

Built on Ancient Roots

The religious use of peyote is very ancient. Tribes in northern Mexico used peyote in ceremonies well before Europeans came to the Americas. In the mid-1800s, spiritual use of peyote spread north from Mexico and was adopted by the American Plains Indians, arriving in North America at a time when indigenous people were badly in need of spiritual uplifting and cultural strength. In the last 100 years, peyotism, or the spiritual use or peyote, has continued to spread.

Tribal Truths _____

Mexican peyotism, or spiritual use of peyote, is perhaps best typified by the traditional practices of the Huichol tribe along the Pacific coast of Mexico. Annual pilgrimages to ritually hunt the sacred cactus—the source of peyote—are still a central part of tribal myth and ceremony.

Native American Church and the Peyote Road

Most of North American peyotism is associated with the Native American Church (NAC), founded in 1918. Approximately 250,000 Natives attend meetings of the Native American Church. The NAC is largely composed of unassociated groups of mostly Native believers organized into local chapters, called moons. Each moon has officers who perform the ceremonies, called peyote meetings, the term for their church services.

Code Talking

The Peyote Road is a way of life for members of the Native American Church. It means living one's life according to the tenets of the Church.

Native Voices

Most Christians talk about God. Native American Church members talk to God.

—Native American Church axiom

Native Voices

It's a great day for members of the Native American Church to finally be able to pray without fear.

—Abraham Spotted Elk, Northern Cheyenne, president of the Native American Church of Wyoming, upon learning of the passage of an amendment to the American Indian Religious Freedom Act permitting the use of peyote for religious purposes.

The leader of a peyote meeting is known as the Road Chief, or Road Man. The Road Chief is charged with overseeing the main elements of the meeting and leading others on *the Peyote Road*, the way of learning to live life well. Although ceremonies among different moons vary slightly, they incorporate many of the same spiritual elements. Central tenets of the NAC usually involve avoidance of alcohol, devotion to family, and right living in general. Metaphorically, those who follow these tenets are said to be on the Peyote Road or following the Peyote Way.

Religious Practitioners or Drug Users?

The use of peyote—a mind-altering substance—is highly controversial. Peyote is classified as a controlled substance, and it is illegal to possess and use it in most circumstances. However, Native Americans have long claimed their right to use peyote as part of their religious ceremonies.

That right was put to the test when two Natives, Al Smith and Galen Black, both of Oregon, were fired from their jobs as drug and alcohol counselors because they used peyote as part of a Native American Church (NAC) ceremony. When they applied for unemployment insurance, the state rejected their request because they had been fired for illegal drug use. Smith and Black took their case to the Supreme Court, and the Court ruled against the Natives, defending the state's right to deny unemployment benefits because of peyote use. However, in 1990, the Court suggested that Oregon pass a state law protecting the use of the drug in traditional ceremonies.

To address this seeming lack of support for Native religious practice, in 1994 Congress passed an amendment to the *American Indian Religious Freedom Act*. The amendment guarantees the rights of Native Americans to possess, transport, and use peyote in the course of traditional religious ceremonies.

Code Talking

The **American Indian Religious Freedom Act** was passed in 1978. The act protects and preserves the traditional religions of Native Americans, and the policy of the United States "to protect and preserve for American Indians their inherent right of freedom to believe, express, and exercise the traditional religions" of American Indian, Eskimo, Aleut, and Native Hawaiians. The act allows access to religious sites, the use and possession of sacred objects, and the freedom to practice ceremonies and traditional rites.

The amendment to the American Indian Religious Freedom Act was a great victory for Native American religious rights. However, it is only one of many battles that Native peoples have had to fight to ensure that their religious rights are not violated.

Put Those Bones Back!

Imagine that someone visited the cemetery where your great grandparents' remains are buried and dug them up. Now imagine they took those remains—without anyone's permission—and displayed them somewhere for public viewing! Or cut them up for scientific research. Or sold them to a collector. How would you feel? Most people would be very angry and upset. After all, those bones belonged to someone once, and they were placed there by relatives as a permanent resting place.

American Indians don't have to imagine how they would feel about such grave desecration—they already know, because this kind of thing has been happening to their ancestor's burial sites for a long time. Making matters worse, many Native religions hold that when a burial

Tribal Truths

In enacting NAGPRA, Congress attempted to "strike a balance between the interest in scientific examination of skeletal remains and the recognition that Native Americans, like people from every culture around the world, have a religious and spiritual reverence for the remains of their ancestors."

is disturbed, the spirit of the individual is likewise disturbed and doesn't rest as was intended when the person was first buried. Yet for years scientists, anthropologists, traders in antiquities—to name just a few—have been desecrating Indian graves.

Although Native Americans can do little to right the wrongs done to their ancestors while they were still alive, they can protect their remains. And they have made great strides in doing so. As a result of decades of activism to protect the burial sites of their ancestors and to recover the remains and sacred cultural objects in the possession or under the control of federal agencies and museums, Native Americans finally achieved victory. On November 23, 1990, President George Bush signed into law the Native American Graves Protection and Repatriation Act (NAGPRA).

Dignity for the Dead

The act is designed to lend dignity to the remains of those who have passed from this world into the next. As legislation, the act provides a vehicle for tribes …

1. To repatriate American Indian remains and cultural items that were stored in museum and agency warehouses, or were on display as exhibits.

2. To prohibit, with limited exceptions, the intentional excavation of American Indian graves and cultural items.

3. To suppress illegal trafficking in American Indian remains and artifacts.

When burying their dead, Indians placed many objects with the body to ensure that the individual had access to the spiritual representations of those objects. Women, for example, often were buried with their cooking utensils, and weapons were sometimes included for men to take to the hereafter. These funerary objects are sacred, and NAGPRA provides a method for tribes to have those, along with human remains, be returned to the tribes for proper disposal.

> **Tribal Truths**
>
> Some tribes, like the Navajo, would prefer not to have the return of their ancestors' remains or funerary objects. Their beliefs teach that the spiritual essence of a person can cause harm if the living come into contact with objects associated with the dead. They have a term for this kind of circumstance: "Ghost Sickness."

NAGPRA permits tribes to repatriate the skeletal remains of known ancestors that are housed in museums and other repositories for proper reburial. Facilities that receive federal support in any way, shape, or form must comply with the regulations. NAGPRA is a unique statute because it considers, for the first time in federal legislation, the Native American perspective on the proper treatment of their ancestors.

NAGPRA hasn't entirely solved the problem of grave desecration. Several questions haven't been resolved, including how to treat "culturally unidentifiable ancient remains" found on federal lands. Furthermore, some scientists believe that the act hinders future research about Native peoples by removing from scientific hands possible sources of study. Scholars point out that NAGPRA is short-sighted by not recognizing that, in the future, technology may develop techniques for learning a great deal more about Native peoples than is now possible, but without the physical remains of those people, those possibilities will be lost.

However, the act has made it necessary for the scientific community, museum curators, and others to work with Native peoples to seek a mutual understanding. The enactment of NAGPRA is historically significant because it represents a fundamental change in social attitudes toward Native peoples. Today, the preservation of the traditions of Native peoples, and in particular their sacred ways, are legislated and legalized. For the first time in 100 years, the federal government protects those practices and seeks to protect the integrity of the past, our ancestors, and their sacred ways.

Yet, there are greater threats than the theft of grave goods or burial remains. Many non-Indians—and Indian people as well—are exploiting Native ceremonies for profit and personal gain.

Prophets for Profit: American Indian Religion and the New Age

In recent decades, the New Age movement has taken the spiritual world by storm. In particular, New Agers have seized upon Native American religious traditions as a means of achieving self-fulfillment. Although Native peoples have no problem with people finding greater meaning in their lives, they do object to practices that exploit their spirituality, including the following:

◆ **Native people who franchise religious ceremonies.** These are Indian people who profess to be spiritual leaders and will conduct ceremonies and pseudo-rituals on behalf of paying customers. Such Indian people take advantage of non-Indians' gullibility and lack of knowledge to offer

> **Tribal Truths**
>
> Some non-Indians believe that all Native peoples are intimately familiar with all Native practices and ceremonies. However, spiritual charlatans frequently have no real calling, nor have they endured the long apprenticeships usually required of medicine people in Native culture.

some sort of spiritual guidance, for a price, of course. These individuals will go anywhere, anytime, to accommodate their clientele—even holding sun dances in the ballroom of a Ramada Inn in London! They are exploiting non-Indians for financial gain, but non-Indians don't always know it.

♦ **People who profess a tribal identity but cannot substantiate that connection.** Usually these people claim to have been raised by an Indian grandmother who passed on traditional knowledge. When confronted, these individuals are often elusive and vague. That is not to say that some people who possess little Native ancestry are scam artists. Those who attempt to profit from their ancestry are certainly suspect, however.

♦ **Non-Indians who are familiar with Native ways and who pass themselves off as experts.** They may have spent a few weeks with a Native person, and based on that experience, claim to have "studied" under a medicine person. Usually they make the claim to having been adopted by the spiritual leader. They see nothing wrong with cultural "borrowing."

Many Native Americans have been offended by the mockery these bastardized versions make of their sacred ceremonies. Some of the incidents Indian people find most offensive include sun dances held on Astroturf, sweats (sweat-lodge ceremonies) held on cruise ships with wine and cheese served, and sex orgies advertised as part of "traditional Cherokee ceremonies." Others make even more specific promises; for example, one workshop guarantees that you will retrieve your own personal power animal in a trance.

Native Americans have noted the bitter irony of these plastic shamans profiting from the degrading, twisted versions of Native American rituals while many indigenous people still live below the poverty level.

Ancient Tales

Some non-Indian people believe that spiritual fulfillment is as easy as buying a book on Native religion from the local bookstore. It is a part of the fast-food influence on religion, drive-through salvation. Others study Native philosophy and only adapt the parts that are convenient. For many, spirituality is like ordering off a Chinese menu; a bit from column A and some from column B. What they don't realize is that a person truly dedicated to Native religion lives his or her life according to *all* beliefs of the religion.

New Age Rationalizations

The question becomes even more complicated when non-Indians exploit Native traditions and practices for profit. Many new-age practitioners charge others to take part in pseudo-religious ceremonies and get rich writing books espousing Native values. These non-Indians justify their actions by stating, falsely, that Native spiritual leaders charged for their services, so for them to do so is not inconsistent to Native practices. The Native Americans were not a capitalistic society and their religions do not incorporate capitalistic ideals. A true medicine man or woman would not even think about making someone pay to learn information.

Code Talking

True spiritual leaders don't make a profit from their teachings, whether it's through selling books, workshops, sweat lodges, or otherwise. Spiritual leaders teach the people because it is their responsibility to pass what they have learned from their elders to the younger generations. They do not charge for their services.

—Andy Smith, Nez Perce

So What's the Harm?

Some non-Indians don't see any harm in the New Age "commodification" of Native spirituality. They perhaps accuse Native peoples of some sort of racism, saying that Native peoples want no whites to take part in Native practices. Certainly, some Native peoples believe that the rituals and ceremonies, having a supernatural origin, were meant for only one tribe or one people. Many other Native peoples welcome a sincere curiosity that non-Indians express about Native ways. Many Native peoples are likewise tolerant of and even welcoming to those who might want to experience Native spirituality. There is no harm in a sincere quest for knowledge.

But much of what New Age practitioners do is insensitive to Native culture. In traditional societies one must earn the right to perform or participate in sacred ceremonies. Other rituals have specific rules and prohibitions that must be followed. New Agers often do not know or follow such regulations. It would be as insensitive for someone who doesn't have the proper training to perform a sweat lodge ceremony as it would be for a non-Catholic to dress like a priest and perform a baptism or the administer Last Rites.

The harm is not one that can be easily described or understood. It is not an earthy concern that has Native peoples leery of New Age use of Native religious practices. The real concern is that there is great power in Native ceremonies. When someone who doesn't understand that power attempts to access it, there is no telling what great good or great harm can occur.

Spirituality Out of This World

There's nothing wrong with being curious about what Native peoples believe and to find out about their religious rites. However, those who believe that anything—even spiritual knowledge—can be bought and sold are wrong. Spirituality must be gained by heart-felt study and be experienced as a part of a life's journey. Spirituality is not an instantly redeemable coupon good for one free ride around this universe!

The Least You Need to Know

♦ Native Americans have a renewed interest in their traditional beliefs.

♦ The Native American Church, which was chartered in 1918, uses peyote to induce spiritual visions.

♦ Congress extended protection for the use of peyote for religious purposes by amending the American Indian Religious Freedom Act.

♦ The Native American Grave Protection and Repatriation Act allows tribes to retrieve human remains and funeral objects from museums and other institutions.

♦ The New Age movement, sometimes aided by Native peoples, has appropriated Native beliefs and ceremonies, often for profit and personal gain.

Stand Up and Be Counted: American Indian Population Facts

The population of Native peoples in 1500, in what is now the United States, can never be known for sure. Some scholars estimate that there were as many as 60 million Native peoples in North America, while others believe there were only about 2 million.

Since about 1820, the U.S. Bureau of Census has counted Native peoples. More recent censuses have been more accurate, although many scholars believe that the number of Native peoples is much higher because of under-reporting and limitations of the census count. One change made for the 2000 census is that a person can claim duel ethnicity, that is, white and American Indian, whereas, in past censuses, a person could only check one box.

The Bureau of the Census estimates that there will be over 3 million Native Americans in 2020 and more than 4 million by 2050. Native Americans have been the fastest-growing major minority group in the United States since the 1960 census.

The following tables break down these population numbers for you.

Native American, Eskimo, and Aleut Populations, 1492 to 2002

Year	Population
1500	5,000,000 to 15,000,000 (estimated)
1800	600,000 (estimated)
1820	471,000
1847	383,000
1857	313,000
1870	278,000
1880	244,000
1890	248,000
1900	237,000
1910	291,000
1920	261,000
1930	362,000
1940	366,000
1950	377,000
1960	552,000
1970	827,000
1980	1,420,000
1990	1,959,000
2000	2,400,000
2020	3,100,000
2050	4,400,000

Native American Population by State, 1990*

State	Population
Oklahoma	252,420
California	242,164
Arizona	203,527
New Mexico	134,355
Alaska	85,698

State	Population
Washington	81,482
North Carolina	80,155
Texas	65,877
New York	62,651
Michigan	55,638
South Dakota	50,575
Minnesota	49,909
Montana	47,679
Wisconsin	39,387
Oregon	38,496
Florida	36,335
Colorado	27,776
North Dakota	25,917
Utah	24,283
Kansas	21,965
Illinois	21,836
Ohio	20,358
Missouri	19,835
Nevada	19,637
Louisiana	18,541
Alabama	16,506
Virginia	15,282
New Jersey	14,970
Pennsylvania	14,733
Idaho	13,780
Georgia	13,348
Maryland	12,972
Indiana	12,836
Arkansas	12,773
Nebraska	12,410
Massachusetts	12,241
Tennessee	10,039
Wyoming	9,478

Native American Population by State, 1990*   (continued)

State	Population
Mississippi	8,525
South Carolina	8,246
Iowa	7,349
Connecticut	6,654
Maine	5,998
Kentucky	5,769
Hawaii	5,099
Rhode Island	4,071
West Virginia	2,458
New Hampshire	2,134
Delaware	2,019
Vermont	1,696
District of Colombia	1,466

Complete population counts for the 2000 census are not yet available.

Top 25 American Indian Tribes in the United States, by Population, 1990

Tribe	Population
Cherokee	369,035
Navajo	225,298
Sioux	107,321
Chippewa	105,988
Choctaw	86,231
Pueblo	55,330
Apache	53,330
Iroquois	52,557
Lumbee	50,888
Creek	45,872
Blackfoot	37,992
Canadian and Latin American	27,179
Chickasaw	21,522

Tribe	Population
Tohono O'Odham	16,876
Potawatomi	16,719
Seminole	15,564
Pima	15,074
Tlingit	14,417
Alaskan Athabaskans	14,198
Cheyenne	11,809
Comanche	11,437
Paiute	11,369
Osage	10,430
Puget Sound Salish	10,384
Yaqui	9,838

Glossary

Anasazi   From the Navajo language meaning "Ancient Ones." They are one of the oldest cultures in the American Southwest, and are perhaps best known for their cliff dwellings, the most famous of these being Mesa Verde in Colorado.

atlatl   From the Aztec word for "spear thrower." The atlatl is a short stick that serves as an extension of the arm, thereby giving the thrower more distance and power.

band   Subdivision of a tribe. It is a local group of people who join together in search of subsistence; it can be made up of related families.

blood quantum   A method of determining Native American ethnicity by meeting the required amount of Native blood in one's ancestry.

carbon-14 (C-14)   A test that measures existing radioactive carbon in an organic artifact to yield an approximate time when that organism lived.

clan   Kinship reckoning through a line of common descent, either through the mother's side (matrilineal) or father's side (patrilineal).

culture   A way of life of a group of people—the behaviors, beliefs, values, and symbols that they accept, generally without thinking about them, and that are passed along by communication and imitation from one generation to the next.

culture areas   Geographic divisions of North America. When tribes share a common environment, their cultures sometimes become similar; therefore, a culture area is a geographic region where tribes have similar cultures.

earth diver myths   Native American creation stories in which the earth is made from a substance brought to the surface by a water bird, such as a duck, or by an animal, like a beaver or otter.

effigy mounds   Mounds created by the Adena-Hopewell cultures to resemble animals or other objects.

emergence creation stories   Native American creation stories in which humans once lived on other worlds, and when those were destroyed, they came to the present world.

hozho   Navajo word meaning, beauty, harmony, and balance. Hozho refers to that state of being that all Navajo try to maintain in their paths of life.

igloo   A type of Eskimo house constructed out of snow blocks.

Iroquois   A language family. The confederation of tribes consisting of the Seneca, Cayuga, Onondaga, Oneida, Mohawk, and Tuscarora. Also referred to as the Haudenosaunee Confederacy.

kiva   A ceremonial room found in the center of a Pueblo village or in cliff dwellings. Inside the kiva were held secret religious ceremonies that only the initiated were allowed to observe.

language family   A group of languages that are thought to have diverged from a common ancestor.

myth   Stories about the deeds and doings of supernatural beings.

Native Americans   People who lived in the Americas before the coming of Europeans or the ancestors of those original inhabitants. Also, American Indians, Indians, Natives, and Indigenous peoples.

Northwest Passage   Water route thought to link the Atlantic coastline with the Pacific. Lewis and Clark unsuccessfully searched for this route on their expedition between 1804 and 1806.

Paleo-Indians   The first human beings to arrive in the New World from Asia. Paleo is from the Greek word meaning "ancient."

potlatch   A ceremony among the Northwest Coastal people used to demonstrate how wealthy a clan was by giving away or destroying all the clan's material assets.

Red Sticks Tecumseh's Creek allies during the War of 1812, so named because Tecumseh had been given a bundle of red sticks to indicate the number of days until a Creek attack on the Americans.

sandpainting A painted design created by healers among the Navajo. Sandpaintings are thought to be curative: Patients absorb the healing energy from the sacred painted designs.

sipapu A depression on the floor of a kiva that represents the "hole of emergence" where humans arose from the underground to the first realm.

shaman A person who is in direct contact with the spirit world, usually through a trance state. A shaman has spirit helpers at his or her command to carry out curing, divining, and bewitching.

sun dance Major religious ceremony of fasting and prayer practiced by many Plains tribes.

ta-ba-bone Shoshoni word for "stranger."

Temple Mounds Large, pyramidlike mounds built by the Mississippian cultures atop which they erected temples.

tipi Conical-shape lodge of the Plains tribes. The word is from the Lakota language meaning "dwelling."

tribe Social group, bound by common culture, history, and culture. In federal American Indian law, a tribe is a distinct political entity with executive, legislative, and judicial powers.

Appendix C

Bibliography

Andrist, Ralph. *The Long Death: The Last Days of the Plains Indians.* Norman: University of Oklahoma Press, 2001.

Boxberger, Daniel L., ed. *Native North Americans: An Ethnohistorical Approach.* Dubuque: Kendall Hunt, 1990.

Brown, Dee. *Bury My Heart at Wounded Knee: An Indian History of the American West.* New York: Henry Holt & Company, 1970.

Champagne, Duane, ed. *The Native North American Almanac: A Reference Work on Native North Americans in the United States and Canada.* Detroit: Gale Research Inc., 1994.

Churchill, Ward ed. *Critical Issues in Native North America* (IWGIA Document No. 62). December 1988/January 1989 ed. Copenhagen, Denmark: The International Secretariat of IWGIA (International Work Group for Indigenous Affairs), 1990.

Debo, Angie. *A History of the Indians of the United States.* Norman: University of Oklahoma Press, 1970.

Deloria, Vine, Jr., ed. *American Indian Policy in the Twentieth Century.* Norman: University of Oklahoma Press, 1985.

Fleming, Walter C., and John G. Watts, ed. *Visions of an Enduring People: A Reader in Native American Studies* (Second Edition). Dubuque: Kendell Hunt, 2000.

Iverson, Peter, ed. *The Plains Indians of the Twentieth Century.* Norman: University of Oklahoma Press, 1985.

Jackson, Curtis E., and Marcia J. Galli. *A History of the Bureau of Indian Affairs and Its Activities Among Indians.* San Francisco: R & E Research Associates, 1977.

Mankiller, Wilma, and Michael Wallis. *Mankiller: A Chief and Her People.* New York: St. Martin's Press, 1993.

Matthiessen, Peter. *Indian Country.* New York: Penguin Books, 1984.

McLuhan, T. C. *Touch the Earth: A Self-Portrait of Indian Existence.* New York: Simon & Schuster, 1971.

Mihesuah, Devon A. *American Indians: Stereotypes and Realities.* Atlanta: Clarity Press, 1996.

Nabokov, Peter, ed. *Native American Testimony: A Chronicle of Indian-White Relations from Prophecy to the Present, 1492–1992.* New York: Viking, 1991.

Neihardt, John G. *Black Elk Speaks: Being the Life Story of a Holy Man of the Oglala Sioux.* Lincoln: University of Nebraska Press, 1979.

Nichols, Roger L., ed. *The American Indian: Past and Present, Fifth Edition.* New York: McGraw-Hill, 1999.

Niethammer, Carolyn. *Daughters of the Earth: The Lives and Legends of American Indian Women.* New York: Macmillan Publishing Co., Inc., 1977.

Pevar, Stephen L. *The Rights of American Indians and Their Tribes: American Civil Liberties Union, Handbooks for Young Americans.* New York: Puffin Books, 1997.

Prucha, Francis Paul. *The Great Father: The United States Government and the American Indians* (2 vols.). Lincoln: University of Nebraska Press, 1984.

Prentaz, Scott. *Tribal Law.* (Native American Culture. Jordan E. Kerber, series ed.) Vero Beach: Rourke Publications, Inc., 1994.

Tannenbaum, Beulah, and Harold Tannenbaum. *Science of the Early American Indians.* New York: Franklin Watts, 1988.

Thornton, Russell. *American Indian Holocaust and Survival: A Population History Since 1492.* Norman: University of Oklahoma Press, 1987.

Tiller, Veronica E. Velarde. *Tiller's Guide to Indian Country: Economic Profiles of American Indian Reservations.* Albuquerque: BowArrow Publishing Company, 1996.

Time-Life Books. *The Spirit World.* Alexandria: Time-Life Books, 1992.

Utter, Jack. *American Indians: Answers to Today's Questions.* Lake Ann: National Woodlands Publishing Company, 1993.

Waldman, Carl. *Atlas of the North American Indian.* New York: Facts On File, 1985.

Index